CREATIVITY IN
TEACHING

CREATIVITY IN
TEACHING

Invitations and Instances   *edited by* ALICE MIEL

Teachers College, Columbia University

Wadsworth Publishing Company, Inc.

Belmont, California

371.3

m1 E

FOREWORD

The word *creative* is not new in educational literature. It came into frequent use in the late twenties and early thirties when educators chose it as a label for their versions of better teaching. The adjective was applied not only to teaching that departed from tradition, but also to children's writing, art, dramatics, dance, and music, when those forms of expression were considered unique and original. The word has continued in use, at a popular level, in this sense.

Creativity, as a concept abstracted from a particular context, began to receive wide attention and close scrutiny in the fifties. In a collection of summaries of selected literature in psychology and psychiatry relating to creativity, almost half of the selections are dated from 1950 to 1959, although a period of nearly one hundred years is covered.[1] Eight of the twelve symposiums and surveys of the literature on creativity listed in the collection were published in the fifties.

Those of us who undertook to compile this book were led to a renewed and intensified interest in creativity by observing human responses to crowded living, to the standardizing influences of mass media of communication, and to pressures related to anxiety about international relations. We saw creativity as a way of responding that is available to all human beings and that enables them to cope with increasingly complex problems, conditions, and opportunities. In particular we saw creativity as a way of lifting

[1] Morris I. Stein and Shirley J. Heinze, *Creativity and the Individual* (Glencoe, Illinois: The Free Press, 1960).

v

teaching from the humdrum it sometimes becomes and of making it the exciting and satisfying venture it may so well be.

We noted the mounting interest in creativity on the part of psychologists, scientists, and representatives of business and industry. Those individuals were exploring the meaning of creativity and were gaining more understanding of the creative process as it applied to their fields of human activity. We felt that the teaching field could profit from similar attention.[2]

The Development of an Idea

A first step was for several of us to assemble for out-of-hours, free-flowing discussions at three different national conventions, using invited guests as added sources of ideas. During the course of the discussions, possible outlines for a book were made and remade, and results of reading, conferring, and mulling were shared. Finally, plans were made for a one-week author seminar for the exchange of ideas needed as reinforcement of our individual preparation for writing in this field.

The seminar was held in September 1958. Francis Shoemaker of Teachers College, Columbia University, served as consultant to the group for the first two days. After our discussions with him, we agreed on an almost final outline, accepted assignments, prepared and shared chapter outlines for critical review by the rest, and made a start on writing.

Following the seminar, the authors exchanged manuscripts, met with the editor singly or in small groups, and held one last session at a national conference. The editor assumed responsibility for final checking with authors and for assembling the total work.

The Naming of a Book

The book did not come into focus all at once. In order to arrive at a clear statement of purpose, we declared what we did *not* intend to do. For example, we decided early *not* to confine ourselves to teaching for creativity in the arts. In fact, we soon decided *not* to address ourselves in any central way to teaching *for* creativity in children and youth. Fostering creativity is, of course, one large and important segment of the responsibility of educators in a democ-

---

[2] It is interesting to note that in the entire set of nearly 350 summaries included in Stein and Heinze, *op. cit.*, no reference could be found to creativity in the field of teaching.

racy, but it is not their total responsibility. Rather, we decided to focus on the teacher's creativity as he works toward the whole range of purposes of the school or college. We were confident that creativity in teaching would result in opportunities for young people to learn to be more creative, but we chose to illuminate the concept of creativity *as applied to the teaching function.* Thus we titled our book *Creativity in Teaching.*

Appraisal of a Book

We decided to make the book a symposium, each chapter of which was to be developed by the author as he saw fit, within our agreements as to the general task to be accomplished by the chapter. No attempt was to be made to write a unified book with each piece flowing into the next. Rather, each chapter was to be a unit with its own integrity. This has meant that each author has had to develop his view of creativity to the extent necessary to establish a basis for his discussion. Thus, the chapters emphasize different aspects of the creative process and employ slightly different terminology. We believe that the reader will nevertheless find some degree of consistency in the book.

It is not easy to maintain a strict focus on creativity in teaching, particularly in chapters where the author is dealing with teachers at work with children and youth. At these points, it is hoped, the reader will see creativity in teaching reflected through activities in which learners are engaged.

While we have not illustrated all aspects of creativity in teaching, we have given some "instances" to clarify points we were making and we have extended, directly or by implication, many "invitations" to the reader to think with us about the concept of creativity in relation to the teaching process.

Always the most difficult judgment to make in connection with a product one is creating is that of deciding when the product may be made public. In the case of this book, we realize that we run some risk in publishing at this time in an area that has had so little exploration. We realize also that there is little agreemeent on what teaching itself is. Serious study of the function of teaching is proceeding at various points in this country and elsewhere at the present time. Is it appropriate to probe into creativity in teaching when both processes are so little understood?

Our belief is that we may throw light on both creativity and teaching by examining each as related to the other. We feel, also, that it may be possible to prevent creativity from becoming another meaningless catchword in education if many teachers will join in reflecting on the deeper meanings of the term. Therefore, we offer our symposium at this time as a way of opening the topic for wider consideration and, hopefully, as a way of encouraging research and experimentation.

Part One of the book is devoted to a discussion of teaching as a creative process. Part Two deals with creativity in teaching in relation to three selected aspects of design. Part Three treats conditions fostering creativity in teaching, discussing in turn pre-service teacher education, administration and supervision, and self-education of teachers for enhanced creativity.

The authors are indebted to publishers who kindly granted permission to quote from their copyrighted materials. Due credit is given at appropriate points in the volume. We wish to express appreciation also to the colleagues, friends, and members of our families who have shown interest in this project and led us to new sources of information. We are indebted also to the teachers who furnished some of our illustrative materials and to our secretaries, who helped us in the production phase. To Louise Berman of the University of Wisconsin, Milwaukee, goes credit for major work on the annotated bibliography. The following teachers kindly contributed descriptions of teaching quoted in this book: May Bell, L. B. Cherrington, William P. Colbert, Audrey Dickhart, Jane E. Edwards, James N. Finch, Helen Fogg, Frank Fucarino, A. Edith Grasso, John W. Hansen, David Long, George Loukides, Manus H. O'Donnell, Dorothea Wein Partch, Marvin Pursinger, Abby S. Rodell, Carla Sue Rucker, Myrtle Townsend, Kaye Trimmer, Joan Weinstein, and Harriet Wilson.

ALICE MIEL

CONTENTS

ix

PART ONE

PART ONE

TEACHING AS A
CREATIVE PROCESS

Teaching is only one of five specialized functions making up the modern complex known as the profession of education. Administration, supervision, guidance, and curriculum development also are functions to be performed by members of a professional staff. The wholeness of the educative process is such that commonly any one member of the profession exercises each of the five functions to a greater or lesser degree. For example, a teacher is performing an administrative function when he provides easy access to paper and other supplies. He is carrying on a supervisory function when he enforces rules during a fire drill or maintains order in his class. He is exercising a guidance function when he makes a plan with a parent whereby a student will have a place to study at home. He is exercising the function of curriculum development when, by himself or in conjunction with others, he plans that the pupils will study Africa or take a trip to a factory or help solve a school problem. Only part of the time is he "teaching."

WHAT IS TEACHING?

Since not everything a teacher does is teaching, what actions are unique to the teaching function?

In past centuries, while education was on the way to becoming a profession, teaching was studied with little reference to learning. In our own century, the "scientific movement" and preoccupation with study of child growth and development combined to put an emphasis on learning that all but closed off for a time the study of teaching as such. There has been a revival of interest in recent years in the teaching function itself. Since the modern student of the teaching process has the advantage of a fuller understanding of the learning process than did his predecessors, the outlook for a crisper and fuller understanding of teaching seems bright. At present, however, there is no generally accepted definition of teaching.

For purposes of this book, we, the authors, must take a stand. Before we can discuss *creativity* in teaching, we must state what *we* mean by *teaching*.

To explain teaching it is helpful to begin with a subsidiary but crucial function, curriculum development. As exercised at the classroom level, this function is so closely connected with teaching that to separate them except for purposes of analysis is impossible. The two functions often occur simultaneously.

We take as our definition of curriculum the *complete range of opportunities for educative experience provided under the auspices of an educational institution*. Curriculum development is a process of making decisions on the nature of the opportunities for experience to be provided—for whom, when, how, and under what circumstances. Also included are decisions on how results are to be evaluated. A teacher makes many of the most important of these decisions, but he is not thereby teaching.

Our position is that a person is teaching when he is *mediating* between another person and his world. To mediate is to be *instrumental* in another person's experiencing of his world and in his search for meaning.[1] Thus, teaching is participating at the actual point of another's experience. It takes the form of helping the indi-

---

[1] Leonard Kornberg in *A Class for Disturbed Children* (New York: Bureau of Publications, Teachers College, Columbia University, 1955), p. 3, writes: "The gathering of what is real (and not fantasy or error) between persons, the facilitation of events so that the world is shared between persons, is, I believe, the task of teaching children."

vidual to gain access to cultural material pointing to a world to be experienced, cultural material which consists of all the facts and the artifacts, the modes of feeling and the values, the skills and the processes, the theories, the questions, and the ways of developing new knowledge that humanity has found useful enough to carry forward to the present. It takes the form of helping the individual to make differentiations and structurings within his experiential field and to organize those parts and wholes in meaningful patterns.

Notice that we are not here discussing "good" teaching; we are trying to capture the essence of the teaching function, whether exercised well or poorly. Teaching is always the implementation, directly with learners, of some kind of curriculum decision. The specific aspects of the mediating function, teaching, may be listed as:

1. Structuring and restructuring a setting to make opportunities for experience available to learners.
2. Pointing to possible experiences to be had in the setting created, or otherwise inviting learners to avail themselves of opportunities for experience.
3. Participating with an individual or group in clarifying or otherwise improving guidelines for selecting opportunities for experience.
4. Serving as a model in interpersonal transactions, or otherwise fostering educative interaction among peers and people of other age groups.
5. Helping an individual or group to use time, space, equipment, and materials.
6. Helping an individual or group to abstract from experiences information, values, skills, and processes.
7. Helping an individual or group to interpret and evaluate experiences. The mediating function, teaching, is exercised basically through communicating in verbal and nonverbal ways—offering, explaining, showing, reinforcing, raising questions.[2]

---

2 Those who may be speculating as to the proper place for the "teaching machine" in education may wish to examine this list with the machine in mind. At what points is there a possibility of turning over part of the teaching function to a mechanical device? What new insights into the teaching-learning process may research on the programming and use of teaching machines produce?

Of the five educating functions, teaching is the first responsibility of the teacher; it is the central concern of no other person in education. However, the present arrangement, in which functions are shared by many and exercised at the point of need, will probably continue in American education, for the arrangement is a useful one. Placing responsibility for several professional functions in one individual lends flexibility to the use of personnel, and thus makes possible more economical and efficient deployment of a school staff. Therefore, a teacher must be prepared to exercise individual judgment in meeting situations in order to maintain proper emphasis on his major assignment and in order to maintain mutually supporting relationships among his varied functions. He can work out those relationships more intelligently and creatively if he grasps the essential character of each type of responsibility he carries. It is especially important that he have clear understanding of the nature of his teaching function.

WHAT IS CREATIVITY?

The creative process has been described as "relating previously unrelated things." [3] It appears to be a deliberate process of making a new combination or patterning of materials, movements, words, symbols, or ideas and somehow making the product available to others, visibly or otherwise. [4] Some people apply the word "creative" to a process only if the resulting product is recognized by competent individuals as outstanding. The medical researcher Hans Selye, for example, has proposed as criteria, "It must be true, it must be generalizable, and it must be surprising." [5] Others believe the quality of creativity has been shown if the individual has made something *new to himself* that is satisfying and in that sense useful to *him*, if he has related things that were previously unrelated in

[3] See *Creativity: An Examination of the Creative Process,* ed. Paul Smith (New York: Hastings House, Publishers, Inc., 1959), p. 18.

[4] On this point, Dore Schary, author and film producer, speaking at the Fifteenth Annual Conference on Higher Education in Chicago, March 8, 1960, said: "To me, the creative spirit generates in the mind, crystallizing a private, individual experience which can have meaning, expression and importance only if it is then shared."

[5] Quoted in *The Third Research Conference on the Identification of Creative Scientific Talent,* ed. Calvin Taylor (Salt Lake City: University of Utah Press, 1959), p. 291. In this section of the report a summary of work on the criterion problem is presented. The essential criteria named are "social novelty" and "breadth of application."

his experience, and if the product is "surprising" (that is, new) to *him*.

The authors are disposed toward the latter view. When we say we desire for everybody, including every teacher, the experience of creating, we mean creating newness from the standpoint of the individual. We wish to emphasize that the process of making something new must at some point be a deliberate one in order to be labeled creative. This point may come after an intuitively fruitful act, however. In agreemeent with Selye, we believe that the product must be "true"; that is, it must be constructive (leading in the direction of growth and life) as opposed to destructive (leading toward damage and death). However, we have some reservations about the criterion of generalizability or usefulness to others. Rather than to label a particular process of making something as either creative or uncreative, we prefer to judge it as falling on a scale between *somewhat* creative and *highly* creative, depending upon the degree of usefulness of the product.

We are convinced that a democratic society stands to benefit from a view of the creative process that encourages each person to engage in it to the extent of his ability. The possible *by-products* (joy of living and creating, self-esteem, growth) are valuable to the individual and to his society, whether or not the product created constitutes an original contribution (is "surprising").

In short, we believe that creativity is a quality which each human being is capable of exhibiting in his living. Individuals differ, however, as a result of both nature and nurture, in the amount and kind of creativity they display. Furthermore, we believe that creativity can be enhanced in most individuals and thus can increase in our society as a whole if we put into practice in education what we now know about conditions fostering creativity and if we continue to study the creative process in operation in many types of endeavor.

WHAT IS CREATIVITY IN TEACHING?

Teaching is a nonrepetitive process.[6] No two groups of learners are ever the same; nor is one class the same from day to day. The world around the classroom changes constantly; the teacher him-

6 See Edwin Reeder, *Supervision in the Elementary School* (Boston: Houghton Mifflin Company, 1953), pp. 6–15.

self changes. The teacher has abundant opportunity to "be creative" in the way he deals with all of these changing conditions. If he deliberately rejects the alternative of falling back on an unthinking, habitual response and instead consciously makes a decision based on examination of the old and the new factors present in a situation, he is engaging in a creative process. If he makes an unusual response and if it is one that will help other teachers to take more constructive action in a similar situation, the teacher may be said to have shown more creativity than he has shown before or than some other teachers have shown.

We do not believe it is possible, nor do we advocate it as desirable, that a teacher aim to teach creatively at all times. It is not easy to take the risks and bear the discomfort of uncertainty. A teacher must discipline himself to the hard work involved in putting polish on a new teaching style. Yet he is the one who experiences the pleasure of having created. Therefore, the teacher himself is the one to decide how much he can tolerate at any one time and what efforts are worth the cost. He must select the points at which he will work creatively and, just as deliberately, select parts of his program in which to operate for a time in a routine way.

It is to be expected that some teachers will engage in a creative process more often and more successfully than others. It is not assumed, however, that teachers may be divided into two groups, the creative and the uncreative.

When an individual is trying to do something creative as a teacher, what is the product? It is clear what the product is *not*. It is not people, for teachers do not mold people as if they were clay. The "product" of the teacher's creativity is *opportunities* for individuals and groups to experience and learn.

What media are used to create such opportunities? What is malleable or plastic? If learners are not to be manipulated like puppets, what can be manipulated by a teacher? The media to be manipulated in teaching seem to be time, space, things, and the people, including the teacher himself, from whom the individual or group may learn. The teacher can manipulate the bearers of the culture, that is, he can arrange an environment that either includes or excludes certain people and things and that extends certain invitations to search and to experiment. The teacher also can vary the character of his mediation between the children and the culture at several points—when goals are being set, when information is being processed, when human interaction is going on, when evaluation is in progress. Creativity in teaching can thus be judged by the quality of opportunities actually provided by a teacher for young people to have educative experiences.

In writing this book we have tried not to use creative teaching merely as a synonym for "good" teaching. We happen to be confident that creativity in teaching breeds good teaching practices, but not all would accept our judgment or our criteria for determining what is good. Many kinds of teaching are called good by someone. What one might consider good another might consider bad or uncreative or both. It seems best to avoid confusion by not equating goodness in teaching with creativity in teaching. We wish to propose that teaching behavior fashioned in deliberate response to the components of a situation be called creative. With such a definition considerable agreement among observers should be possible.

In Part One of this book three authors present their views of creativity. As one way of showing how pervasive is the quality of creativity in human living, Peggy Brogan takes us straight into a classroom, then into a home, and then out into a wider world. Arthur W. Foshay next presents a reasoned analysis of the creative process, showing implications for teachers in fostering creativity among learners as well as in themselves. A third writer, Evelyn Wenzel, points out how a teacher may judge the extent of his own creativity and how he may increase that creativity through finding meaning in his teaching and living.

ABOUT THE AUTHOR...*Peggy Brogan has taught children and college students in Glencoe, Illinois, in Bronxville, New York, and in New York City. In her writing one always meets real people, for she reaches out toward the world with all her powers of sensitive response, as she invites her readers to do. Creativity is part of her life, just as it is a part of yours.*

Among Mrs. Brogan's *writings are* Helping Children Learn, *written with* Lorene Fox (*World Book Company, 1955*), *and* More Than Social Studies, *written with Alice Miel (Prentice-Hall, Inc., 1957). As a professional educational consultant, her work has varied from assisting a county school system in changing its arithmetic program to helping a private school to develop in one unified process a curriculum and a school plant.*

1 THE CASE FOR CREATIVITY

It is a time for wondering and observing and figuring out. Eight-year-old Peter has drawn a picture of an invention to improve the world. Several of his classmates stand around the table where he has been working.

"What's it supposed to be, Pete?" asks Larry as he edges in closer to get a better look.

"Can't you see?" says Phyllis, pointing. "It's a new place for bicycles to go. Not on the sidewalk and not on the street."

"A new place for bicycles," muses Charlie, his mind playing around with the idea. "A new place for bicycles. A place without cars. A place without people walking. Boy, I hope it works."

"It can't work," interjects Stanley. "How can there be a place just for riding bicycles? You've got eyes and can measure. Anyone can see that the space is all needed for the sidewalk and the street."

"Let Pete show us, Stanley. He might have something there. Come on, Pete. Show us."

As Peter begins to explain his drawing, Mrs. Wilson moves over toward the group. This is a time for a teacher to be on hand. Perhaps the children will need help as they begin to explore Peter's new idea. She glances around the room at the other children—some in groups, some working alone. It is 9:30. Half an hour remains in this early morning work period—half an hour for the children to. work on things and ideas that really matter to them.

"No wonder it's their favorite work time," thinks Mrs. Wilson. "They come into school with their ideas already in the making and they get so much done. I wonder if more of the day should be given over to this kind of free work time." She sits down to listen to Peter's explanation.

"Well, you know what this is," Peter says as he holds up his paper and points to a long strip that is sketched in with silver-gray crayon. "This is the regular street where the cars go."

"Yes, and where you weave in and out on your bike if you ride in the street," comments Mike.

"And here is the sidewalk where the people go and where most of us ride our bikes."

"Why didn't you draw some little kids getting knocked over, Pete? That would have made it real."

"Little kids! What makes you think it's just little kids that get knocked over? You should hear what my dad says about the bicycle riders."

"And this," says Peter, pointing to a narrow stretch between the sidewalk and street, "is the new place for bicycles. It looks narrow on this little paper, but there's plenty of room for passing and going two ways."

"Is it raised, Pete?" asks Charlie. "That's a neat idea. I can see me now. Sailing down the right-of-way."

"I didn't think of raising it, Charlie. I just thought of the cars with their own place for driving and the people with their own place for walking and the bicycles with their own place. And I drew it in a picture."

"Well, it's a mighty stupid picture," mutters Stanley half to himself as he rises to leave the group.

WELCOMING CREATIVITY IN THE CLASSROOM

Mrs. Wilson's mind has been actively at work during the children's discussion. She recognizes this as a time when creativity is in the air. And she knows it is not only in the affairs of children but in the affairs of all mankind that, when something new is offered, it is a time for wondering and observing and figuring out—a time for welcoming creativity as a part of living.

Mrs. Wilson senses the exciting implications in Peter's drawing.

"It can very well be," she muses, "that this is how humanity will reach new heights. It is entirely possible that Peter will not stop with picturing his own better way for cars and bicycles and pedestrians to move about with increased safety and freedom. Dreaming up a plan for traffic on overcrowded streets can be a forerunner to dreaming up new ideas for an overcrowded world— ideas encouraging untapped human resources to come into their own and inviting people to picture themselves in other than warlike human relations."

Mrs. Wilson is justified in thinking along these lines. Peter lives in a world where he is surrounded by newness. New information. New inventions. New problems. And he gives evidence that he is a boy who can think creatively. He does not look to other people for answers to problems that are his. He figures out fresh answers for himself, answers that provide better ways of dealing with the newness in his world. Without this creative ability, he would remain at the mercy of all that is going on around him, finding his life lived for him.

Considering Output and Intake in Creative Communication

Mrs. Wilson's thoughts return to the concerns of the moment, and she ponders the children's responses to Peter's new idea. Here she has both output and intake to consider. For it is not only Peter's creative product that matters. There is also the ability of the children to take in something that is new. There is Larry's open curiosity, Phyllis' ability to see the new idea for what it is, Charlie's way for playing around with the idea, for visualizing how it would work, for improving the idea with his own inventive thinking. And then there is Stanley's response to consider.

This is not the first time Stanley has turned down new ideas. Such behavior is quite characteristic of Stanley. It isn't that Stanley doesn't use his mind. He has intelligence but he uses it in certain defined ways when he responds to other people's ideas. He seems to have learned to use his mind to figure out why things *can't* work, why new ideas don't make sense. As he learns new skills in school, he uses them to protect a closed-in world. In the case of Peter's idea, Stanley quickly used arithmetic to tell himself that the idea could not work. He used language skills to pass this information along to the others in the group.

Planning a Daily Schedule To Foster Creativity

In planning her daily schedule, Mrs. Wilson has deliberately allowed for creativity, both her own and that of the children. The early morning work period is an example. All of the facilities of the classroom are available to the children. As each child comes to school he is free to go to work on something that matters to him. He may work alone or with one or more classmates. He may work on something new or something that has absorbed him for several days. During such a work period the children use paint, clay, science equipment, building materials, books, paper, pencils, tape recorders, and projectors. They sketch, build, experiment, read, and work with numbers. And they talk with one another and with Mrs. Wilson, sharing their quests and their discoveries.

Helping Children Think Creatively

Mrs. Wilson cannot plan her questions and answers ahead of time. How is she to know, for example, that Peter will draw a picture of his new idea? She can and does plan her general way for behaving during such work times. She knows that the children will be coming up with new ideas. They will be involving her in ideas and projects that are new to her. She will be asked to stretch her own mind to places where it has not gone before. She plans to take a responsible part in such ventures, whatever they may be. She expects the unexpected.

Not always is it one of the children who makes the suggestion that helps the rest to use their minds to explore the new, to go places where they have never been before. Just as often the suggestion comes from Mrs. Wilson. But right now the teacher is faced with the problem of sensing whether or not Peter needs help in order to keep *his* idea alive. Stanley has made a disparaging remark that may have been hurtful to Peter, who has invented and is sharing an idea. On the other hand, there may be no harm done because satisfaction from communicating a creative idea has come to Peter in the response of a single other person, Charlie. In fact, both of these boys may be receiving the satisfaction of thinking creatively in their two-way communication about Peter's invention. Again, it sometimes happens that communication with a specific person is not what matters at all. To be able to use symbols (in Peter's case, graphic representation) to get the idea down, to express the idea so that it is there for others to see and understand is enough to bring satisfaction.

It isn't only Peter whom Mrs. Wilson must consider in her present thinking. The other children have responded and are thus involved in this particular creative situation. What happens when sensitive children help creative ideas emerge, only to see them dropped by the wayside? How much better for children to see and help creative ideas take root in their own living!

Nor is it only the *now* which Mrs. Wilson must consider. In her eagerness to help the children keep this creative moment alive, she must use special care. When ideas are left by the wayside because of disparagement or neglect, the effect can be harmful. However, very often in creative endeavor an idea is dropped from conscious consideration for other reasons. Then at a later date it reappears —with evidence of interim working, evidence that the idea was not lost at all. For creative ideas are as alive as the people who nurture them. They are born and they grow like other living things. People who would enjoy creativity must learn to look to and respect the timing of the idea that is growing, must learn to respect and consider important factors in the environment into which the creative idea has come.

In the case of Peter's particular invention, Mrs. Wilson knows that she cannot help the children turn the idea into a practical reality in their own community. Not right away, anyway. Desirable as it might be to have this orderly use of space for walking and riding, the people responsible for community planning do not have this kind of project on their agenda. Still Mrs. Wilson knows that it is not a waste of time for children to think as Peter, Larry, Phyllis, Charlie, and the others are thinking right now. These children live in a world that is being shaped in important ways by technology. As citizens of that world, they cannot sit idly by, doing nothing about the problems created by inventions such as bicycles and cars. They must begin early to accustom themselves to being actively involved in doing something about the problems that touch themselves and other people. And, whenever possible, the something that they do must be creative in nature, for the habits of action encouraged by this kind of creating stand a good chance of becoming part of a person's characteristic way of responding.

With regard to Peter's invention, there will be ways to enhance communication of this idea—ways that will grow naturally as the

14

children and their teacher behave creatively. Perhaps, also, other children will want to paint or draw or dramatize their ideas for improving the world. It may be that even Stanley will want to use his imagination to open up his frequently closed-in world. Perhaps Peter will reflect on the problem he has seen and draw other ways to solve it. Or perhaps he will want to make a model of the idea he has already drawn. And of course there is always the possibility that Peter will simply hang his drawing in an appropriate spot on the bulletin board where it will serve as an especially warm reminder, not only to himself but to other children, of one more instance when creativity flowed among them and gave special significance to living.

CREATIVITY IN HUMAN AFFAIRS

When and where and how do people learn to live creatively? Under what conditions do children learn to think new thoughts? make new products? take in the creative thoughts of others? What is so significant about creativity? Why is it so important in human affairs?

It is not a whim, but rather, a deep concern that causes creativity to be placed in a key spot on the human agenda. The human situation in and of itself demands creativity. Consider the conditions into which all are born. An individual comes unfinished into a world that is unfinished and, to each, new. He grows, and so does his world. He is surrounded with the products of thinking and doing as well as with growth and movement and change. He is born with an urge, and also a need, to take an active part in what is going on within and around him.

Exploring and Creating Newness

A child does not wait until he is old enough to attend school to begin his creative adventures. Even a very young child has ways of exploring what is new, of giving meaning to what he finds, and of creating newness on his own. Young Jackie is an example. He has just learned to toddle. Daily he can be seen on the sidewalk in front of his two-family house exploring and changing the world in which he lives. Right now it is the garbage can that claims his attention. Big and shiny and new it stands in the sunshine beside the driveway that separates Jackie's house from that of his neighbors. Jackie likes what he sees. With arms outstretched he moves toward the big shining object, talking happily in his own special language as he goes. He looks—and smiles. He touches—and laughs. Over and over again he touches, laughing all the while. By now a new idea has come. Instead of touching with his fingers he uses his whole hand, and a new sound fills the world. It is no longer the same world that Jackie began to explore just a few moments ago. Now the world has a ringing sound that Jackie has managed to make on the wonderful object he has discovered.

This is a hard moment for Jackie's mother. She has watched his exploration, aware of his personal delight in his discovering and inventing. But garbage cans are not toys for toddlers. Jackie must be told *no*. He must learn that certain objects in the world are not to be explored by newcomers in search of meaning. This mother is sensitive to the effect of *no* in this situation. She wants to help Jackie see that *no* applies only to the garbage can. She does not want him to learn that whole areas of living are closed to exploration, or that there are taboos against exploration itself. She also wants to keep him from attaching bad feelings to his successful and obviously enjoyable experience with creating rhythmic sound. Gently she takes him by the hand and persuades him to move along with her.

Using Old Meanings

Luckily this is not Jackie's first experience with successful exploring and inventing. Already he has learned that people create beauty and meaning in the world where he lives. Of course he cannot express this learning in words. But in his short lifetime Jackie has learned that there are objects in the world for him to explore. And since his mother values creativity, Jackie is going to have, in the near future, several experiences in exploring and creating sound. Already his mother is thinking of the pleasant tinkle of small bells that she can sew to a narrow strip of canvas, and the marvelous boom of a drum she can provide. She can even give him certain kitchen pots and pans to bang together.

Creating New Meanings

But why is this so important? What if Jackie's mother did not behave in this way? Supposing she had been horrified at the sight of Jackie touching the garbage can. Many mothers would have been. And they would have passed their feelings on to their children as they angrily snatched them away—scolding, perhaps spanking. Nor would this be an isolated incident for many children and adults. Many children have daily experiences in being stopped— in attaching bad feelings to their natural urge to find out and try out and make new. They are *told* what things are and what they are not. These children are denied the wonderful and basic human experience of exploring objects with an open mind, a mind that sincerely and rigorously wonders.

A wondering mind is open to the message that the object, be it a person, place, or thing, has to convey about itself. Such a mind will reach toward the object with all powers of sensitive response— seeing, hearing, tasting, smelling, touching. Such a mind will create meaning in encounter with the object. Such a mind will take in new information—information that takes its place with what is already known, thus grounding a particular person's living in reality.

Jackie's learning is not narrowly related to his experience with the garbage can. Neither is it specifically related to the making of some sort of artist. This kind of learning is related to the making of a human being—and the making of a human world. It is the kind of learning that is needed by Jackie and other individuals since they will continually encounter newness and must take personal responsibility for integrating this newness with what they already know. It is a kind of learning that yields sensitive ways for exploring people and places and things.

Encountering Old and New

What does it mean to be alive, to be capable of sensitive response? Human aliveness assumes a kind of reaching out toward the world. Reach out ... pause ... make contact ... pause ... create meaning. This is the human rhythm, a rhythm that is repeated as regularly as breathing. And somewhere within that rhythm there occurs the all-important struggle between the new and what is already known.

Mr. Bennett awakens in the morning ready to respond to his world. Bright sunshine pours in through the window. Mr. Bennett sees this sunshine and immediately brings meaning to the situation —meaning that has been formed in his past experiences with sunshine. The sound of chirping birds also comes in the window. This, too, has meaning.

As Mr. Bennett gets out of bed he hears other sounds coming

from downstairs and he pauses. His two children are talking with their mother. "Probably telling her what they plan to do in school," he thinks. Again, his human equipment makes it easy for him to "know" what the sounds mean. They mean what similar early morning sounds have meant on previous occasions. But suppose there is other meaning in the sounds. His son may be explaining that he is not going to school today because he is afraid of the test in spelling. His daughter may be saying that she is staying home because of a cold. All sorts of things may be going on in the kitchen below. To be in accurate touch with his world, Mr. Bennett must have his mind open to other possibilities. He must pause longer and realize that he cannot be certain of what the sounds mean until he goes downstairs where he can get more information.

Maintaining Awareness of the Unknown

To do this further exploring, Mr. Bennett will have to reckon with the unknown. He will have to let his past experience with downstairs sounds be only partially influential when he encounters today's new sounds. He will have to give attention to signs of the unfamiliar as well as to signs of that which is known to him.

Mr. Bennett is not the only one who reaches out toward the world in the morning. Everywhere, awakening people are reaching out to another day. If they have been fortunate in their life's experiences, they hear more than the familiar practical message in the sounds about them. If they hear rain, they hear it not merely as something that will water the crops or require rubbers or tie up traffic. It is true that rain does water crops, require rubbers, and tie up traffic. But how much more there is in the message of the rain! For people who have learned to respond to their own inner want for sensory contact with the world, what glorious moments can come with the early morning rain—or sun, or wind, or any of the sights and sounds and smells and relationships of the new day.

What message does a sunset have for a person with inquiring eyes? What meaning is there in a towering building? a spider's web? a bit of prose? an absorbed child? And what does it mean when two people—or two nations—encounter each other? What do their eyes and ears take in? What awareness have they of newness? of significance?

PEGGY BROGAN

REACHING OUT TOWARD THE DAY:
A TEACHER

When Mrs. Wilson awakens and reaches out toward the day, she thinks about the children with whom she will be spending it. At first her mind plays lazily and happily with the various patterns the children make in their work and play—Leo and Mike moving toward one another as they have been lately; Peter and Charlie exploring Peter's invention; Becky and Patsy painting on a common piece of paper, with Becky beginning on the left, Patsy on the right; Ben lost (and in a very real sense found!) in his new delight in working with clay. Mrs. Wilson thinks, too, of the game the children have invented, "Jets in the Universe"—the lovely game where countless jet planes and planets are played out in dance. Planes spin and spin around a given planet simply for the joy of spinning; a planet spins and spins around itself, apparently for the same kind of joy.

The teacher's mind moves on to exciting language work times when the children come to know their power as human beings in beginning to create with words. Then Mrs. Wilson begins to wonder. What new designs will begin to take shape in the day that is just beginning? What patterns will be formed by personal and interpersonal inquiry? What beauty lies in wait? What new information will be organized within the day's interaction? When will the teacher be an interested onlooker and when a participant?

By now Mrs. Wilson is up and moving. There is work to be done, work that matters. She thinks fleetingly of the world of so many current science fiction writings—a new and imaginative world where, disappointingly, even in the faraway future people are behaving in destructive patterns. A world where men in the most exciting space vehicles fail to capitalize on new potentialities, finding nothing better to do than to use up their energy fleeing from one another, playing outmoded games of cops and robbers. But that is not the world of Mrs. Wilson. Not on this new day that is just beginning. Here is a world where people *do* find better ways to pattern their meanings and movement, a world where human nature is invited and helped to expand into new life-fostering possibilities.

Mrs. Wilson does not begin her day as she does simply because she is a teacher. Powerful inducements of many kinds persuade teachers to interact in ways that are quite different from this teacher's behavior. Some teachers' manuals discourage teachers from wondering about and looking forward to the newness in each of their pupils. Many of these manuals tell teachers exactly what to look for, and, in many instances, exactly what to say to the inquiring human beings with whom they interact in school. For example, teachers are conditioned *away from* the significant new words that come into the lives of growing children. Instead, they are given lists of supposedly "new" words to teach—words selected by authors far from the specific encounters of a teacher's specific class. Grouping procedures also put blinders on teachers' eyes— blinders that cause them to shut out human *uniqueness* as they picture children in "high," "middle," and "low" groups. Other pressures work in the same direction. Public demands would have teachers look at children as "scientists" in international competition, as "gifted" and therefore destined to follow certain prescribed courses of study, as "slow" and therefore condemned to follow other predetermined learning rituals. No, to be a teacher does not necessarily mean that one is encouraged to reach out toward living as Mrs. Wilson does.

Mrs. Wilson's behavior expresses her deliberate and basic commitment to living. She is not a person to be swept along by any current that happens to move in her direction. Alone and with others, she creates useful currents as she goes. She recognizes that in living, just as in teaching, there are pressures tending to mold people into passive, unthinking roles. Mrs. Wilson recognizes that in human nature itself there are potentialities for these humanly unrewarding roles just as there are potentialities for creative living. She recognizes that each person determines his life pattern in the choices that he makes. And, whenever possible, Mrs. Wilson chooses firsthand encounters as a basis for creating her important meanings.

In order to fulfill their wants, human beings have to *care about the meanings they create.* When the invitation comes, as it always does, to settle for meanings that are old and familiar and second hand, the individual has to *want* to respond also to the everpresent invitation to explore for his own new meanings. He will not forsake what is known but will integrate it with what he has freshly discovered. That is the function of creativity in living. It is part of the human birthright—something to know and want and value, something to add enjoyment and vitality to everyday encounters in the adventure that is living.

ABOUT THE AUTHOR ... Arthur W. Foshay has many interests—music and talk, people and writing, art and comparative education, research and children. He began his career in education as a teacher and elementary school principal in California.

Since coming east, Mr. Foshay has concentrated increasingly on curriculum research. With Kenneth Wann, he conducted and reported on action research in the Springfield, Missouri, public schools (Children's Social Values, published by the Bureau of Publications, Teachers College, Columbia University, 1954). Later he headed the Bureau of Educational Research at the Ohio State University. Mr. Foshay has served as executive officer of the Horace Mann–Lincoln Institute of School Experimentation at Teachers College, Columbia University.

2 THE CREATIVE PROCESS DESCRIBED *

As teachers, we become concerned with creativeness as we examine the products of the child's work in school. It is obvious that most children, most of the time, simply imitate what others have done. Of itself, this is neither good nor bad. Imitation has served the children well before they came to school. The basic lessons of infancy are learned through imitation: speech, "manners," some aspects of locomotion, much play. We continue to ask children to imitate in school, because we teach in the main by precept and example ("this is the way you do it"). It should not be surprising, therefore, that when we ask that children be imaginative, as in painting or sculpture, they respond by being imitative. Any organism, confronted with a new situation, responds to it by running through its existing repertoire of behaviors. Children respond to a new demand in a known way—imitation.

What a child produces is the result of the process he uses— his mode of attack, or style, which is determined by his vision of the product. Presumably, the same terms should characterize both the style and its product. An imitative product would probably come from an imitative intent and an imitative process. A creative product would come from a creative intent and process. The child who imitates has set for himself a goal like "let's see whether I can

* Note: The author wishes to express gratitude to Frank G. Jennings for his assistance in developing this chapter.

do it, too." The child who creates has set for himself a goal like "let's see what I can make of this."

One generalization follows: that product and process are interlocked in some way; that it would be unproductive to think of one apart from the other. It would be unproductive, for example, for a teacher to attempt to foster a creative process without attending to the amount and the quality of the product. The product must be taken to be a part of the process—a sort of summary of it. Moreover, to set standards for the product without reference to the process would in all likelihood lead to mere imitation. For, as we have observed, it is the process that is imitative or creative. Rollo May has insisted that creator and creative act are inseparable: ". . . we cannot speak of a 'creative person'; we can only speak of a creative act." [1] May's "act," of course, is a totality, a whole process, which includes the product. Let us consider what takes place during the creative process. [2]

THE CREATIVE PROCESS

To discover the nature of the creative process, we must examine the way those considered creative go about their work. This has been done repeatedly, through biography and autobiography. [3] More recently, it has been done through the close examination of diaries, correspondence, and rough drafts of work that later was completed (as, for example, in the Garrod edition of Keats' notebooks, in which one can almost observe masterpieces in the act of being created). New research techniques permit such observa-

[1] Rollo May, "The Nature of Creativity," in *Creativity and Its Cultivation,* ed. Harold H. Anderson (New York: Harper & Brothers, 1959), pp. 65–66.

[2] For the formulation of the creative process around the concepts of openness, focus, discipline, and closure, I am indebted to Ross L. Mooney of The Ohio State University. However, he should not be held responsible for my development of this formulation. For a statement of Mooney's view, see his "Groundwork for Creative Research," in *The Self,* ed. Clark Moustakas (New York: Harper & Brothers, 1956), pp. 261–270.

[3] There appears to be a generally "European" view of this kind of research, and a generally "American" view. The "European" view is that great creative geniuses are beings apart from the rest of us, and the purpose of research on creativity, following this assumption, is to permit us better to appreciate these great men. The "American" view, which I shall take here, is that great men and lesser men differ only in degree. We study great men in order to detect hints of their attributes within ourselves. We know Da Vinci, and ourselves, better when we recognize something of Da Vinci in ourselves.

tion to be carried out on students of various ages, including little children and graduate students. Such study has been made urgent by the demand for creative people in every branch of human effort. Engineers complain, for example, that the engineering schools produce, in the main, mere draftsmen. "The basic criticism is that most of these men are not capable of original creation and design." [4] What is needed, to respond to such charges, is a way of thinking about the creative process that makes it possible to recognize and account for creative behavior as it occurs.

There are four major aspects of the process which, taken together, seem to account for creativity: openness to one's own experiencing, focusing of one's experiencing, the discipline of one's actions to work out the focus, and closure—bringing the work to an end.

OPENNESS

The first requirement for creativity is that one deliberately open one's self to new experience. The first problem is that of letting in the data—all the data—so that creative forms may be developed. What is required is that one learn to take an open, unstructured look at the data available. The landscape artist looks at his landscape not as a scene but as an undifferentiated mass of colors and shapes. The scientist seeks first simply to describe what is present. The teacher, studying a child, first observes. Openness involves suspension of judgment, since to judge is to structure. One must suspend habitual judgments, habitual interpretations, in order to be open to experience.

To take an unstructured look at things, a person must have a kind of inner peace. Carl Rogers describes openness in these personal terms: "This is the opposite of psychological defensiveness, when to protect the organization of the self certain experiences are prevented from coming into awareness except in distorted fashion. In a person who is open to experience, each stimulus is freely relayed through the nervous system, without being distorted by any process of defensiveness. Whether the stimulus originates in the environment, in the impact of form, color, or sound on the sensory

4 Harold F. Clark, "Teachers' Salaries and the Cost of Living," *School Executive,* 79, No. 1 (September 1959), p. 22.

nerves, or whether it originates in the viscera, or as a memory trace in the central nervous system, it is available to awareness." [5]

Rogers might have said "definition" where he said "defensiveness," for the two function equally to block openness. Creative behavior involves new definitions of the commonplace. Old definitions, old stereotypes, get in the way. They cause one to do no more than to rediscover what one already has defined.

Being open is being able to involve all of one's self with all that is not one's self, but within one's view. It requires a lowering of the usual defenses and an abandoning, for the time, of the usual definitions. Is it a surprise that such openness is rare? To abandon definitions and to lower defenses is to expose one's self to threat. What is allowed to come in may become disorganizing, even destructive to the self.

This "threat" is recognized by creative people. To cope with it, they sometimes engage in preparatory rituals: they may arrange their materials elaborately, or dress in a certain way, or sing. The purpose of such behavior is to become sufficiently disengaged from run-of-the-mill reality that openness, and thus new perceptions, becomes possible.

Two other notions, by Guilford and Pepinsky, may be helpful here. Guilford considers creative thinking to be a subclass of thinking in general, and makes a distinction between "convergent" and "divergent" productive thinking.[6] His "convergent" thinking is that which is directed toward a single correct answer, as in the mathematical problems most familiar to nonmathematicians. Divergent thinking, on the other hand, "involves searching around or changing direction. It does not necessarily mean flying in the face of convention, but it frequently leads to unconventional results. . . . It can be said that creative people are more likely to excel in the divergent-thinking abilities."

Next to Guilford's two ideas, let us place two others, offered by Pepinsky: the percept-bound and the concept-bound. Pepinsky describes a student in the School of Fine and Applied Arts at The

5 Carl Rogers, "Toward a Theory of Creativity," in *Creativity and Its Cultivation*, ed. Harold H. Anderson (New York: Harper & Brothers, 1959), p. 75.

6 J. P. Guilford, "Can Creativity Be Developed?" An address prepared for presentation to the Pacific Arts Association, April 1, 1958 (mimeographed). Guilford has discussed the concept of divergent thinking in a number of places, but his discussion of it here is more understandable to the nonpsychologist than are his other discussions.

Ohio State University.[7] "The student cooperated in a psychological evaluation that included the Rorschach and the Wechsler-Bellevue. . . . In addition, she was observed in a studio course. . . . With striking consistency, she responded to each (Rorschach) blot by picking out salient details in it. She used these as a basis for organizing the entire blot, drawing often on remote instances in her experience to yield a concrete and vivid image . . . she did not hesitate to force particular details in the blot to conform to her image." The clinicians in the group, without reference to the observations of her art work, made the following predictions among others:

> That, once having established the image, she would have difficulty in modifying her perception, if circumstances called for a change.

> That she would have difficulty in adapting to other situations (e.g., interpersonal) that demanded a change in "plan."

The point here is that this student approached the ink blots determined to make a structure out of them, and proceeded to do so at once. The openness we have been describing was not present. That is why she "did not hesitate to force particular details in the blot to conform to her image." Pepinsky then continues with his argument: "[A person] may be required to follow one of two lines of thinking. (a) He may be required to test his theory against his experience, and to revise the theory to conform with experience that the theory does not account for. (b) He may be constructed so that he must test his experiences against his theory, and . . . reject those experiences that do not fit the theory." [8] The first kind of thinking is called "percept-bound," the second "concept-bound." According to this notion, the tendencies toward being concept-bound that exist within us would inhibit our ability to be open to unusual perceptions in what we saw, and thus would reduce our ability to be creative. Being percept-bound, on the other hand, would imply the same "openness to experience" we have been discussing here. That is, a person would have to "let

[7] Harold B. Pepinsky, "Cogito, ergo. . ." *Journal of Counseling Psychology,* 2, No. 4 (1955), pp. 285–289.
[8] *Loc. cit.*

it all in" in an unstructured way before he tried to structure it or to theorize about how it was to be interpreted.

This "letting it all in" is implied in yet other concepts. One of these is "tolerance of ambiguity," the ability to suspend one's need for order and certainty. Another, described by Hilgard, is the ability to "unfreeze" one's perceptions—the opposite of "functional fixation" (a habitual way of regarding things), or a rigidity of interpretation of events.[9]

Perhaps enough has been said to illustrate the way in which the category openness fits the speculations of a number of thoughtful people. It should be observed that a great deal of what is said about creativity has to do with openness. Even Osborn's "brainstorming" can best be understood as an attempt to give social sanction to openness.[10]

Being open requires that one arrange one's self so that much more detail than usual can be perceived. A person can seek the habit of openness deliberately; or he can be taught by another to be open. What is necessary is that one seek raw, unmediated experience, confident that he can make something of it. One must be able to assume that raw experience has aesthetic, or intellectual, or spiritual possibilities; that it has potential form, surface, and order. Someone once asked an unlettered sculptor how it was that he took a piece of wood and made such beautiful horses. "It's easy," said the artist, "I just cut away what ain't 'hoss.'"

Of course, merely being open is not enough. If we were merely to *take in*, there would be no product, no creation. Like dilettantes, we would seek experience, but we would take no responsibility for making something of it. There is a rather widespread tendency among educators as well as others to act as if openness were enough. The responsibility of anyone who attempts to be creative is to create and to expose his product to some kind of public examination. No product, no complete process.

Implications for Teaching

Children, to be creative, must be permitted to risk themselves. It follows from our comments about defensiveness and definition that

9 Ernest Hilgard, "Creativity and Problem-Solving," in *Creativity and Its Cultivation,* ed. Harold H. Anderson (New York: Harper & Brothers, 1959), p. 168ff.

10 Alex F. Osborn, *Applied Imagination: Principles and Procedures of Creative Thinking* (New York: Charles Scribner's Sons, 1957), pp. 227–258.

a teacher must be supportive enough in class so that children will, at the very least, not have to deal with the teacher's uncertainties while they try to cope with their own. Children, to be creative, have to act as if they could handle themselves in such a way as to be open to their experience. They have to act as if solutions could be achieved; as if the "hoss" could be made.

This sort of behavior is no longer common by the time a child reaches school. Much has happened, by then, to teach him that the safe course is the best course, and that he is safest when he imitates, and most exposed to danger when he tries things on his own. To say the least, the teacher must try to provide conditions that are conducive to risk-taking. There is more, however; there is a discipline to such risk-taking. Children have to be taught to open their minds and keep them open, to survey many possibilities before they act.

Examples abound of teachers doing this, though they might use terms other than "openness" and "creative process" to describe what they do. One way to start the creative process is simply to ask that children separate question-raising from answer-giving. Here is an example, drawn from a second grade in Ann Arbor: [11]

> TEACHER: "Could you offer some questions we might find answers for in our study? Later on, we will call on you to help us out with the answers, but now what are some of the things you think we ought to know?. . ."
>
> MARGO: "My name is Margo, and I wanted to know how the moon got to be so high. . ."
>
> KAREN: "I know the answer to that."
>
> TEACHER: "Perhaps we ought to think of other questions now. We'll think of the answers as we talk about the different things."

For an experienced teacher, such an exchange is commonplace. Something like it takes place whenever a class is asked to explore possibilities: to be open to a number of questions before they settle on one. From the point of view of openness, this kind of interchange has a crucial place, for it is at this point that the children are

[11] From the 1959 Yearbook of the Association for Supervision & Curriculum Development, *Learning and the Teacher* (Washington, D. C.: National Education Association, 1959), pp. 11–12. This example is slightly edited by the present writer to make apparent the teacher's attempt to promote open examination of possibilities.

ARTHUR W. FOSHAY

shown how to keep their minds open to a number of possibilities long enough to let them in. The same sort of thing happens, of course, in art. It can happen in the writing of prose, or of drama, or in the making of a dance. It can happen in preparing reports to the class or the teacher, or in organizing an excursion. It can happen, that is, at every point in school where the teacher and the children can view a universe of events as open possibilities. Wherever the teacher's intent is that children compose their own response, it is possible to teach openness. It can happen even in reading, as the French have known for a long time. Their basic device, the *explication de texte*, requires first that the text of a masterpiece be placed in its proper context (they call it *location*), then that it be examined very closely for choice of words, images, style, and content. Inference (what we might call interpretation) comes only after prolonged and disciplined openness to what the text is, in itself—its "is-ness." [12] The French are not noted for approaching experience openly; they are self-critical of their *apriorisme*. The *explication*, however, whatever the abuses it is subject to in the hands of an unimaginative teacher, must be viewed as an orderly, disciplined approach to openness. One must first let the text in; then one may draw inferences from it and speculate about its meaning.

FOCUS

Having let in the reality, one must compose it. "Openness" and "focus" are both parts of the creative process, but it would be a mistake to view them as "steps" or "phases." They are not that clearly sequential. Since openness may bring on a feeling of being overwhelmed, as by an overbright light, one mediates, accommodates, adjusts one's self at once—even as the eye does to light.

The movement from openness to focus may be thought of as an alternation in which one lets in some data, tries a structure on them, lets in more data to test the structure, then more, and more still. This alternation may go on for some time. Probably, for most of

[12] See Raymond Cortat, *L'Explication de Texte* (Paris: Editions Bourrelier, 1957), especially pp. 57–70, which may be translated and abstracted as follows: "In placing a text in its context and studying its composition, we come to its heart. Placing the text in its context gives us a panoramic view of the passage as a whole . . . study of its composition permits us to discover the paths into it which, each ramified in turn, already lead us to a mapping out of the text. Now it is up to us to push our exploration forward . . . to penetrate still further the secrets and charms of the underbrush. . ."

us, the period of "openness" is brief, fragmented, and recurrent. In any case, the alternation between openness and focus goes on, with successively briefer periods of openness and longer periods of focus, until a satisfying focus has been achieved.

A focus is a proximate test of the possible meaning of some data. My way of managing my openness is my focus. James Joyce closes *The Portrait of the Artist as a Young Man* with a peroration that catches both the spirit and the process of moving from openness to focus: "Welcome, O Life! I go to encounter for the millionth time the reality of experience and to forge in the smithy of my soul the uncreated conscience of my race."

Optically, things are in focus when they are differentiated; outlines are clear; background and foreground are clearly distinguishable. A creative attempt to focus implies a deliberate attempt thus to refine the data that have been let in. The attempt may be made consciously or impulsively, intuitively or by insight. It is not likely to be done by obeying habit or consulting authority, on the one hand—or by a purely unconscious response on the other, since it does require deliberate control. What one seeks to do is to bring what is unconscious to the level of consciousness, where it may be managed.

It is well to remember that focus is an internal subjective affair, since what is really focused is one's own experience. The astronomer's hypothesis (his focus) about a heavenly body has no effect on the heavenly body, but it has a considerable effect on the astronomer. A man is what he has made of his experience. When we relate ourselves to what is external to us in the manner we have been describing here, what we really create is a portion of ourselves. The product is truly self-expressive (that abused term!) but it is also evidence of self-generation. In anticipating a product through giving focus to raw experience, we create our own image. "For a moment in one aspect, for a lifetime in many, experience may achieve lucidity and vividness, intensity and depth. To effect such an intensification and clarification of experience is the province of art. . . . Art is the name for that whole process of intelligence by which life, understanding its own conditions, turns them to the most interesting or exquisite account. Any art, properly important, would be, as Aristotle pointed out, politics. Its theme would be the whole of experience; its materials and its theater the whole of life. . . . It is for purely accidental reasons that the fine arts have been singled out to be almost identical with Art." [13]

Focuses are the innumerable ways of ordering experience. They include the entire repertoire of human response, from verbal-syllogistic to pure organic response. They represent our ways of dealing with the wholeness of things.

A child has many experiences with such wholeness. You see him entranced with an ant colony, or lying face down, "hanging on" to the spinning earth, with arms and legs spread wide to get a better grip. Consider, as focus, the address of Tommy Sellender, Fourth Grader:

> Thomas Willard Sellender, Jr.
>   31 Oak Street
>   Elmville
>   Johnson County
>   Wisconsin
>   United States of America
>   North America
>   Western Hemisphere
>   World
>   Solar System
>   Milky Way
>   Universe
>   Under the Hand of God

To focus what is otherwise undifferentiated is to put it in order. This is often done by seeking similarity between the new data and what is already known: to seek analogy, a metaphor, "a base in theory," and the like. Tommy used yet another approach to comprehending the All—location. By locating Tommy, he hoped (inarticulately) to locate the universe, and even God. This he did by seeking an order consisting of successively larger contexts, each in relationship with all the others, and all of them in relationship with himself. The relationship between a datum, like Tommy, and its context may be dynamic, involving some kind of tension; it may be trite, hackneyed, or inappropriate (i.e., untrue to the *proprium*—the self).

Ordering involves giving form, whether the form is represented by Tommy's categories or an artist's composition. A focus, once achieved, is a structure, whether the structure appears as a

13 Irwin Edman, *Arts and the Man* (New York: Mentor Books, 1949), p. 10.

conceptualization, an idea or a theory, a composition or a categorization.

To say these things is to say something about learning, for learning is often considered as a process of differentiation. The undifferentiated response of an infant is like the naïve response of anyone confronted with a new, vast, overwhelming, tremendously detailed experience. A number of people, sightless since birth, have received sight through surgery. These people report that what they see when they first open their eyes is a swirling mass of light with no apparent meaning. They ordinarily retreat from the experience, returning to the known world of touch, smell, taste, and sound. Why, after all, learn that a certain visual pattern is to be called "square" when one can detect this immediately by feeling for the corners? Only when they find ways of making order out of the chaos of light can these people make use of their sight.

To be creative, we have said, means to make form out of what is formless. He who makes the form is the creative one. Education for creativity, therefore, must equip learners to make forms, both by acquainting them with existing forms (thus making analogies available) and by giving them opportunity, encouragement, and practice in the actual making.

It is worth noting that very little has been written on focus directly, though considerable attention has been given to one aspect of it—hypothesizing. Even hypothesizing, however, has been treated in too narrow a fashion for our purposes here. What is required of us teachers is that we develop a clear notion of the process that leads to an appropriate focus. It is not enough to know the properties of a good hypothesis. An hypothesis is usually taken to be an early act in the drama of inquiry, preceded by an analysis, and followed by a test. There is a strong resemblance between the method of inquiry so described and the creative process as we describe it here.

Methods of inquiry may be applied to all kinds of fields, including the subjects usually taught in schools. Some have thought such inquiry inimical to the creative process, for they have seen it as a search for the logic of a subject, a logic which then was used to determine learning sequences without the awareness of the student. A search for the logic of the subject in which students participate intelligently can be most creative. The creative possibilities of a subject are lost, and its logic destroyed, when schools substitute formalism for forming, when the learner is presented with pre-analyzed subjects as if the analysis *were* the subject, when the logic of the subject is to be taken as something given, not something to be worked out by the student.

Let us consider an example. History is one of the most intriguing of all the disciplines, both because of its scope and because of the phenomena it treats. What is more exciting than the attempt to account for the great events of the world of men? What could be more important than the attempt to clarify antecedent and consequence in the past, to gain perspective on the present and the future? This is what history does, as a discipline, but it is not what we have usually tried to do in school. Instead, we have learned a great deal of information *about* history, and (it may be asserted) *about* other important fields of knowledge, too. The alternative has always been present, but seldom acted upon. We could have been learning how an historian creates history, how a mathematician creates mathematics, how a scientist creates science. Instead, we have taught facts and ready-made interpretations in the name of history, computational schemes in the name of mathematics, prosody for poetry, grammar for writing, and so on. Our academic tradition does not favor teaching children to be open to experience, then to focus it. Even our intelligence tests fail to take this crucial ability into account, as Calvin Taylor has pointed out.[14] Other studies by Torrance and Getzels report that the abilities related to creativity tend to be unrelated to or to have only a low relationship with the types of items entering into our current tests of intelligence.[15] If high IQ is used to locate high talent, only thirty per cent of those with high creative ability (as measured on a test devised for the purpose) will be found. There are more people by far, according to these studies, who have relatively high "crea-

[14] Calvin Taylor, "A Tentative Description of the Creative Individual" (dittoed, University of Utah, November 14, 1959). Note the following: "A sizeable number of scientists on the job were interviewed by Allen, after which he asked them to arrange 28 dimensions of the mind relevant to success on the job in physical science in rank order according to their judged importance on the job... About five or six of these characteristics have been included in traditional tests of intelligence. All but one of these traditional intelligence factors ranked below 20th in the list."

[15] E. P. Torrance, "Explorations in Creative Thinking in the Early School Years: A Progress Report," and J. W. Getzels and P. W. Jackson, "The Highly Intelligent and the Highly Creative Adolescent: A Summary of Some Research Findings," in *The Third University of Utah Research Conference on the Identification of Creative Scientific Talent,* ed. Calvin W. Taylor (Salt Lake City: University of Utah Press, 1959).

tivity" scores and relatively low "intelligence" scores than there are people who are "high" in both ways.

Since our intelligence tests measure that which contributes to high achievement in schools, these studies indict not only intelligence tests, but also the schools as we ordinarily conduct them.

We have used certain terms as if they were equivalent to our term, focus. Let us review them, and see whether they suggest what is implied for the teaching of creative behavior. To focus is to differentiate, to impose a form on things. The focus may be the painter's composition of his painting, or the scientist's hypothesis. It may take the form of an analysis so that the independence or the interdependence of parts may be revealed. It may depend on thorough exploration, as in the French *explication de texte*, or disciplined scientific observation, as in the close examination of an object, or the close study of a child by a teacher. In any case, it is an attempt to grasp phenomena as if composition, or ordering, were possible. The focus is an early fruit of a transaction between a man and his environment, in which the man has first looked at the environment as if it were open and unstructured, and has similarly opened as much of himself as he dares; his focus, we have said, is his plan for continuing the transaction.

The focus proceeds by an alternation between openness and trial structure; and is achieved when one can anticipate the creative product to his satisfaction. One says to one's self, "If I take this focus, I am likely to produce this kind of product, and this kind of product would be satisfying." Acceptance of a focus involves a commitment to a definition of the outcome of one's work.

Implications for Teaching

We must confess, as teachers, that we have stopped far short of helping children to learn how to focus their own experiences. What we have done, historically, is to provide children with prefocused data in all kinds of fields. Now, information is necessary if children are to know something of the possible focuses that may be made. One does not achieve creativity out of simple ignorance. However, to supply information alone—the historical purpose of the school —is to do nothing about the development of creativity. Perhaps this is why school marks, IQ's, and college degrees tell so little about the creative abilities of people. What is required is that as teachers we give specific attention to the act of focusing experience. We do not know very much about how this can be done, but some of what we already do know may be useful for this kind of learning.

Focus involves ordering experience, we have said. When do we ask children to order their experience? We do it (or we can) when we ask them to give a book report, provided we ask them to report their *experience* of the book, not merely to prove that they have read it by reciting the names of the chief characters, the author, publisher, and so on. This latter widespread and meaningless practice invites fraud, in any case.

We ask children to give form to their experience when they use art media, too, unless we ask them only to copy. Since elementary school art is such an obvious case, I shall not elaborate upon it here, except to emphasize its importance, and to call attention to the fact that in most schools it is the only field in which we genuinely invite creative behavior.

We invite focusing of experience when we require a report of it, whether oral or written. The familiar social studies report is the typical example. Most children remember reports they have given quite vividly, just as most adults remember their term papers, chiefly because they had to organize and state them. Good, mediocre, or poor, they are personal creations.

There are very few examples from the other fields taught in school. There could be more, of course. In science, we could be asking children to account for phenomena, but so far this is only beginning to appear in the new proposals for elementary science. The same thing is true of the new mathematics programs. A generation ago, there was a brief excursion into music composition in the elementary schools—the "creative music" movement—but it was quickly overwhelmed by the demand that children learn to read music, to hear masterpieces, to perform under direction, not that they compose or freely interpret music. Yet it may be asserted that every school subject has such creative possibilities, since every subject is itself the result of creative endeavor. What is required is that we teach "sciencing," "mathematicizing," and so on, and that the information in these and the other fields be made available (taught) for the purpose of discovery, not merely for passive learning.

DISCIPLINE

When the focus has been achieved, production is begun and carried out in a disciplined way. The aspect of the work behavior of creative people that is most apparent to others is their discipline.

Having considered possibilities, the disciplined composer works for hours, even days, on end. The scientist cannot leave his laboratory; the painter perseveres; the inventor conducts hundreds of experiments; the writer shuts out his family.

The creative ones are aware of what we are calling "discipline" here; they consider it as adopting a way of working that is appropriate to the focus they have committed themselves to, and as a rejection of distraction. Distraction by others is not what bothers them most at this point, however; it is the distraction from within themselves—"inner noise"—that is most destructive. After he is committed to a focus and a disciplined way of working, the artist frequently must deal with the distracting notion that he should retreat and go back to reconsider his focus, or go all the way back to the beginning and start over. What he has to do is to work hard and unremittingly. Such work is not necessarily joyful; it may be exceedingly unpleasant. Artists of all kinds speak of it as if it were simply hard work—"the seat of the pants to the seat of the chair." The chief discipline the creative individual is aware of is self-discipline.

In the colloquial sense, "discipline" connotes inhibition, limitation, rigor, ordering, codifying, following the rules, being accountable, being responsible. It means all of these things to the creative person. To adopt a disciplined way of work involves accepting the focus as limiting (i.e., defining, in the literal sense) and as providing the means for ordering experience, thus as providing rules, or a code, so that the artist's work may render a responsible account of his focus. For nobody knows better than the artist that his work will be subjected to the examination of harsh critics—himself and others like himself. The product renders the focus into public space, where the pressure for conformity is very great. However, the artist's task is to remain true to the decision he has made (his focus), and thus to himself. He is answerable to himself first of all; hence his feeling of responsibility. The artist has to take himself with utter seriousness, as humanity-as-it-might-be. His commit-

ARTHUR W. FOSHAY

ment to the public is to disclose himself, through his product, as a human possibility.

We may consider disciplined work as a part of the creative process that mediates between the focus and the product, just as we might consider focus as mediating between raw experience and disciplined work. One works with an end in view—the product, which is to be judged as good in the degree that it conveys to the artist (as a representative of other people) the meaning the original transaction had for him.

Except for the fact that the actual working out of an adopted focus is the most obvious part of the creative process, we might not deal with discipline at this length. In a sense, all of the process is work, but the disciplined "working out" is the penultimate work, the climactic act in the drama. It is not so anxiety-laden as the earlier aspects of the creative process, nor is it usually subject to public censure or even public apathy. We live in a work-centered culture.[16] When the artist "stops dreaming and goes to work," the culture can award him respect. One is at peace when he is actually producing. Being at peace, he can work hard and long, for he has survived the self-doubt of the earlier parts of the process, and circumvented the tendency of the social group around him to impose its structures. If he can resist the temptation to retreat by going back and starting over, he has freed himself to work.

Implications for Teaching

What of the teacher's responsibility here? If one can assume a well-focused student, the teacher's responsibility when the student has "gone to work" is to keep out of the way except as tools are needed, and to see to it that the student is not interrupted by others. Ideally, children thus at work should be allowed to continue at their own pace until the work is completed. In practice, we violate this with bell schedules, irrelevant demands, or sheer pressure to "get on with it." As is true in the earlier aspects of the creative process, school as we conduct it does not favor the kind of unremitting work that a creative person must learn to carry on.

We do make some provisions, however, if only by accident. The

16 This has been extensively discussed recently. See, e.g., Hannah Arendt, *The Human Condition* (Chicago: University of Chicago Press, 1958). Lewis Mumford dealt with it earlier in *The Condition of Man* (New York: Harcourt, Brace and Company, Inc., 1944).

high school study hall is one example. Actually, study hall is an administrative convenience, the result of an accident in scheduling, not planned for the purpose of providing uninterrupted time for work. But a certain amount of uninterrupted work does go on in study halls. If we really believed unremitting work to be desirable as a part of the creative process, we would greatly increase our provision for independent, individual study. As things stand, the school requires of the student that he flit from one field of activity to another—in high school, every forty minutes or so—so that he can cover many subjects. Such scheduling amounts to an institutional conspiracy to prevent creative behavior. For most students, the genuine engagement with one's work that a creative focus requires is effectively ruled out of the school year. Even homework is cluttered with fragmented assignments so that long periods of work on a single topic are unusual or impossible for most serious students.

What has happened is that in school we have stereotyped "hard work" as imitation, memorizing, "doing assignments," preparing for tests, and the like. The kind of hard work that the creative person carries on—self-defined, self-imposed, unpredictable except in the terms of his focus—is not generally acceptable in school. As Torrance points out, ". . . it was found that the highly creative are considered less desirable as pupils, less well known by the teachers, less ambitious, and less studious and hardworking. [Torrance has already indicated that the highly creative children in his study achieved as much on the standardized achievement tests as the others did.] . . . My guess is that these highly creative children are learning while they appear to be 'playing around,' possibly through manipulative and/or exploratory activities which the teacher tries to prevent." [17]

CLOSURE

One of the most important aspects of the creative process is its end. One may ask, "How does an artist know when to stop?" Knowing when to stop is a great virtue, whether one is writing, making a speech, or conducting research. At some point one stops the work

17 E. P. Torrance, "Current Research on the Nature of Creative Talent" (unpublished manuscript, Minneapolis: Bureau of Educational Research, University of Minnesota, 1959).

and announces that the product—the aesthetic object—is finished. How is this achieved? There is nothing about a painting of itself that tells the artist that he is finished, that further tinkering will blur the effect. There is nothing about a research project that tells the researcher that he is finished; there is always one more question to be asked of the data, one more implication to be explored. Even in writing the report, there is the feeling that one more revision of the text would give it more shine, make it more creditable. When do you stop?

Creative people stop when their criteria are met. Being creative, however, their criteria are personal, not imitative. It is interesting that most of these criteria are aesthetic. It is easy to understand that the painter, or the novelist, uses criteria like symmetry, parsimony, elegance, harmony, or their opposites. It is perhaps more surprising to hear a physicist explain that his theory is right because "it's elegant."

Two things may certainly be said about the decision that the product is finished: the decision is arbitrary; it is personal. In order that such judgments be made, the creator must give himself permission, or have the courage, to make the judgment for himself, and to submit it for public examination. His judgment may be (a) the product is finished, (b) it is not worth finishing and should be destroyed, (c) it is not finished but this is all that the creator can do with it now. In any case, the judgment is his, and his alone, or else the product is not his.

Since creative behavior involves a heavy investment of self, from beginning to end, the act of closure may be regarded as an act of self-discovery. It may well be a prideful discovery in a legitimate sense. It may also be a discovery of one's limits, but in no denigrating way. It is good to go to one's limits, to exploit one's strength fully, to "go all out."

Implications for Teaching

What does the teacher do with respect to closure? For one thing, he must teach the learner that the judgment is his own. The child who asks the teacher whether his work is finished must be answered with "Are *you* satisfied?" or with some variant of the request that the child look in on himself. It takes courage to stop. Throughout the creative process there is a sense of risk, even of dread. Great courage is required all the way (except, as has been indicated, during the "working out" of the focus). The sources of this courage are to be found in the general stability of the creator, in his feeling of competence, and most especially his feeling that the public (the teacher in the case of the school child) will base its judgment on criteria that are relevant to the purpose he had in mind during the creative process.[18]

There are, of course, some exceptions to the generalization that the decision to stop is arbitrary. Some projects have built-in terminal points, yet are creative. In the classic evaluation scheme, the researcher decides in advance that he will be satisfied when a certain predeclared product has been achieved. If one wished to invent a device, he might predetermine the specifications to be achieved, and stop accordingly; the clockmaker will be satisfied if the clock keeps time within certain tolerances. Much more frequently, however, the point of closure is implied by the focus adopted but is not fixed by it. Probably, the more complex and novel the effort, the less fixed is the point of completion, and the more responsive it is to purely aesthetic criteria.

The creative process as we have described it here is a process intended to produce something—an object, an idea, a course of action. The process cannot rise above the transaction between self and environment which is its first aspect. It cannot rise above the daring of the person who undertakes such a transaction. We live in a society which seeks the fruits of creative effort, but often denies the validity of the creative process. The question is whether the school, which is a faithful mirror of that world, will provide what the creative process requires. In the current power struggle, as one sixth grader said, "If it won't put up a missile, you can't teach it." Novelty in the fundamental approach to teaching is frequently discouraged while, in the name of experimentation, the restrictive, inhibiting tradition of pedagogy is being reinforced— this at a time in our national history when it is apparent that creativity is required for our very survival.[19] Some hope is to be derived from the widespread interest in creativity and the creative process, of which the present book is an expression.

18 See James Thurber's *Here Lies Miss Groby* for a bitter, though humorous, account of Thurber's anger at a teacher who didn't accept Thurber's purpose in a school incident.
19 This problem is treated in an article by the author, entitled "What Is the Message?" which appeared in the *Saturday Review* for February 13, 1960.

ABOUT THE AUTHOR ... Evelyn Wenzel has found meaning in teaching throughout her career, and her interest in creativity dates back to her earliest work ("Creativity: An Inquiry," mimeographed doctoral dissertation, Teachers College, Columbia University, 1955). At that time the literature was only beginning to reflect the wide interest in creativity that is growing today. Miss Wenzel approached the problem partly through self-reports of creative individuals in the arts and partly through observing herself in the process of exploring media entirely new to her. Since completing her study, Miss Wenzel has continued her interest in the subject, applying her insights to the teaching field in such articles as "Teaching—Pattern or Design" (Educational Leadership, February, 1956).

Miss Wenzel has taught in public and campus schools in Kentucky, Ohio, and Indiana and has served on the staffs of Syracuse University and the University of Florida, Gainesville, where she has continued her special interest in language arts and children's literature.

3 FINDING MEANING IN TEACHING

This chapter offers a special kind of invitation. It invites you, as a person who teaches or is interested in teaching, to take a look at your own creativity. Perhaps you are insecure and fumbling at being creative. Perhaps you lift a skeptical eyebrow at the very mention of this word that has become overused, loosely used, and for many even "loaded." Perhaps you suspect that you are not creative and that there is little hope of your becoming so. To all of you, as persons interested in the process of your own living, this chapter is addressed.

Such an invitation—to look at yourself—demands a commitment from you. To understand why this is so, we must look back to the views of creativity suggested in Chapters 1 and 2.

We can be told what things are and how to behave toward them. We can be trained to follow the rules. We can be taught to listen, to accept, and to prefer safe enclosures. If this is the way we learn to make sense for ourselves out of the world around us, we are denied the experience of exploring, discovering, and creating meaning out of ourselves through our own experience. We are establishing habits that are likely to be life-long—habits of giving first priority to meanings that are established by others and of denying or distrusting our own. Thus, to be creative is to establish meaning in a particular kind of way.

And so this chapter—and indeed this whole book—asks that you bring yourself, your experiences, your thoughts, your feelings, with you as you read. For a book cannot tell you how to be creative. It may cause you to see something differently, or to do something you have not done before, or to understand better what you have been doing all along. At best, a book can only start you off on a way of your own and be a resource to you as you go ahead. It can do little, compared to what you yourself must do. And perhaps in the very process of relating yourself to what you read—agreeing, disagreeing, pausing to reflect where points seem relevant, skimming over what makes little sense to you now, rereading to see how the ideas "feel" later—you will be taking a first step toward creating meaning for yourself, toward becoming better acquainted with yourself as a person and as a teacher. For, says Carl Rogers, ". . . the real self is something which is comfortably discovered *in* one's experience, not something imposed *upon* it." [1]

How far you go beyond this first step is largely up to you. As a person, in a sense, "chooses" to live and indicates this choice by the way he takes care of certain basic needs, so a person must "choose" to live creatively. Before you can so choose, you must somehow know the difference between living that has little or no creative quality and that which has some degree of creativity in it. Moreover, the conditions in the world around you must not make the choice too difficult.

This chapter, then, will attempt to influence your choice, will invite you to build your meanings more creatively as a person and as a teacher. It will make use of two somewhat different approaches to thinking about creativity and teaching. The first examines a commonly accepted assumption that we can look at teachers and children and classrooms and make some judgments about the creativity of the teaching and learning going on. The second is based upon the assumption that an important part of understanding creativity lies in *feeling* the process in ourselves.

[1] Carl Rogers, "What It Means To Become a Person," in *The Self,* ed. Clark Moustakas (New York: Harper & Brothers, 1956), p. 202.

LOOKING AT CREATIVITY IN TEACHING

What can we tell about the creativity involved in teaching by *looking at* teachers as they work with children and with fellow teachers? Here are three teachers, described as they might be seen, not in one observation, but over a period of time, by children, parents, and fellow teachers. As you read, you are invited to recall teachers you have known, from your own school experience as well as from your adult contacts with teachers, because these are only three of many that could be described. We are attempting here to look at teachers and at teaching as most people experience them. Then we shall examine, more closely than ordinarily is done, the nature of the creativity of each.[2]

Teacher A

This teacher's classroom is the showroom of the school. It is bursting with interesting and attractive materials that suggest both the process and products of children's learning. Things are always going on and both teacher and students are excited and enthusiastic.

This teacher can always be counted upon to engage the attention and enthusiasm of visitors, and the teachers who come to watch are fortified with many clever ideas to try out in their own classrooms. Teacher A thrives on assembly programs, open houses, and demonstration teaching, and his performances are the outstanding ones in the school.

There is little duplication in his teaching program from year to year, for he seems to have a steady flow of ideas and is quick to capitalize on the unique qualities of changing situations. Everything that happens can become teaching material for him. He seems competent in areas other than teaching, and people frequently comment on the versatility of his talents.

He fans creative sparks in many children and they may perform in his room as they never have before and may never again. They are likely to remember this time as the most exciting and challenging of their school experience. Because of his enthusiasm and many ideas, Teacher A may, likewise, fan creative sparks in those of his fellow teachers who are clever enough to make use of his

---

2 Adapted from a technique used by L. Hobelman in "Three Creative Teachers," *Clearing House* 32:161–162, November, 1957.

ideas or who may be challenged to compete with him. They, too, may view the time they taught with him as a memorable one in their teaching careers. On the other hand, he may threaten teachers with less ability and interest in teaching, or those less secure in their own abilities which may be very different from his.

Teacher B

This teacher has an interest or a "specialty" in one area. (It may be in a subject matter field—history, arithmetic, literature—or a hobby—stamp collecting, travel, flying—or a combination of these.) This teacher can deal with his specialty or incorporate it into his teaching in such a way that this area comes alive for his students. They look forward to being in his classroom for the particular kind of experience they know awaits them there. Much the same kind of thing may happen year after year, yet it always seems new and freshly exciting to both students and teacher.

It is characteristic of this teacher that other areas of his teaching are drab and routine. Just as one plot of irrigated land stands out fresh and green in a land of monotonous brownness, so the inner wellsprings of this teacher seem to flow fitfully and to quicken his teaching at certain points only.

Visitors to this classroom may come out either charmed or indifferent, depending on what part of the program they have chanced to sit in on. Other teachers in the school tend to be tolerant, amused, or occasionally critical of his "overdoing a good thing," but they are seldom really threatened by him.

Most of us probably can remember a teacher of this kind. Adults, recollecting school experience, often describe him:

> As often as once a week, Miss Owens became a real character from history. "One hand in his vest and one behind his back," just like the picture in our history book, she entered the room. She spoke Napoleon's words, ripped out his orders . . . and then, from exile, sadly looking back at his beloved country, disappeared—into the cloakroom. On another day she was Columbus going from place to place to sell his idea. . . Miss Owens was for us Paul Revere, Sir Walter Raleigh, Pocahontas, Woodrow Wilson, a child on the Mayflower. Strangely enough, when I made my way over the cobblestones at the palace of Versailles many years

later, it was Miss Owens I recalled as she wobbled on her desk chair impersonating Marie Antoinette riding over the cobblestones.

Miss Owens didn't know much about geography. So every night we read page _____ to page _____ for homework and we wrote the answers to the questions at the end of each chapter.

. . .

I can remember that my third grade teacher had just returned from Mexico and was bursting with new stories and ideas. She had decorated the room with many of the country's products, brightly colored costumes, and beautifully dressed dolls... The whole situation made such an impression upon me that for years afterwards I hoped to visit this country some day.

. . .

Miss K., my first grade teacher, must have gotten a tremendous bang out of Christmas. One morning during the week before Christmas, we came to school to find our classroom completely disarranged. Miss K., fully as wide-eyed as her first graders, had only to suggest and we believed—Santa Claus had been there!

She must have worked for hours the night before to prepare this moment of delicious excitement for us. Year after year she did it, for my younger brothers and sisters, and later for my own children. And its magic never failed, even with her advancing years and the increasing sophistication of succeeding generations of first graders.

Teacher C

Unlike his predecessors, this teacher does not photograph well. He is not easy to catch with a camera, for he hardly shows in a classroom full of children. You rarely see him performing, for he watches more than he is watched, listens more than he talks, and perceives rather than questions. It is the students who show and are heard in this classroom. They seldom can be seen doing the same thing at the same time, and the variety and volume of the sounds they make are sometimes a matter for discussion in the teachers' room.

The classroom itself is not attractive in an immediately observable way; that is, it does not present an over-all effect of conspicuous neatness or beauty, though a closer look may reveal both of these qualities in spots. Evidence of students' work and interests are everywhere, but there is little in the way of formal exhibiting of the tangible products of learning. The room somehow has a disordered, dog-eared look and feeling that goes with being vigorously used and lived in.

Visitors to this classroom make a wide range of responses. A few are highly critical, some are indifferent, and many are confused to some degree. It takes unusual awareness to get the feel of the teaching-learning process going on, but those who do feel it are very enthusiastic. Getting ideas and answers to questions from this teacher takes time and patience, for he is more a learner than a knower and seldom has answers for those who seek quick help. Parents in a hurry to solve children's problems must learn how to listen and to learn from him. Those observers who linger or return to seek out this teacher are richly rewarded. At critical times they uphold him staunchly, for this teacher attracts disciples. Along with these, perhaps in equal number, are those who find it difficult to understand the reason for such devotion.

Students of Teacher C respond in individual ways. They are more likely to experience learning than to feel they are "being taught," and it is almost inevitable that some are much more sensitive than others to the nature of this learning. Some become deeply devoted to this teacher during their time with him, others do not appreciate him until later years, while still others scarcely remember him.

The same devotion or indifference may be noted among fellow teachers. When this teacher keeps in the background and is cautious about stating his ideas, he is not a threat to anyone, because nobody feels inferior to him. When he is articulate about teaching, he poses a serious threat to some teachers because his ideas are highly individual, often nonconforming and unorthodox. He feels that he is different from the others and he occasionally suffers periods of doubt and uncertainty about himself as a teacher. It is difficult to judge his influence on the total school program. While he enriches professionally those teachers and administrators who individually seek him out, few desire or aspire to emulate him.

Three Teachers Compared

Here are three "good" teachers. That is to say, they all view teaching as more than a routine job, derive satisfaction from it, and are generally respected (as teachers) by co-workers and parents. *Yet each shows creativity in somewhat different ways.*

If, as you were reading, you were reminded of yourself or of teachers you know, it may be because most teachers who are reasonably adequate in their jobs have in them something of each of these teachers. They have their moments when they are unexpectedly, even accidentally, creative. They stumble upon creativity rather than plan for it or experiment with inviting it. It is possible, even, that many teachers who bear some resemblance to Teachers A, B, and C never identify these qualities in themselves as creative.

To see insightfully and discriminatingly so as to recognize differences among creative teachers—particularly subtly shaded ones —is hard. To respect these differences is even harder. Yet the recognition and valuing of individuality in the creativeness of teachers is an important first step for all of us concerned for our own creativity as teachers.

Teachers A, B, and C look very different as teachers, their classrooms feel different, and whatever it is that constitutes their creativity has its origin in very different personality structures. Teacher A probably conforms most closely to the popular conception of the creative teacher. Many teachers have tried to emulate him, and, although unable to achieve the same total effect, have nevertheless made use of many of his ideas and techniques.

The disadvantage of our tendency to so stereotype the creative teacher is that creative qualities that show less spectacularly are likely to be obscured, to be therefore less valued, and so to go unrecognized and unencouraged. At the risk of oversimplifying, we might say that the fault lies not in Teacher A, but in a culture that likes to package and exploit a product that sells well. Under the label of "the creative teacher" he has been advertised widely and has sold well.

Do we value Teacher A less if we value Teachers B and C more? Perhaps Teacher B is not undervalued as a teacher so much as unidentified as creative in his own unique way. He has, as a matter of fact, enjoyed a kind of renown as a "natural" teacher. He was, perhaps, more prominent and more valued in the days preceding four-year professional teacher preparation programs. He is the person who chose to teach primarily because he loved children and began teaching with little more than this love to sustain and instruct him.

Teacher C probably has been least often identified as creative because he differs rather conspicuously from the popular picture of the creative teacher, as well as from the childlike, "natural" one. At the present time he may not even be recognized as particularly "good" except in the minds and memories of more sensitive students and co-workers. His particular uniqueness seems to lie in the climate of his classroom and in his relationship with his students. The intangible nature of "climate" and "relationships" makes them more appropriately sensed or felt than seen. It is understandable, then, that Teacher C is not readily judged, in his own way, creative.

CLOSER EXAMINATION
OF INDIVIDUAL CREATIVITY

Once we are able to overcome to some extent the rigidity of our vision, we may be better able to see creativity where it was not visible before. If we look again at Teachers A, B, and C, we may be able to see them, not so much as more or less creative teachers, but as teachers, each in his own way, possessing some *creative qualities*. We see, also, that each confronts somewhat different problems as he attempts to discover and to develop his own creative potential.

Teacher A, for example, shows many qualities that research has identified as characteristic of behavior that is creative: originality, flexibility, fluency of ideas, unwillingness to duplicate his own or others' behavior, sensitivity to materials and opportunities, and a dedication to his work. There are, however, some things about him that we do not know from this description, that we would need to know before we could say whether or not he is realizing his full creative potential *as a teacher*. Can he, when necessary, stand aside and let students discover or does he feel that they must be shown? Does he trust the ideas of others as well as his own? Is his concern with what happens inside himself and his students or merely with performances? Does he value his students' achievements as learning for them or as enhancement for himself? That is, does he avoid manipulating students for his own purposes?

The creativity of Teacher B shows spottily in his teaching. To some of his teaching he brings originality, imagination, and spontaneity. But much of his teaching is uninspired, and even in the area of his specialty he shows a willingness to duplicate. We would need to ask about this teacher some of the same kinds of questions we asked about the first one, for he, too, seems to get more satisfaction from doing himself than from letting students do; for showing them rather than letting them discover.

There are, however, some interesting and important differences between these two teachers. It would be unfair to suggest that Teacher B is concerned with self-enhancement at the expense of children's growth or that there need be concern that he exploit them. The description of this teacher as a child among children, while oversimplified and perhaps sentimental, is not entirely inappropriate. For the nature of his particular kind of creativity is not unlike the spontaneous, unselfconscious kind characteristic of children. Perhaps it is partly because he is unknowing about it himself that he is unable to use it consistently in his teaching. So further questions present themselves concerning this teacher. Does he know what he is about? Does he have some degree of intellectual understanding of his job? Can he go beyond his own and his students' enjoyment of certain activities to deeper perceptions of the learning values involved? Can he relate his ways of working in one area with those in another?

Teacher C shows creative qualities that are quite different. His classroom and his manner with children are not orthodox or conforming, and the devotion accorded him implies a dedication to his work. There is much, however, that is not understood about the creativity of this teacher. The questions we would raise are somewhat different from those asked about the other two. Does he understand his own teaching process? That is to say, does he analyze his teaching behavior or does he rely upon intuition—his "feel" for the right thing to do at any particular moment—and show unconcern, even resistance, perhaps, to studying what he does? Can he communicate about his teaching to others? Does he have sufficient personal security and confidence in his own abilities to remain unthreatened by the misunderstanding and disapproval of his unorthodox classroom?

It is easy to look at teachers working with students in class-rooms. It is a temptation to make quick judgments about the kind and degree of creativity involved. The above descriptions and analyses of teachers and teaching suggest that:

1. To label "creative" any one kind of teacher is to over-simplify the concept of creativity.
2. Creative potential appears in different ways in dif-ferent people.
3. The starting point in understanding and developing creative potential is with the creativity that exists, wherever and however we find it.

We have ample evidence from studies of creativity now being made that "looking at" creativity from the outside, while helpful and illuminating, is not enough. Creativity must also be felt or sensed or appreciated, by a process that is more aesthetic than mental or analytical. The rest of this chapter, therefore, will suggest some ways that each of us may go about "comfortably discovering" increased meaning in teaching.

FEELING CREATIVITY IN TEACHING

Sometimes a word seems to be just right for a particular pur-pose. It may be a simple word, an old word that we have used many times and with never a thought that suddenly one day it would "light up" for us and dispel the shadows in which we were groping. Thinking now about teaching, about how creative involvement with teaching may be a way of finding meaning for ourselves, the word *care* as defined and used by the Overstreets, seems right:

> It is in the capacity to *care*—to care intensely about some-thing beyond the limited self—that we seem to find our best clue to what mature individuality is. For it is through our *caring* that self-knowledge and self-acceptance are brought into creative collaboration with the form of life we call devotion: self-giving.[3]

The authors go on to point out that the capacity for caring

> —is a trustworthy clue to the truth or falsity of the self image. (Keeps a person from trying to be what he is not.)

3 Harry and Bonaro Overstreet, *The Mind Alive* (W. W. Norton & Company, Inc., 1954), p. 112.

—makes for selective habits of seeing. (Jesus "saw" as a carpenter, not as an Einstein.)

—maps the area of willing self-discipline. (Provides spontaneous reasons for getting over humps of inertia.)

—determines inconveniences a person will suffer and risks he will run.

—determines sources of joy, strength, and companionship. (Consider the "relaxed alertness of good shop talk.")

Caring in this sense becomes a truly integrating force in our living. What we care for and how much we care for it, therefore, are important to examine when we are seeking to become more knowing about our own creative energies.

Three kinds of caring seem appropriate for us to look at: caring about teaching, caring about children, and caring about ourselves.

Caring—About Teaching

No other job in the world could possibly dispossess one so completely as this job of teaching. You could stand all day in a laundry, for instance, still in possession of your mind. But this teaching utterly obliterates you. It cuts right into your being: essentially it takes over your spirit. It drags it out from where it would hide.[4]

Thus a teacher speaks about her caring for teaching, a teacher of young children in an overcrowded, ill-equipped school in New Zealand.

What does it mean, to care about teaching?

Caring about teaching—inquiring of oneself: "Why do I choose to teach? Why do I continue to teach? What is teaching doing for —or to—me?" These are pertinent questions, necessary ones for those concerned with teaching as creative experience. The self-assessment involved in answering such questions periodically is a necessity if, as Marie Rasey puts it, a person wants to lead a life rather than be led by it.

People's decisions to teach grow out of motivations as numerous and varied as the people who make them. There are the practical, tangible reasons: convenient hours, reasonable salary as supple-

---

4 From *Spinster* by Sylvia Ashton-Warner. Copyright (C) 1959 by Sylvia Ashton-Warner. By permission of Simon and Schuster, Inc., p. 9.

mentary income, opportunities to earn extra money, and, particularly for women, the advantages all of these present when one must rear a family.

There are other reasons, less tangible, that for some people may count more significantly than these. Teaching is particularly able to satisfy certain needs—needs that we may or may not be fully aware of as influencing our decision to teach: a need to help others, to mother, to dominate, to be looked up to, or to advance on the socioeconomic scale. There are other satisfactions that we are very much aware of, that grow out of seeing students enjoy learning; of watching them receive honors of various kinds; of seeing their liking for school as evidenced in school spirit and high morale among students, staff, and parents; of receiving expressions of gratitude from parents and students who "feel helped"; and of receiving even wider recognition in the form of "Best Teacher" awards.

All of these are in some degree "respectable" enough reasons. Most teachers identified as "good" have chosen to teach both because it is a pleasant way to earn a living and because they are aware of some degree of satisfaction in doing it. But what have these to do with *caring* as defined above? Can teaching that grows out of these motivations help us know ourselves, give ourselves, enjoy ourselves to the depths suggested by the Overstreets? Or provide the spiritual refreshment and release that the New Zealand teacher finds in it?

It may be that a few who choose to teach do so because of a powerful sense of self-direction or destiny. They teach, perhaps, for much the same reason that an artist paints or a dancer dances —because they have to. Such teachers probably can no more help teaching than Beethoven could help composing. They may or may not be rich in material things or be recognized or honored, but such rewards are of marginal importance to them.

For most, "caring" as referred to above does not spring full blown out of adolescent dreams. Teachers probably must *learn* to care, and this learning may go on over a period as long as a teaching lifetime. They cannot know in the beginning stages of preparation or of actual teaching what is in it for them. They may feel satisfactions of various kinds, but may only now and then catch glimpses of some qualities of the experiences of teaching that make it self-fullfilling. Compared to other satisfactions, these are the least tangible, as difficult to describe as the qualities of creative experience itself.

Renewal through teaching. One quality that seems characteristic of creative teaching experience is that it is a means of growing, that it is more energy-giving than depleting. It renews even as it exhausts.

There are many energetic teachers, and their energies may be fed from varied sources: sheer physical exuberance, travel, hobbies, artistic activities, homemaking, and many more. Such people may renew their energies by stepping out of their teaching roles. For so many hours a day and so many weeks a year they work as teachers; outside this time they re-create themselves in various ways not related to teaching.

Or they may bring their hobbies, interests, and talents into the classroom and get satisfactions from using them in connection with their teaching. And renewal may come as much through these channels as through the act of teaching itself. We saw in the descriptions of Teachers A and B the possibility of this kind of renewal.

The line between renewal from nonteaching activities and renewal or re-creation *through teaching* is indistinct indeed. Teaching experience that is itself renewing or self-fulfilling seems to be characterized by "high points," by moments of awareness that things are different, that exactly the right point is reached for meaning to emerge for students, for the teacher, or for both. Such a moment comes for Mrs. Wilson in Chapter 1 when she "senses the exciting implications in Peter's drawing." It comes in a different way for Anna, the New Zealand teacher:

> It is the last hour in the afternoon. . . Sensuously and accurately I vibrate and respond to the multifold touch of my Little Ones. . . I am made of their thoughts and their feelings. I am composed of sixty-odd different pieces of personality. I don't know what I have been saying or what I will say next, and little of what I am saying at the time. It is a potent drunkenness, an exhilaration, and it is one that does not leave depression in its wake.[5]

It comes, too, for all of us in small ways and in important ways. We may be only vaguely aware of high points, perhaps see them

[5] Ashton-Warner, *op. cit.,* p. 22.

in no way related to creative experience. Yet, how many of these moments can a backward look recall—moments of heightened enjoyment, of clarity emerging from the cloudiness of confusion, of ideas pouring out, dovetailing, and finally falling into place as a completed plan? Enjoying stories, savoring together the memory of a walk, a trip, or a surprise visitor; pausing to enjoy the smell, taste, look, sound, and feel of things going on right now; laughing together over something, or over nothing much—all describe moments when teaching touches us deep inside and we are not quite the same again.[6]

Seeing the wholeness of teaching. Another quality that seems to be important when we are looking at teaching as creative experience involves seeing whole-part relationships. Suppose a teacher is teaching first graders the very beginning stages of handwriting. He must know something about the range of differences among six-year-old children in ability to control small muscles. He must be able to simplify the process of forming individual letters so that children can achieve some degree of success in their early attempts to write. He must know about the varying abilities of first graders to attach meaning to the hieroglyphics adults call writing. He must have in mind the relationships of these letters to words and of words to ideas, and be aware of the role that writing plays in communicating ideas.

This is to say that teachers must know a great deal in order to teach so "simple" and taken-for-granted a skill as beginning letter formation. Their *whole* knowledge must range all the way from discrete, specific "basic skills" of teaching to an over-all perception of the relevancy of one aspect of the teacher's job to the advancement of mankind. Creative teaching involves *both* skill and art, so integrally bound together that when we separate them in our thinking and in our practice, we do so at great risk to the concept of creativity.

This wholeness of the process of teaching is hard to see and to talk about. At no point is the difficulty more evident and more frustrating than when a young person is going through the process of learning how to teach. Those who work with prospective teachers have long been concerned with the place of "methods" courses in teacher education programs that hope to nurture creativity

6 See A. H. Maslow, "Cognition of Being in the Peak-Experiences," *Journal of Genetic Psychology,* 94:43–66 (March, 1959).

in students. All teachers need to master some "basic skills": how to get a class quiet when necessary, incorporate a wrong answer into a discussion, make a learning step in long division understandable to children, and provide for individual differences in a spelling lesson. But the sum of skills is not an art, and skills used creatively are different from skills used mechanically.

And yet, if we move for a moment away from teaching, we find artists in many fields referring to this wholeness as they talk about the nature of their own creative process. The initially conceived whole is referred to by one artist as "the initial vision," by another as "the informing idea or spirit . . . which holds all the elements in place."

When we view teaching as art, or as creative process, we might say that the artist teacher does not lose sight of the goal as he teaches all of the parts that are necessary to reach it. It means, more specifically, that in any one teaching-learning situation, the teacher who is an artist has control over not just the many discrete bits of knowledge and skills that he needs, but he has a "vision" of the whole job to be done that strongly influences his choices of method and materials. Teacher educators are much concerned with what it is that helps teachers envision the totality of the teaching process.

We know that the complete cycle of the creative process includes the consumer as well as the producer, the appreciator as well as the creator. The person who looks at a painting or listens to a symphony participates in the process of their creation as he is increasingly able to perceive the original vision of the artist or composer. And so the wholeness of the teaching process should be felt by those on the *receiving* end of creative teaching. Skills learned creatively are perhaps different from skills learned mechanically. Thus, while the teacher does not verbalize with children about the above-mentioned components of his own understanding of the teaching of beginning letter formation, children learning to write under such a teacher may catch a glimpse of the meaning and significance of the writing process.

Most "good" teachers are both artists and craftsmen. They have had to learn skills, and they find that these skills often serve them well when creativity is at low ebb. A person who is much of the time unable to be creative presumably would need to be provided with a technique for every situation that could arise. Someone has said that creativity begins where know-how leaves off. It is often at this point that one person gives up because he has no answer, while another finds himself improvising, discovering answers, and using skills he did not know he had. So, the technician gives way to the artist.

The process of teaching the proper combination of circle and straight line that makes the letter "d" seems very distantly related to the plays of Shakespeare, which we can enjoy today because someone once *wrote* them down. It takes imagination to see this relationship, but it is the degree to which such imagination exists that makes the difference between the skilled technician and the artist teacher who has mastered the skills demanded by the nature of this particular medium.

"What difference does it make, just so he learns his letters?" asks the person who has never had his imagination kindled by a teacher who not only knows children and "how to teach," but who has, also, an image of the wholeness of his job.

Creative experience through teaching may be something we do not even know we want when we choose to try teaching. Most of us, if we have some degree of sensitivity, learn the feel of creativity as we teach, at first accidentally, perhaps. Later, as our insights into the teacher's role deepen, we begin to see and feel more satisfactions and pleasures than at one time we had believed possible. If these satisfactions are important enough to us, we begin to make plans—conscious choices—that increase the chances that the satisfactions will occur on other than accidental bases.

Being highly sensitive and aware, making value judgments and choices—all are essential ingredients of teaching as an artistic process.

Caring—About Children

Asked "Why do you think you want to teach?" a young person almost invariably includes in his answer, "Because I like children."

Teachers rich in experience with children smile and wonder what it really means to "like" children. Can you like children when, for the seventh time in a day, you have told them to stop shouting, to work for five minutes without asking a question, not to play too close to open classroom windows, not to talk during rest time, not to wrestle in the lunch line, not to paste without spreading paper first?

Can you like children when they won't learn what you have so carefully planned for them to learn, when they can't think of anything to write about, when they miss the same words over and over, when they forget, put off, argue, and defy you?

Can you like children when they are dirty, when their noses run, when they smell, when they use offensive language, when their parents thwart your every attempt to "help" them?

"Of course," you say, for these are but scattered clouds that obscure momentarily the bright sunshine of childhood. Most of the time, most children delight us with their spontaneity, their outspoken honesty, their capacity for becoming interested in almost anything, their ready giving of trust and love.

Loving children, liking children, enjoying children—such terms are loosely used by adults. When we ask for more precise meanings, we find that answers are often contingent upon whose children, where, under what circumstances, to what degree. For children being most truly themselves are very likely making life uncomfortable for adults. Many cultures, including the "teacher culture" within our own society, have worked out their own unique ways to insure that children, growing up, do not disrupt adult life too drastically.

The experienced teacher, smiling at the young person's reason for wanting to teach, knows that, in a sense, "liking," "loving," and "enjoying" are not quite the right words to use when we talk about a teacher's way of seeing children. As the beginning teacher who *likes* children lives with them and grows in awareness of all of the shadings of difference in meanings behind their behavior, he learns to *care* about children in new kinds of ways.

What does it mean to care about children *as a teacher?*

A character in a recent story, in the process of looking at herself in relation to her social work, ". . . knew that she had to see, touch, and talk to people in order to care about them—that was all there was to it." [7] Similarly, we might say that one basic necessity in a teacher's caring about children is that he not only see, touch, and talk to them, but also smell, taste, hear, and feel them. "Touch" is too mild a word to cover the multitudinous variety of contacts

[7] Nadine Gordimer, "Something for the Time Being," *The New Yorker,* 35:26–31 (January 9, 1960), p. 28.

a teacher has with children in any one day. A poet, a philosopher, an absentee parent, or a college professor may love children in the abstract, but a teacher's caring about children must survive the shock to the senses that children *en masse* can produce with endless variety.

More is involved here, however, than trial-by-ordeal. To tolerate the tremendous energy of children is not enough. A teacher must be able to *appreciate* children being children, to see purpose and beauty in their noise and movement, to understand how wide open their senses are to receive meanings from everywhere, even from such taken-for-granted objects as garbage cans. The New Zealand teacher shows in abundance this kind of caring for children as she dreams of an ideal school:

> The image that jostles forward ... is one of an infant room that has achieved the organic order; a seed-bed where children grow and expand and bloom, where there is an end to don'ts and bells... It's a noisy, happy place with much free coming and going through the door. Children dance spontaneously like leaves in the wind and learning is a matter of preference.[8]

Teachers of older students, too, must be appreciative of qualities that nonteachers merely tolerate: corny jokes, teen-age lingo, tough-guy swagger, the unpredictable lightning-like changes from childhood to adulthood and back again to childhood, temporary addictions to sentimental stories and tear-jerker programs, and assumptions of superiority and know-it-all that they may never feel again. There are probably no more versatile appreciators of children and young people than teachers rich in experience of living close to them—and liking it.

Another quality that seems to define more precisely the nature of a teacher's caring about children is the *respect* that he shows for them. Teachers show respect for children in many ways. Some ways are easy to see, are relatively easy to teach and to learn. They differ not too much from ways we show respect for each other as adults.

But there are more subtle evidences of respect that a teacher *as*

8 Ashton-Warner, *op. cit.,* p. 43.

a teacher shows for children. Perhaps some examples from the New Zealand infants' room can illustrate a few:

> [Anna has lost her patience and slapped a boy for making noise like gunfire. Then she regrets her action deeply and ponders:]
>
> A boy drawing his guns with the appropriate gunfire: what could be truer expression? It is a powerful creativity from the very storeroom of his being. . . Heard as an explosion of inner pressures, seen as the flowing of an impulse, the noise, as a sound, becomes endurable. It is no longer an ugly sound that hurts me personally, but just the sound of a boy drawing madly at his guns and supplying the spit of the bullets.[9]
>
> [Mark's mother refuses to buy some materials he needs in school. Anna impulsively buys them for him herself. Afterwards she concludes:]
>
> A little boy . . . should never be allowed to experience a conflict of loyalties between his parent and his teacher.[10]
>
> It's time to let my fearfully noisy youngest ones go. . . True, the bell hasn't said so, but . . . this lordly bell is being flouted these days . . . emotional time is taking over from bell time.[11]

Here we see examples of some of the ingredients of respect for children—respect for their ways of telling us about themselves, respect for their relationships with others outside of school, respect for the built-in time demands of children that so often do not coincide with adult kinds of time parcels.

Respecting children in ways such as these assumes a rare and sensitive kind of communication going on at all times within a classroom. Communication in this sense is quite different from the kind we are all familiar with and use in many ways: exchanging greetings and using other conventions of social intercourse, asking and answering questions, making announcements, giving directions, writing notes, raising hands, snapping fingers, scolding, praising, and the like.

To communicate as fully as possible demands a kind of responsiveness between the teacher and his students that, on the part of

9 *Ibid.,* p. 36.
10 *Ibid.,* p. 72.
11 *Ibid.,* p. 116.

the teacher, involves physical, mental, emotional, even spiritual sensitivity. Such sensitivity may be partly "natural" for some teachers, but for most it comes about through a combination of "common sense," professional training, and experience. To be able thus to sense the meaning of what children are trying to tell us, not just through the literal meanings of their words, but through their bodily movements and facial expressions, their noises and their fantasies, their picture making and their playing, and even their silences—this is indeed teaching art of the highest order.

> A rainy, rainy Thursday . . .
>
> Seven . . . is shouting in a ring of his enemies. Tame . . . is reading exhaustively to himself. Mark . . . is copying pages and pages. Hohi . . . is dreaming on the mat, and the Twinnies, with a ukulele between them, are singing together. And Waiwini is working out a private dance step upon a table . . .
>
> A rainy, rainy, rainy Thursday and I talk to them all day. They ask ten thousand questions in the morning and eleven thousand in the afternoon. And more and more as I talk with them I sense hidden in this converse some kind of key. A kind of high-above nebulous meaning that I cannot identify. And the more I withdraw as a teacher and sit and talk as a person, the more I join in with the stream of their energy, the direction of their inclinations, the rhythms of their emotions and the forces of their communications, the more I feel my thinking travelling towards this; this something that is the answer to it all; this . . . *key*.[12]

Caring about children—as simple at first as liking and enjoying them. Later, *learning* to care in other ways—appreciating and respecting children and responding to them. Thus do we as teachers increasingly gain control of our medium and to that extent become better equipped to enhance the creativity of our teaching.

Caring—About Ourselves

We conclude with the most basic of all considerations—our caring for ourselves. For self-respect, self-trust, and self-love underlie our capacity to respect, trust, and love others. Just as, at the beginning of this chapter, we suggested the necessity of stripping away our stereotyped thinking about creativity in teachers, so now we urge

12 *Ibid.*, p. 59.

that each do the same in looking at himself. Here are suggested three things to remember, and three questions to ask.

Everyone has creative potential. There are many studies of creativity going on today, some of which assume the possibility and the necessity for sorting out creative from noncreative people. This assumption is adequate for the purposes of studies where creativity is being defined in a special way.

But there are other kinds of studies that define creativity differently and more usefully for our purposes. A good example is A. H. Maslow's study of self-actualizing people, that is, people who are making the fullest use of their own potentialities. He refers to the way his study has changed his own view of creativity:

> It definitely discourages the either-or, all-or-none approach to creativity which is now so wide-spread and which amounts to a dichotomous separation of sheep from goats, creative from noncreative, those who *are* from those who are not. Instead it tends to see more or less creativity in every person, if only as a suppressed potential, and asks the questions, "Why was it lost?" "How much is left?" "How much can be recovered?" [13]

Such a concept of creativity is refreshing for those of us interested in teachers and teaching. The lack of an easily identifiable product makes teachers more comparable to the creative parents and homemakers studied by Maslow than to artists, musicians, and poets. To be relieved of the strain of pointing to a tangible product when we talk of creativity is heartening indeed.

The second encouraging contribution from Maslow, of course, is the realization that we all have something to start with, if only from having once been children, for he likens the creativity he has examined to the expressive, spontaneous, "easy" kind exhibited by all normal children. He calls it "primary creativity," and sees it growing out of play, love, enthusiasm, humor, and imagination and gradually being lost in the process of acculturation. Fortunately, all people do not lose it entirely and perhaps there are ways to recall it even for those of us far gone in sophistication.

Creativity cannot be "copied." When as teachers we are engaged in a self-search for creativity, it is important to resist the

[13] A. H. Maslow, "Creativity in Self-Actualizing People," in *Creativity and Its Cultivation,* ed. Harold H. Anderson (New York: Harper & Brothers, 1959), p. 94.

temptation to judge ourselves by comparing our own creativity to that of the teacher down the hall. We cannot become more creative by copying a creative teacher. A close association and rapport with a teacher who is making use of his creativity may do a great deal to start us thinking and perhaps experimenting with being more creative in our own teaching. But the *form* of creativeness must never be mistaken for its *substance*. If we drink deeply of this idea, it will relieve us of the kinds of guilt feelings we may have because we have not garnished our bulletin boards for parents' night as our neighbor has. Thus we are released to be, in our own way, creative.

You are both a person and a teacher. Third, and finally, try not to separate yourself as a person from yourself as a teacher. For most people, the two are not exactly identical nor, we hope, are they sharply separate. It is not uncommon to find a person with rather a strong creative interest in his personal life, who has not as yet found comparable creative strength in any part of his teaching. Likewise, there are some teachers who have some rather strikingly creative qualities in their teaching but show little creativity in their personal lives. The distinction is relevant here only because it is probably important to examine yourself in both respects. Enriching yourself as a person may make an important difference in the teacher that you are; while the satisfactions you feel from your teaching cannot help but enrich you as a person.

And here are the questions to ask—

What are your areas of strongest sensitivity? To sound out your own creative potential you need to have a certain kind of knowing about yourself. To what kinds of experiences do you respond with some degree of sensitivity? In what directions does your energy flow most readily? When do you accomplish most without the feeling of pushing yourself? In what areas do ideas present themselves most fluently? At what times and on what occasions do your accomplishments tend toward uniqueness?

The spirit of this quality of creativeness might be illustrated by reference to a series of advertisements running in some current magazines. One such advertisement displays prominently a word, FUSTIAN, and invites the reader to "seize the moment of excited curiosity—and consult the dictionary." If you have a particular kind of sensitivity to words, you cannot help yourself. You look up the word. But perhaps you resist the directive very easily, for your curiosity is not in the least excited. If this strange word were to block the meaning of something you were reading, or if its spelling were to block your writing, you would look it up as a practical necessity. But just for fun? Just out of "excited curiosity?" Never. A dictionary for you is a practical, not a creative tool. (Perhaps you suffered the fate of many children who have interest in the dictionary as a place to explore, but who are pressured by adults to make use of it too soon and too exclusively for practical purposes.)

What *does* excite your curiosity? Can you resist trying a recipe when a new magazine arrives? Rearranging a room after keeping things in the same place for a week? Reading a book as soon as it arrives? New ideas? Strange people? Crossword puzzles? Jewelry? Old glass? An unmarked side road?

What kinds of things are especially pleasant and satisfying to you? The sound of words rhythmically joined? The smell of sawdust and the feel of sanded wood? Cleaning an especially dirty house? Feeling the response of an audience to your talk? A sunset? Skating? Dancing? A well-told joke? Remembering?

We are talking here about starting points in self-discovery, about Maslow's "primary creativity," about things that are more play than work for you, that you have a "natural taking to." With this kind of creativity the way you feel about what you do is more important than the success of the outcome or how the quality of the product compares with that of experts or professionals.

It is important, moreover, not to belittle this kind of creativity. It involves elements that research has shown are very much a part of all creativity: ability to play, curiosity, fluency of ideas, spontaneity, sensitivity, and imagination. It is thus a kind of seedbed out of which all "productive" creativity grows.

But more than this, it is our most potent means of *self* discovery. It is only by doing much of what we can freely and spontaneously "give" ourselves to doing that we eventually discover what we "have" to do—not because someone tells us, but because of purposes deep within ourselves.

How do you see problems? We live in an imperfect world, and certainly the teacher's portion of it abounds in imperfection. If the shoots of his creativity are too tender, they may not weather some of the problems and pressures that teachers are likely to have to face.

There are problems of a material nature that seem always to be with teachers in all but the wealthiest school systems. There are shortages of all kinds of materials, equipment inadequate in quantity, decaying in condition. There are children and more children to use the materials and equipment and to fill classrooms far beyond capacity. There are services desperately needed to get children in condition to learn in normal classrooms and to take care of those who have problems that cause them to be unable to learn under overcrowded conditions.

There are problems of other kinds, problems that take the form of pressures on teachers to deny their individuality and to conform to a pattern. There are pressures from students: "Mr. G. never gave us homework last year." "The other classes are going on a trip; why can't we?" From parents: "None of Susie's teachers have given her a good strong background in phonics." "John can hardly wait to get into Mr. C's room next year because of all the work in science he does with students." "One dollar prize to the room with the most mothers at the next PTA meeting." From other teachers: "The noise in her room disturbs my class across the hall." "If we all teach them to keep their notebooks in the same way, it will save time for everyone." "Why don't the elementary schools give them the grounding in grammar we need to teach English in high school?"

There are administrative pressures in the form of testing programs, courses of study, textbook adoptions, and merit rating procedures. And, finally, of course, there are pressures from some kinds of teacher preparation programs that stress standards of appearance and behavior and that advocate methods that are rigidly prescriptive.

Added to these are current pressures put upon all of us, as members of society, to be less conforming, to shun the way of the organization man, to revive the spirit of our individualistic forebears. As teachers in society, however, we are often made aware that the majority group in the community expects us to live our personal lives in a way that conforms rather closely to theirs. The whole question of teachers' freedom to think and to express viewpoints in the classroom is frequently called to our attention in front-page headlines and argued out on editorial pages.

Problems and pressures exist whose number and variety have only been suggested. Some are petty and unnecessary, others are

EVELYN WENZEL

almost inevitable in a complex society. There are interesting differences among people, however, in the way they see problems and in their choices of action or inaction.

A problem is a block of some kind that necessitates a change in behavior. The need to change accustomed ways of doing things is very painful for some people. It may be threatening because they are unsure about whether they can behave differently. For others, the need to change may be seen as merely a nuisance. Such persons change ways of doing things, not because of an inner feeling of necessity to change, but to please someone, or to "look modern." For still other people, change is invention, experimentation, innovation, the lifeblood of teaching. Monotony and repetition are intolerable.

Most of us, of course, do not fit neatly into any of these categories. We may be inventive in finding ways to help a child learn to write a story but be threatened by a change in the system of reporting to parents. What we know of the creative process indicates that in areas of our deepest security, those from which we get most satisfactions, we take problems in our stride. A truly creative cake baker is intrigued and challenged by a not-too-successful attempt to combine three recipes. A child struggling with long division presents a delightful puzzle to a teacher who is intrigued both by arithmetic processes and by the way children respond to them.

This is why it is important for you to look at yourself in relation to teaching and its problems. If too many problems are threatening or frustrating rather than challenging to you, then teaching is almost sure to take more from you than it gives back.

What do you really value? The rewards and satisfactions of creative experience are great, but so are the risks you must take. All creativity poses some degree of threat, of danger, to someone. Facing the possible consequences of your own creativity—of doing what you feel you "have" to do—demands a certain faith and trust in yourself, an ability to evaluate yourself from the inside rather than rely upon the judgment of people around you.

This means, sometimes, not only *being* different, but *feeling* your difference and being willing, if necessary, to take the consequences. It means feeling "out on your own," separated from others, taking sole responsibility for what happens.

Even on the "homely" level from which most of our illustrations have been drawn, we can illustrate this kind of risk: There are parents who take their children out of school for an extended trip ... the mother who paints pictures and never gets the house cleaned up ... the person who loses all sense of time in moments of intense concentration and is late for appointments ... the family that spends money on phonograph records rather than on repairing the roof.

Now it is easy to argue that these are all questionable evidences of creativity. And so they are, *if* they grow out of ignorance, irresponsibility or neuroticism. But there is also the possibility that they *could* have their origins in conscious awareness of values, in putting "first things first." As such, they are evidence of health, of faith in oneself rather than in the dictates of others.

We could cite many examples of teacher-risks that must be taken when behavior is unorthodox in some way. Anna, the New Zealand teacher, refers to them over and over. We can see here the misery and guilt that can accompany nonconforming behavior when faith in one's self weakens while there exists, at the same time, a strong feeling of having to do what one "must" do: [14]

> Face the facts. I'm a poor teacher and all the inspectors to date have proved it. I'm a mass of mistakes, and all of life has proved that... I shouldn't have flouted an order from the Director of Education himself. It's time I fitted in and made myself useful.
>
> But often I feel the noise is too big a price to pay at my age. Not as noise,.. but as this Guilt that persists on my shoulders; born from What Other People Think.
>
> If only I had kept workbooks and made routine schemes and used orthodox time-tables, and stood up and taught from the blackboard with a pointer, and insisted on silence like other teachers, then I should at least have had the confidence of numbers... Sometimes I feel too old to pay the price of stepping out of line; yet I must do what I believe or nothing at all.

Out of "necessities" from within, discovered through the playful, enjoyable, spontaneous experimentation of immaturity, and nurtured by increasingly conscious control of maturity, emerges

14 Ashton-Warner, *op. cit.,* pp. 82, 60, 204, *passim.*

eventually a life style that is unique. Necessities from without are there, too, partially molding and partially being molded by interplay between the person and the world, if the interplay is *creative*. Thus, if teaching becomes a way of creating meaning, emerges a style that is one's own, both in teaching and in living.

PART TWO

PART TWO

ASPECTS OF DESIGN IN TEACHING

A human being who is open and involved, who is investing himself in life and learning, is the hoped-for outcome of the educative opportunities that a teacher is instrumental in providing. Creativity in teaching may be exercised in the designing of those opportunities. Using the "raw" materials of teaching—time, space, people, and things—a teacher creates his designs, arranging (ordering and re-ordering) those ingredients of education in a constant flow and in an intermingling way.

This part of the book treats of three aspects of design: (1) responding in interaction with individuals and groups, (2) developing content with individuals and groups, and (3) organizing interrelated uses of time, space, and materials.

RESPONDING IN INTERACTION WITH INDIVIDUALS AND GROUPS

This aspect of design is derived from one item in our earlier statement of function: A person is teaching when he is "serving as a model in interpersonal transactions, or otherwise fostering educative interaction among peers and with people of other age groups."

The basic phenomenon in the classroom is a pattern of interaction among human beings. Between a teacher and any one child there is the possibility of one set of interpersonal relationships. Add one more child and the number of possible sets of one-to-one relationships is increased to three: Teacher to Child A, Teacher to Child B, and Child A to Child B. Adding a third child means adding three to the total; adding a fourth means adding four more. A progression in this network of relationships begins to emerge:

Number of Pupils with a Teacher	Number of Possible Sets of One-to-One Relationships
2	3
3	6
4	10
5	15
10	55
15	120
20	210
30	465

When one considers that the great number of possible group interrelationships is not included in this progression, it is small wonder that teachers often find troublesome what seems to the outsider like a small change in group size. Whether a class is large or small, there are two important considerations: (1) the sensitivity with which a teacher responds to the spoken and unspoken signs that someone needs help or understanding or direction and (2) the quality of the interaction that the teacher encourages among members of the group. In discussing teacher response in the interactive situation in Chapter 4, Marie Hughes develops as a key thought maintenance of integrity in all the various human relationships possible in a classroom. Since teachers deal with events in process and in a complex patterning, and not with one event at a time in isolation from other events, opportunities for creativity in this part of the designing problem are exciting and important.

Kornberg has captured the drama and the beauty of such designing in discussing his experience in teaching disturbed children:

My children's violence stripped away all extravagant growth of academic theories, and the root was this: they faced me not as pupils, not as grades, not as kinds of immaturity, but as children living their histories of being hurt and nourished by the world. They faced me with that and I could not impose on that or exchange for that any meaning of my own. I could only listen and answer. I could act so that a history grew between us, a facing and being faced, a continuum of our contact with the world. In this the world's "lesson" would be transacted, not as some dead object or one-sided fantasy, but as a meaning in encounter, as that which confronts each of us in our difference.[1]

DEVELOPING CONTENT WITH INDIVIDUALS AND GROUPS

Another part of the teaching function, central to mediation between the child and the world, is development of content. A person is teaching when he is "helping an individual or group to abstract from experiences information, values, skills, and processes."

The word *content* is commonly used as a synonym for subject matter. When a person says, "This course has no content," he likely is implying first of all that the course has no content that he considers worthy. Second, he probably means that those planning and teaching the course are not aiming at the acquisition of subject matter—that is, *informational* content—by learners.

We believe that in the dictionary sense of *subject matter*, "subject of thought or study," no experience can be empty of it. We do not wish to restrict the word *content* to information, however. We believe that an experience contains potential learnings of four sorts —ideas, feelings, skills, and approaches. Content to be developed with children and youth, then, includes meanings and ability to live one's meanings. The term *meaning* is here used in its fullest and deepest sense of ideas with value dimensions.

In naming this aspect of design in teaching, we were influenced by a research report by one of the authors. The term *development of content* in the research study is a category defined as "response to the data placed in the situation by the children." A section of the

[1] Leonard Kornberg, *A Class for Disturbed Children* (New York: Bureau of Publications, Teachers College, Columbia University, 1955), p. 2.

report shows the function the teacher may perform in this connection:

> The functions that are placed in this category [development of content] are those that elaborate and explore the structure or problem that is under consideration. It may not be amiss to think of them as the heart or core of the business of the school. The teacher who performs these functions is directly helping the child with his learning and search for meanings. He is responding to him within the situation and with an appreciation of the meaning the child is bringing to it. The teacher, in responding in this manner, "opens windows" for the child. The teacher is a resource; he is, also, a learner, an explorer *with* the child.[2]

From further discussion in this research report we infer that creativity in teaching, from the standpoint of development of content, begins with inviting and listening to responses of learners for cues as to information they already have and that which they seek. It continues with observing the variety of ways in which young minds work. The aim is to encourage learners' interest in content and to invite use of a variety of mental processes, such as expansion and association of ideas, comparison and inference, and the testing of ideas through personal involvement.

It was not the intent of the writers of the report to restrict consideration of development of content to response by a teacher to topics *introduced* by learners. Important as it is to deal creatively with such opportunities, teachers have a further responsibility to make content available that might not otherwise come into the experience of the individuals in a specific class. Neither task is an easy one. Both require great understanding of children and youth in general and accurate assessment of the particular individuals in a teacher's charge. Both require sensitivity to clues that help a teacher to judge how fast and how far to go and in what direction. In Chapter 5 Jeannette Veatch and Alice Miel address themselves to this dual responsibility with relation to development of content, an aspect of design in teaching that calls for more and more creativity on the part of a teacher as man's information mounts and his need for order and meaning increases.

2 Marie M. Hughes and Associates, *Development of the Means for the Assessment of the Quality of Teaching in Elementary Schools* (U.S. Office of Education Cooperative Research, Project 353, 1959), pp. 69, 144.

ORGANIZING INTERRELATED USES OF TIME, SPACE, AND MATERIALS

The third aspect of design in teaching derives from this item as we have stated it: A person is teaching when he is "helping an individual or group to use time, space, equipment, and materials."

Time was the first of the raw materials of education to be the subject of intensive research. Studies of time utilization reach back into the last century. Early approaches concentrated on time allotment for various subjects in the curriculum and there was little attempt to see interrelationships within a complex of factors. Much of the concern with space has revolved around the physical plant for education—school buildings and grounds. The movement on this score has been from allotting a number of square or cubic feet per pupil to designing in such a way that the most appropriate spaces for educative experiences may be available. Another advance has been the extension of space for education through field trips.

Developments in the area of instructional materials and equipment have been so rapid that it has been difficult for teachers to remain informed as to availability of new tools for their trade, let alone discover proper uses of them and build skill in their utilization. Teachers had scarcely learned what radio might do before television came along and the scrambled textbook is an example of a recent challenge to both the familiar textbook and the workbook.

A big part of creativity in teaching appears to lie in finding, with learners, the best and most mutually reinforcing uses of a multitude of tangible things, both new and old, and of planning uses of time and space in relationship to these sources of ideas. Prudence Bostwick devotes Chapter 6 to this large area of creativity.

INTERRELATIONSHIPS IN DESIGN

Although each chapter in this part of the book has its own special focus, it has been impossible to maintain sharp boundaries. While Marie Hughes places a strong emphasis on the education of the feelings of children as she deals with integrity in human relationships, she cannot avoid considerations of integrity in idea content. Prudence Bostwick, too, in illustrating the various uses of time, space, and materials gives further examples of development of content in all aspects—feelings, ideas, and skills. She also reflects in her sketches the maintenance of integrity in relationships, as do Jeannette Veatch and Alice Miel in their illustrations. This spilling over from one apsect of design to the other seems more fortunate than unfortunate, for it but emphasizes anew the wholeness of teaching.

Another kind of boundary the authors of Part Two have not been able to maintain is one separating the role of the teacher from that of the student. Again, this is not unexpected and not unfortunate. Whether one chooses to focus on one role or the other, the necessary interrelationships are in the picture, implicitly if not explicitly. We believe, however, that the profession will continue to be hindered in understanding the role of the teacher if the role remains hidden. We believe that the profession will not learn the part a creative teacher takes in education unless more of us are willing to describe carefully the teaching role in each instance of classroom interaction. We need to study the consequences of various instances of entering in and of holding back—the consequences of various types of questions, statements, and other means of giving structure to a situation. It will be useful to distinguish between actions on the part of a teacher that deny learning opportunities to children and youth and actions that facilitate independence in learning.

The four authors writing for this part of the book have deliberately put the teacher in the center as a person designing in a creative field. The reader is invited to speculate on the effect of teachers' actions as reported in the three chapters that follow. He is invited also to think of the three aspects of design in teaching as possible starting points in making his own teaching more creative.

*ABOUT THE AUTHOR ... Marie M. Hughes has long been an avid consumer
of educational research reports and a person who "reads anything she can get
her hands on" when interesting new ideas come forth. For the past several years
she has been immersed in the subject of creativity—reading, writing, speaking,
reflecting on her own experience for further illumination of the concept. In the
course of a sizable resarch project* (Development of the Means for the Assessment of the Quality of Teaching in Elementary Schools, *U.S. Office of Education Cooperative Research, Project 353, 1959), Mrs. Hughes gained further
clues to differences among teachers who are more or less creative. Observations
made in connection with that study furnished much of the material for her
chapter in this book and reconfirmed a belief that integrity is a prime factor
in constructive teacher-pupil relationships. Mrs. Hughes taught and supervised
in Michigan, New Mexico, and California before joining the staff of the
University of Utah.*

4 INTEGRITY IN CLASSROOM RELATIONSHIPS

Teaching, with its thrills, its anxieties, its puzzles, and its rewards, is complex and all-encompassing. An observer in a classroom
is likely to become a part of its prevailing current and mood—be it
one of anxiety, of quest, of boredom, of discovery, of contempla-
tion, or of frustration. A recent visit to a third grade, a busy class
made up of thirty-one children and their teacher, was especially
rewarding. The children were working singly, in groups of twos
and threes, and in one group of four. They were writing, reading,
sewing, completing individual projects, cleaning the hamster cage,
observing the snake, practicing French. This catalogues only a
part of their activities during a free choice period.

The French group behind the piano worked earnestly to learn
the vocabulary of the day and review as much as they could
recall. One boy, Russ, spoke exceptionally well. His leadership and
corrections were accepted by the group. Ann had real difficulty
with her pronunciation but Russ was patient and allowed her
to try again and again. In fact the three other members of the
group were also solicitous, offering their support and corrections.
As each one decided that he had worked enough on his French,
he left the group until only Russ and Ann were left. Ann persisted
in trying and Russ corrected her. Then he resolved the situation

by saying, "I'll tell you what, Ann, tomorrow you wear a lot of blue and I'll help you describe what you have on." Thus freed, Russ got himself a book and sat in the library corner, but Ann took a piece of paper and drew a picture of herself as she would be tomorrow, wearing a blue polka-dot dress, blue ribbon, and blue socks.

Now and then the observer was permitted a brief moment within the mysterious world of childhood. For example, one boy left a group of three with whom he was working to speak with another boy who apologized as he left the members of his group by saying, "This is very confidential." The two boys placed their heads close together and the bearer of the message whispered audibly, "Tommy has the right answer to number four and you said that you would get it first." The receiver of the news sent a savage glare to the offender across the room, made a threatening pass or two with his arm, then all who were involved returned to their former activities.

The teacher responded to those who came for help or reassurance:

> BOY: "I made this for the bulletin board and there is no room for it."
> TEACHER: "Is there another place you might put it? We would like to have it."
> GIRL: "Ed won't let me help him with his reading."
> TEACHER: "Has Ed asked you to help him now?"
> GIRL: "He is in the puppet theater with some others."

The teacher waited a minute without comment. Then the girl said, "I guess he'll ask me sometime like he always does." And off she went stopping on her way to straighten the library table before stretching out on the rug with her book, a hamster on her shoulder.

Many times the exchange between children and teacher could not be heard. The teacher was seen getting materials, helping a child with his school committee report, spelling words, admiring work, laughing with a group sharing something hilarious.

One little episode with the teacher stands out. Jane followed the teacher for a second or two until she caught her attention. Upon noticing her, the teacher said, "I'll be with you just as soon as I get the paper for Pete." When she was free she addressed Jane. "What may I do for you?"

JANE: "I want a title for my story. I don't have one. Give me one."

TEACHER: "Let us sit over here. I'll read your story to you and maybe that will give you the title."

The teacher read the story carefully, showing complete interest. When the reading was finished, the little girl said, "I don't have a title." The teacher replied, "What is your story about? What did you write?" The little girl replied, "About a girl, an April girl." Then with triumph she announced, "That is my title, 'An April Girl.' "

TEACHER RESPONSIVENESS AND CREATIVITY

In the classroom reported, the teacher made a variety of responses as she interacted with the children. Those responses influenced relationships all around. A teacher's creativeness is exhibited to a significant degree in the nature of the response made to children or youth in this process of interaction. Rogers has defined the creative process as *"the emergence in activities of a novel relational product, growing out of the uniqueness of the individual on the one hand, and the materials, events, people, or circumstances of his life on the other."* [1]

A teacher interacting with children is confronted with the new meanings they are building and the meanings they are expressing. Each response of the children has a freshness that says it has not occurred previously, at least not for them. No matter how many children of the same age one has met, lived with, or taught, this one and the next one are new, and the new formulations with which they are responding must be met with new formulations on the part of the teacher. *Responsiveness* is the material with which the teacher creates; the *product* is the meaning that emerges from the interaction. One is instantly aware that the product is not something that one can hold, taste, measure, hang on the wall, or otherwise exhibit; instead, what can be seen is the smile, the renewed vigor with which the problem is attacked, the sage nod of the head, the light in the eye. What is heard is the next question,

[1] Carl Rogers, "Toward a Theory of Creativity," in *Creativity and Its Cultivation,* ed. Harold H. Anderson (New York: Harper & Brothers, 1959), pp. 69–82.

the statement of insight or understanding, and the boast to a classmate of now knowing and understanding. Lou LaBrant relates an incident of a secondary student who, at the close of a conference with the teacher, called to her friends and said, "Come here, I have the most beautiful thing that does just what I wanted. It's magic!" She was talking about the use of a colon in her writing.

There are times when the product does not present itself even in these forms. The *meaning* to the child and the new relationship that he is formulating cannot be easily identified. Sometimes as teachers we wait in vain for the cues that tell us of our success or nonsuccess. This is our reality, with which we learn to live without frustration. Teaching requires a long-range view.

TEACHER RESPONSIVENESS, INTEGRITY, AND CREATIVITY

Responding in interaction with children and youth as a part of their organized education is one aspect of design in teaching, the aspect selected as the focus of this chapter. Of the several qualities in teacher responsiveness that may be considered marks of creativity in teaching, none seems more fundamental than maintaining integrity in the relationships of the human beings involved in the educational enterprise.

All children possess creativity. It is a part of their inheritance as human beings. Creativity, like other aspects of an individual's potential, must be nurtured.

Creation implies some problem to be solved, something that arrests the attention of the individual to which he can give of himself and his own uniqueness. The "something" may be an emotional response; it may be an image of what might be; it may be a different pattern of relationship. Millard writes that, "to create means to endow with meaning a personalized experience." [2] Rogers suggests that for the creative the "locus of evaluation" is within the individual. In the last analysis, it is his own judgment that he did or did not do what he wished to do.

A first grade child, intent on painting an iris, asked the teacher, "Is my stem too long?" The teacher answered, "How do you want

[2] Cecil Millard, *Child Growth and Development* (Boston: D. C. Heath and Company, 1958, revised), p. 181.

it? How does it seem to you? You could try another one and decide what you feel about it." [3]

A fifth grade boy had drawn the inside of the university field house on a large sheet of paper and with surprising detail. There were row upon row of empty bleachers surrounding the basketball court which contained one lone figure poised with ball in hand. The art supervisor, inspecting the drawings, stopped and said, "You haven't filled the space. Here let me show you." Whereupon he picked up a crayon and added figures to the court and bleachers. As he turned his back, the child tore his paper with as loud a sound as the paper would make. He was sent out of the room but was heard to say, "I was all alone. I was practicing and it was a little scary."

The nurture of creativity and the lack of such nurture can be identified in these two episodes. Under conditions such as those identified in the second example, the danger is that children will not rebel but rather will learn not to expose themselves, not to share their feelings. They may learn to ask, "What do you want us to do?" They may learn to orient themselves to the authority figures in their lives, to discover what is expected and to do it.

If individuality is to be cherished, if the child is to gain confidence in himself and learn to respect and like himself, if the child is to become or even approach that which he is potentially capable of becoming, his own "core" of uniqueness and his right to be himself, as he is and as he chooses, must be cultivated and respected. Otherwise he cannot create, for, as an individual, he cannot maintain his own integrity.

What is integrity and how is it maintained in classroom relations? For the purpose of this discussion, integrity is used to denote an active quality in the relationships of teacher and child, child and child, or child and group, that facilitates the process of integration within the individual and the group. The observer of the third grade classroom described at the beginning of this chapter saw many aspects of integrity. One element in the classroom that promoted integrity was that of *mutuality*. The children

[3] To an older child, the reply might have included some principles of relationships of height of flowers to container or vase. They might be stated as ways evolved to help people decide such questions, then the suggestion made to try it and see if it helps "you to do what you want."

were helping one another. Of course, there was not absolutely perfect mutuality (one boy with three new erasers refused to loan one to another), but the working together was apparent in their organization for practice, for example, in the French language. It was found in some of their group writing. It was seen in the aid the teacher gave the class in getting books and paper, in supporting the requests of the children.

The dictionary uses the word *unity* as a synonym for integrity. When we look at the synonym for unity, we find such words as solidarity, integrity, and union. Union, in turn, means the "property or character of a thing that is a whole composed of many elements or parts."

The third grade class had attained a unity and mutuality in the common goal of wanting to learn and wanting others to learn. The children spelled words for one another. One measured a picture mounting for another who had difficulty in getting it straight. They took on responsibility for the housekeeping of the room, for example, the straightening of the library table and the cleaning of the hamster's cage.

Another element of integrity in interpersonal relationships is that of individuals' respect for one another, as persons with some right of choice and some "core" that must be kept inviolate. It is of interest that the first dictionary definition presents integrity as the "state or quality of being complete, individual, or unbroken; entirety; an unimpaired state."

The teacher maintained the integrity of the little girl's effort when she was asked to give a title for the story. Her reply was, "I'll read your story to you and maybe that will give you the title." There was respect shown for the story by the care with which it was read. There was aid offered but the story remained the *child's own story*.

The teacher protected the right of the one child to choose not to have help with his reading at a particular time, although it was clear that he often did ask for help. She knew that a period of the day set up for personal choice of activity loses its integrity when children are thoughtlessly asked to change their choice.

The report of the third grade classroom given in these pages does not do justice to the flow of activity and purpose that bound the school days together. Many activities in the room pertained to what had happened or what was being planned for the coming days.

Integrity, then, is the quality of relationship that keeps unimpaired the child's relationship to himself, to others, and to the objects and situations he meets. This quality in relationships fosters mutuality within the classroom group.

Mutuality is most appropriately built on the common desire to learn, to do, to understand and control the environment. Mutuality grows out of the aid children give one another as they go about their business of learning. It grows out of shared activities, and out of expression of personal feelings. A classroom of such mutuality is able to accept and cherish the differences among its members. Mutuality is *not* built on the practice of pitting children against one another; it is not built on the denial of aid one to another; it is not built with the requirement of standardized, stereotyped responses; it is not built on the denial of expression of personal reactions; it is not built on the practice of grouping children in such a manner that any member or group occupies a continuous position of inferiority in relation to the remainder of the group. These are all practices that jeopardize the integrity of the classroom relationships.

Children growing up under conditions of mutuality that give support, respect for individuality, and some opportunity for self-direction, develop into persons with a sense of social responsibility.[4]

TEACHER RESPONSIVENESS, INTEGRITY, AND OPENNESS TO EXPERIENCE

As we search for a clearer understanding of the creative process, we find general agreement among investigators that the more creative individual views the world, its situations and objects, in ways that go beyond those of clichés and accepted schemata of the culture. He stores and reorganizes his impressions, concepts, facts, and ideas. As he invents, forges new relationships, builds new theories, composes new songs, and otherwise creates, he *invests some of his own uniqueness in the work*. Schachtel says, "What is essential for the artist is that he experiences and expresses more precisely, and

    4 See A. W. Brown, A. W. Morrison, and G. B. Couch, "Influence of Affectional Family Relationships on Character Development," *Journal of Abnormal and Social Psychology,* Vol. 42 (1947), pp. 422–428.

without being blindfolded by the sociocentric view, what happens in his encounter with the world or some aspect of it." [5]

What human relationships make possible this kind of development of openness to experience? According to Schachtel, the problem of *creative experience* ". . . is the problem of the open encounter of the total person with the world, that is, with some part of the world." [6]

He goes on to describe the quality of the encounter that leads to creative experience.

> The quality of the encounter that leads to creative experience consists primarily in the openness during the encounter and in the repeated and varied approaches to the object, in the free and open play of attention, thought, feeling, perception, etc. In this free play the person experiences the object in its manifold relations to himself and also tentatively tries out, as it were, a great variety of relations between the object thus approached and other objects, ideas, experiences, feelings, objects of imagination, etc. [7]

It is probably true that not all experiences (encounters with the persons and objects of the world) can be creative in this sense. It is certain, however, that most teachers would covet for all children a preponderance of creative experiences within the school situation.

Children who encounter the world with their full senses learn to trust and respect their own reactions. They build for themselves a mine of impressions that give depth and meaning to life. A teacher who furthers such encounters often has to be somewhat flexible, always sensitive to the meaning for children, and always striving to maintain integrity in relationships.

A teacher of young children in a southwestern city took her group to the small park by the river, which at that time was the only public patch of green grass and shade trees in the city. Brown sand and sun-baked clay were all that was known to these children. Teacher and children had planned to read a story, to play some singing games, and to play ball at the park. Upon arrival at the park, the children tumbled out of the cars and threw themselves upon the grass. They savored it through their feet and their

[5] Ernest G. Schachtel, *Metamorphosis* (New York: Basic Books, Inc., 1959), p. 244.
[6] *Ibid.*, pp. 240–241.
[7] *Ibid.*, p. 241.

hands. They allowed the coolness to envelop them as they stretched out on the grass, lying motionless for many minutes. They ate the fresh grass blades. They traced the contours of the land with their fingers. They somersaulted and jumped. They raced and shouted, always coming back to the ground to clutch the coolness, the greenness, and the freshness of this oasis of grass and shade to their bodies.

The remarkable thing was not only the manner in which the children absorbed the "encounter" with their world, but the flexibility of response the teacher made to them in not once imposing the preplanned program upon them. They did not listen to stories nor play organized games. Green grass and shade were too new to them. In the succeeding weeks the children organized and expressed their reactions to this experience in their drawings. The drawings were exceptional in detail and mood. The joyousness and aliveness of the children were felt by those who looked at the drawings.

There are many levels of encounter in the sense of multiple relationships of thought, feeling, and perception. These may be illustrated by an episode in a second grade classroom, demonstrating again the responsiveness of a teacher to the diversity of meaning a situation may have for children. This second grade had an aquarium of tropical fish. One morning when the children came to school only one fish was alive. Such an accident is surprising and upsetting to children. To understand, handle, and organize the experience, the teacher and children talked about the toughness of the fish that survived. They decided his story should be written. Together over a period of a few days the second grade wrote the story. Copies were made for each child. The librarian, the principal, the custodian, and other friends were each given a booklet with the story of this very tough fish with which the young authors expressed such a feeling of identification.

TUFFY

Once there was a little tropical moon fish. His name was Tuffy. He was about one and one-half inches long with black tail and fins.

One day in September Tuffy came to live in Room 118 of the Stewart School. It was in the Second Grade. Tuffy's home was a very nice home for a fish. It was a glass aquarium. Some water plants helped to make the aquarium attractive. There was a light over the top to keep the water warm. Tuffy liked to be warm.

Tuffy had many friends in the aquarium. His special friend was another moon fish. It was Tuffy's mate. Another friend was a little catfish that looked for food in the gravel. A beautiful angel fish was a friend too. There were two neon-tetras that were very colorful.

There were guppies in the aquarium too, big guppies, little guppies, and middle-sized guppies. There were many big and little snails. Tuffy liked snails. They helped with the housekeeping in the aquarium. Tuffy also liked the children in the second grade room, and the children liked Tuffy. They took turns feeding the fish.

One day one of the neon-tetras and the beautiful angel fish died. Tuffy did not know why. Neither did the children. Tuffy felt bad.

Day after day went by. Tuffy watched the children work and play. And the children watched Tuffy. One day someone put goldfish food in the aquarium. Tuffy looked at the food. He was too wise to eat too much of it. Some guppies ate too much and died. So did Tuffy's mate. Tuffy missed his mate very much but he played with his other friends and soon got over it.

One day some men came in and put a new electric plug in another corner of the room. Now Tuffy's home could be moved to the science corner by the window. He liked it there very much.

Winter came. The nights were very cold in Room 118. Tuffy shivered. His friends shivered too. He did not like to be cold, but he lived through it until the children and the teacher moved his home down closer to the radiator. Now Tuffy was comfortable and happy night and day for a while.

January passed and February came. February 20th was a hard day for Tuffy and his friends. The heat in the building accidentally went off. The room got very cold Wednesday night. Tuffy shivered again. He looked around for the warmest spot in the aquarium and there he stayed until morning.

MARIE M. HUGHES

In the morning the teacher came in early. She found the room very cold so she opened the radiator full blast. No heat came. She went to the principal's office to find out what was the matter. The principal called the University heating plant and a man said he would take care of it.

The children came to school. Room 118 got very warm. Tuffy and his friends got warm. The teacher opened the window. After school she shut the window but forgot to turn the radiator partway off. The teacher and the children went home.

The next day was Friday, February 22. It was George Washington's birthday. There was no school. The teacher did not come. The children did not come, but the heat still came. The room got very, very warm. Tuffy tried to find a cool place. Tuffy was hot.

He felt ill. He could hardly breathe. Tuffy was worried but he didn't know what to do. His friends didn't either. It was afternoon when the teacher came in to feed them. She found all of the fish dead except Tuffy. He was struggling very hard to keep living.

She opened the window, she turned down the radiator, and she moved Tuffy to another fish bowl with just-right water. Tuffy was safe. He began to feel better.

Tuffy had been very, very warm. Tuffy had been very, very cold. Tuffy was brave. Tuffy was tough. Tuffy lived through hard experiences in Room 118.

THE END

Children who participated in writing the story of Tuffy had an opportunity to increase their awareness of relationships with their environment and to express their own feelings. In a sense they felt heat, cold, loss of friends, and recovery with Tuffy.

A secondary student, through the sensitive response of the teacher, experienced an awareness of another dimension. The chemistry class was asked to write a research paper on any aspect of chemistry that interested them. One young man came to school early in the morning to tell the teacher that he was going to write on bacteriology.

TEACHER: "What do you think of as bacteriology?"
STUDENT: "Aaah oh, well, you study something with a

microscope." (*Then—real enthusiasm*) "I know the greatest guy who goes up to the university and he is in bacteriology. He thinks it's great!"

TEACHER: "You admire this student who is studying bacteriology?"

Then followed an extended monologue on the virtues of the university student. Out of this expression the student gained further awareness of his attachment to his friend. He discovered that he did not know anything about bacteriology; however, he wanted to know more about his friend's work. Space does not permit the full record of this exchange with the teacher. Plans were made to interview not only the friend but others. Some books were given him, among them several biographies. In the end he wrote a very personal paper on how men have worked to solve problems of mankind; the qualities of these men were identified; and lastly, much thought had been given to the work yet to be done. This proved to be the most interesting paper written by any of the sixty students taking chemistry. It was highly personal, factually accurate, and endowed with the uniqueness of its author; however, it bore few marks of the conventional research paper. It was the teacher's recognition of the meaning in the student's life of his hero worship and his vague reaching out for more knowing and understanding that maintained the integrity of relationship between student and teacher, as well as that of the student with his own purpose and personal environment. This flexibility and understanding on the part of the teacher led to an increase in the awareness of the student of himself, of the activities at the university, of the past, and of the future.

Increased awareness develops with openness to experience. However, new data cannot be admitted and incorporated when conditions become too threatening. One principal recognized this fact and was able to help a second grade boy expand his concept of a situation.

This child often missed the bus and was then brought to school by his mother. However, there came a day when his mother did not have the car and he had to walk to school. He arrived quite late and went directly to the principal's office where he began to fuss about the bus not waiting for him. The principal merely asked, "What might happen to the children on Corner X and Corner Y while the bus waited for you?" The young boy responded without hesitation. "They might fight. They would get cold. Somebody could get sick." "What must you do then, so that all these things won't happen?" With this extension of reality (the walking and the image of other children) the boy acquired new insights and subsequently had no difficulty in meeting the bus on time.

The principal's response to the second grader was nonpunitive, therefore nonthreatening. He did not reprimand but responded in a manner that permitted the child to take in more of his environment, to perceive other relations.

TEACHER RESPONSIVENESS, COURAGE, AND RISK

The very concept of creativity implies something different, something new in the situation. In general, it is agreed by students of the creative process that the more creative individuals among us take calculated risks. They dare to do what most of us would not do. They give evidence of a kind of courage and autonomy that makes it possible for them to try the new, the unusual. How may conditions of development be maintained so that children feel safe enough to explore, to try things out, and to be themselves? [8] Risk taking is, of course, one condition of openness to experience.

A teacher-monitor of a lunch room was attracted one day by a little boy who, with evident enjoyment, moved from table to table visiting with one child and then another. Finally he came to the teacher and said, "Today I came way over here to visit my new friends." The teacher responded within the meaning of the child and said, "It makes us feel good to have friends, doesn't it?" The teacher did not tell him that he was breaking a rule of the school, that one could not come to the lunch room without buying something and eating his lunch. Little Ralph was a timid boy who had experienced great difficulty in finding a place for himself in the new group in a new school and town. The teacher sensed the meaning

---

8 In a recent biography by Elizabeth S. Sergeant, *Robert Frost* (New York: Holt, Rinehart and Winston, Inc., 1960), Robert Frost is pictured as a man who wrote the way he saw things. In the writing of his poetry, he has ignored the style, content, and way of looking at the world expressed by his contemporaries. In expressing his reality, he has enriched reality for all of us.

Although this quality of personal uniqueness and its value can be readily seen and accepted in poetry, it is not so easily accepted in other areas of living. Perhaps we would value expression of personal uniqueness in many more areas if we would take longer looks at the possibilities opened by such expression.

of his adventure to him. He had summoned up sufficient courage to cross the street, enter the lunch room, and initiate contact with the other children. For him to continue to reach out and try things, this effort had to remain successful.

As a child or youth searches for his own meanings, attempts to test himself, and organizes his experience, he raises questions and gives his answers in nonstereotyped and unconventional ways. There is some evidence that we, as teachers, are unaccepting and discouraging of such behavior.[9] To illustrate:

A fifth grade class was making a mural depicting the story of the westward movement. Jack approached his teacher and said, "How do you put a map on the mural? I kind-of want to show some trading."

>   TEACHER: "I don't understand."
>   JACK: "You know, there were places where they traded with the Indians; they followed their maps, and . . . oh, you know."
>   TEACHER: "Why don't you make a few figures and let it go?"

If Jack's attempts to share his vague ideas meet many responses similar to this, will he continue to risk his own ideas and his own thinking?

A third grade class had taken on the responsibility of constructing and filling a large cornucopia with fruit and vegetables to symbolize the Thanksgiving season. Each child had chosen the fruit or vegetable he wished to make. One boy was laboriously cutting out cherries one by one. Said the teacher, "Here, fold your paper like this and you can cut many at one time." The boy explained, "I was making them like my grandfather's. Some of them are very big, some aren't so big, and some are kind of puckered." The teacher replied, "That will take too long. Just go ahead and fold your paper."

The organization of ideas into a form that communicates to others requires skill and effort. The idea, solution, or reaction has to be considered worthwhile by the individual if he is to acquire the habit of continuing his work to the point of usefulness. The

9 J. W. Getzels and P. W. Jackson, "The Highly Intelligent and the Highly Creative Adolescent: A Summary of Some Research Findings," in *The Third University Research Conference on the Identification of Creative Scientific Talent,* ed. by Calvin Taylor. (Salt Lake City: University of Utah Press, 1959).

period of test and retest, write and rewrite, design and redesign, is sustained by the image of what might be; also, by the support, receptivity, and belief of those whom one holds as important to him. Most teachers are, and all teachers must learn to be, worthy of this role of significance to the individual children they teach if they are to be of genuine service to them. Therefore, the nature of the teacher's response to children has much to do with fostering their courage to try out and expand vague ideas. An important element in encouraging children appears to be helping them maintain integrity in their *own purposes*. Acceptance and recognition of children's purposes appears to be requisite to helping children to shift their purposes, when desirable, either by integrating one purpose with a larger purpose or by abandoning a purpose in favor of a new one. For example, in the incident of cutting out cherries, it would have been possible to explore the experience of the child with his grandfather's cherries, then clarify the representative and symbolic character of the paper cornucopia filled with paper fruit and vegetables. The teacher directive, without such exploration and opportunity for insight, rejects the child's purpose. Sensory and affective experience were sacrificed as well.

There are many factors related to the courage and inclination to risk one's self. Thibaut and Kelley have used the concept of cost and reward in their discussion of group membership.[10] They consider the dyad, for example, teacher-child, as the most pervasive of all group memberships. How does the teacher interact with a child to keep the relationship to objects and situations sufficiently unimpaired for the child to continue to reach out, to take unto himself, and to give of himself? If the relationship is such that the child will want, voluntarily, to *re-enter* the situation (reading class, biology laboratory, etc.), the school remains a place where he can keep on learning and developing.[11]

It is difficult and requires creative response for the teacher to work within the meaning of the child in such a way that the cost of the relationship in the situation does not exceed the reward. Actually, the reward must be greater than the rewards of alterna-

10 John W. Thibaut and Harold H. Kelley, *The Social Psychology of Groups* (New York: John Wiley and Co., 1959).

11 It is impossible, of course, to separate the interpersonal relationship from that of objects, since most objects are mediated by persons, and most frequently persons of significance to the child. Someone gets the bicycle, gives permission for its use, helps to steady it as one is learning to ride; or, contrarily, someone refuses to get the bicycle and to aid in the process of learning to ride it.

tive activities (staying at home, playing hookey, dawdling, etc.) or the child will forgo the situation.[12]

Some illustrations from the records of an elementary school librarian may prove helpful. The librarian is the same person in each episode.

A class of intermediate grade children were in the library for their regular period. Tim, a boy new to the school, approached the librarian.

> TIM: "Do you know that book I had yesterday, that *Fur Trappers*, . . . I can't find it but I put it back."
> LIBRARIAN (*after locating the book on the shelf*): "Do you see the difference in the numbers on the spine of the book, 978—921?"
> TIM: "But I'm new to this."
> LIBRARIAN: "That's why we need to talk about it, so books get returned to their right places without getting lost for us. You'll get so you feel quite at home with the numbers."

It is an unanswerable question whether the teacher's response to the child's "I'm new to this" was heard by him as encouragement or as an admonishment. Was anxiety created which would make it more difficult for him to re-enter the library? Would a straight response of encouragement make it easier for him to continue his learning? For example, "You will soon learn how to use the numbers to get and return the books properly. I'll be here to help you."

Joe was a sixth grader who didn't like to read. He scored at the beginning of fourth grade in reading ability. Most of his time in the library he spent reading or looking at easy picture books. The librarian approached him one day.

> LIBRARIAN: "Joe, isn't that quite an easy book?"
> JOE: "Yes, but these kinds are the only good ones."
> LIBRARIAN: "Have you tried any others?"
> JOE: "I tried *Brighty of Grand Canyon* but I didn't like it."
> LIBRARIAN: "Do you like sports stories?"
> JOE: "No, I don't like sports."
> LIBRARIAN: "How about wild animal stories?"
> JOE: "No, I don't like them."
> LIBRARIAN: "Have you read *Friday, the Arapaho Indian*, or *Hooty Owl?*"

12 *Ibid.*, Chapter 6.

JOE: "No, I don't think so."

LIBRARIAN: "Perhaps when you finish this book I could show these others to you."

This interesting exchange began with an accusation, "Joe, isn't that quite an easy book?" In other words, "You shouldn't have such an easy book, Joe." Thus, the relationship began with a handicap or impairment. It is questionable that Joe will voluntarily ask for aid in locating a new book since his own choice was so unacceptable. Had the librarian worked within Joe's meaning, namely that picture books are the "only good ones," a relationship might have been built that would have made it possible (at least easier) for him to receive help from the librarian.

The third example is a straightforward response to the child.

Agnes had difficulty with reading. She did not enjoy it very much and she did not stay with one book very long. At her request, the librarian found a story for her about a kitten. She stayed with the book longer than any other. On her way to the lunch room one day, the librarian was stopped by Agnes.

AGNES: "I've finished my book. I surely like it."

LIBRARIAN: "What book was that, Agnes? I can't remember."

AGNES: "The one you found me about the kitten. It is called *The Tale of the Good Cat, Jupie.*"

LIBRARIAN: "Oh yes, I remember. It is a good one, isn't it?"

AGNES: "When I come to the library tomorrow I want you to find me another one about a kitten, will you?"

LIBRARIAN: "I certainly will. I think we can find a good one."

The next example is an interpretative response and an introduction of a new purpose that appears to be within the meaning the child is expressing. It has a quality of artistry and sensitivity that keeps unimpaired the relationship of teacher and child, the child's relationship to books and to himself.

Bobby, a retarded reader, who exhibited negative behavior generally, had read *One Kitten Too Many*. He came to the teacher and held out the book.

TEACHER: "You seemed to especially enjoy this book today."

BOBBY: "I did, but I don't know how I did it."

TEACHER: "You are really going to be surprised this year at how you are going to grow in the number of books and kinds of books you can read."

BOBBY: "This part was really funny." (*Child opened to a page and held out the book to the teacher, who read.*)

TEACHER: "Tabby sailed through the air. She boxed one of his ears. 'Now are you going to be polite?' she asked. She didn't give him time to answer. She boxed his other ear." (*To child*) "That sometimes happens to us, doesn't it? We get another ear boxed before we can even answer." (*The child exhibited a wholesome grin, which wasn't usual.*)

TEACHER: "Here's another book that is funny, *Feed the Animals*. Let me share some of this with you." (*The teacher read from the book, which describes a feeding situation for animals in the zoo and has a puzzle page.*)

TEACHER (*after reading three or four pages*): "Do you notice that the last four lines are always the same? 'Guess the animal before you open the flap. You might be surprised.'"

If the teacher-learner situation is to be one that the child will voluntarily want to retain and to re-enter, he must perceive it as one that furthers a goal or purpose he has accepted for himself. When the integrity of his purpose is maintained, the reward in the relationship exceeds the cost, and for the most part is more rewarding than the alternatives open to him.

TEACHER RESPONSIVENESS, ALTERNATIVES, PROBLEM-SOLVING

It has been observed that the formulation of alternatives is a creative act. The manner in which a teacher responds to children may permit the seeking of several possible solutions to a problem or it may compel adherence to a preconceived answer or way of doing things. If the development of creativity is to be sought, then, of course, the teacher will encourage alternative approaches by the children.

A return to the third grade reported in the first part of the chapter yields an illuminating illustration. When the observer entered the room, many children in the group had turned in donations of fifty cents for a school project and "50¢" was written nineteen times on the board. The teacher suggested that the pupils add the column to check on the accuracy of the sum they were taking to the office. "There are many ways to do it," she remarked. A few minutes elapsed and then she asked, "How much money should we take to the office?" Several correct replies of $9.50 were heard and one reply of $9.80.

> TEACHER: "Does anyone want to tell how he went about getting his answer?"
> CHILD I: "Well, twenty fifty cents would be ten dollars. We had nineteen so fifty cents less made $9.50."
> CHILD II: "Two fifty cents make a dollar so I counted this way. Wait a minute, I'll show you." (*This child went to the board and carefully bracketed two fifties and then two more fifties until he was down the column with one left by itself. He counted the nine pairs and wrote $9.50 as the answer, remarking*) "If I had had another fifty, I would have had ten dollars."
> CHILD III (*boasting*): "I counted by fifties; that made it easy."

Several children said that they just added. "That's a way we can always use; shall we do it together?" This teacher response appeared to bring in any stragglers and to legitimatize the "regular" way. Her final remark to the group was, "We found many ways to solve this problem."

This third grade teacher's response to the diversity in ways of working a problem was in contrast to that of a fifth grade teacher who, with the class, was looking at some pictures and asked, "What do you see?" One boy replied, "They have all the stuff in containers." To this the teacher responded, "That's a fancy word you are using; why don't you just say cans?" Different words and different ways of saying things offer great opportunity for alternatives. Most of us may be able to remember our embarrassment as children when the teacher responded to our contribution with, "That isn't what I was thinking." With such a response, the child finds it necessary to forgo his exploration of content and begin to guess what the teacher wants.

It is not the purpose of this section to discuss content as such, since that is done elsewhere. It is desirable, however, to attempt to clarify the relationship of teacher responses to the intellectual explorations and purposes of children. Once more, illustrations may prove more useful than exposition.

A teacher was presenting a lesson on the use of the foot rule. She said, "Today we are going to use the middle line between the figures. What is it called?"

CHILDREN: "One-half."
TEACHER: "All right. Today, just use the middle line."

As the lesson progressed, some children reported on the quarter or the third. In each case the child was correct in the report of his measure and in each case he was admonished that today only the middle line was to be used.

Such tight structure of a lesson discourages children from using what they already know, and does not maintain the integrity of their right to know more and explore. The discovery of better ways to meet individual differences is a measure of the creative ability of any teacher.

A sixth grade boy of ninth grade reading ability did no reading unless forced into it. He would not participate in the "silly reading class" with the state-adopted reader. Finally, he admitted to the teacher that he wanted to learn something about the mind. Said he, "I don't have any other ideas now. All I think about is how the mind works but I don't know." The teacher brought him two college introductory psychology books and some high school physiology textbooks. The boy went to work. Later his activity sent him to the library on his own. In the end, he prepared and presented to his interested classmates illustrated lectures and demonstrations on the eye and the ear. At the close of the year, his reading gain from September was between three and four years. He was the only sixth grader in the district with a reading score of ninth grade in September who gained appreciably; moreover, he became a considerate and thoughtful member of the class.

The offbeat question that surprises a teacher is often an attempt to organize the material under consideration into a more comprehensive scheme, or an expression of insight into an unsuspected relationship. Without acceptance and exploration with the student, a teacher cannot know of the possibilities inherent in his idea. Even if his idea does not prove to be useful, it may generate an idea in another student. Taylor suggests that we "encourage students to develop their own ideas and to be willing to toss them into the arena of ideas." [13] He suggests that children could then learn the consequences of submitting a new idea—what it means to have it supported, and how to survive its nonacceptance. Taylor's suggestion opens up an interesting field for those who wish to see the creativity of children developed.

TEACHER RESPONSIVENESS AND THE PROCESS OF CONSULTATION

A large number of individuals using the same materials and occupying the same space are bound to have some problems of being together. The solutions to such problems require consultation with those concerned if the integrity of relationship between the young and the authority figure, and among the members of the group, is to be maintained.

An elementary school had a problem with the spinning of tops. These were large tops that were released from a string with a dexterous turn of the wrist. The child who could throw his top in the proper manner so that it would spin for the longest period of time demonstrated real skill and was declared the champion. As some children will, they competed strongly in this activity, with the result that several children were injured by the flying tops. The principal forbade the bringing of tops to school; however, tops continued to appear and owners were difficult to locate. The problem came up in student council, where the children were unanimous in wanting to continue to spin the tops. They recognized the danger of hurting others, especially the younger children, but they wanted to play with their tops. The principal asked, "Do you think of any way you could play with your tops safely?" The first suggestion was that those bringing tops have their recess alone. The children did not find it difficult to enumerate arguments against this suggestion. Someone then proposed that the younger children keep off the big playground. It was pointed out that this penalized a group not interested in throwing the tops. When this idea of consideration for other people got through to the children, someone suggested that the ones who had the tops have a special place to throw their tops. The final solution was a large circle drawn at one

[13] Calvin W. Taylor, "Possible Positive and Negative Effects of Instructional Media on Creativity." Paper prepared for St. Louis seminar, April 1960, on a theory of instructional materials–an ASCD project supported with funds from the U.S. Office of Education.

end of the playground. Those who wanted to try their skill with the tops could stand outside the circle and throw the top into the empty space.

In this episode teachers and children worked creatively in solving a problem of rule enforcement, achieving results that appeared sensible to the children—all within the framework of social responsibility.

Later in the year the same school was called upon to solve another problem of group living. Again the children were forbidden to do something, this time to go over the fence for baseballs that rolled into an alley of less than two short blocks which connected two arteries of traffic. Although the alley was used infrequently, cars tended to speed as the drivers switched from one highway to the other.

As the playground space was small, balls did go over the fence. Children could boost someone over the fence but that child had to walk around to the front to return to the school ground. This maneuver slowed the game appreciably, and the task of determining who broke the rule, the booster or the one who went over the wall, seemed never ending.

The school council, with a committee of ball players, decided that the only way they could play ball without trouble was to build a stile over the fence. A school board member was invited to examine the situation with them. Since the danger of cars remained, he suggested that they petition the city to close the alley during school hours. The children interviewed the residents on either side of the alley to determine their attitude toward closing it. The children prepared properly documented papers and sent them, with a letter of transmittal from the board of education, to the city council. The council consented to close the road.

This action effectively enlarged the playground for all children, improved the ball game, and gave the children a sense of intelligent control over their environment. The experience gave them a view of adults as people who wanted to help them do something they valued—to play ball. There was, in addition, the learning of the actual process of consulting, presenting data, and building a petition. They also learned of the power and authority of the city council in its ability to close the street during school hours.

A university laboratory school received a letter from the building and grounds department requesting them to move their ball diamond because the players were injuring one of the flowering shrubs on the grounds. The letter was read to the student council. Then followed violent protest from the boys, who insisted there was not space to place the diamond elsewhere. Since this assertion could be verified, a committee was organized to measure the playing field and report the outcome. There proved to be no additional space. The boys admitted they were running into and breaking the shrub. How could the shrub be protected? Someone suggested a fence around it. The players were realistic enough to see that they could easily knock the fence down, "anyway it wouldn't look very pretty." Then the solution came. "Move the bush to another part of the grounds." Immediately a gardener in the group informed the others of the care needed by a big shrub if it were to be moved successfully. The group said that they could take turns watering it.

A careful reply was prepared in answer to the letter from the building and grounds department: the boys acknowledged the damage to the shrub; they explained their measurement of the space; they offered the new solution of moving the shrub to another part of the grounds; and they pledged their help in watering the shrub.

The shrub was moved. The boys carried out their part of the bargain. The shrub grew. The boys played ball.

The examination of the consequences of a rule or a solution to a problem in terms of all who are affected by it is an important aspect of implementing the value of "concern for the welfare of all." Vigilance in this manner is a requirement for maintenance of the integrity of the multiple relationships involved. To illustrate:

An eight-year elementary school in an old building had rather large girls' lavatories with doors closing the toilet booths. Since young children as well as older ones used the same lavatory, trouble arose when the young children locked the doors and crawled out beneath them. This presented a problem to the older girls in re-opening the doors, because the lock was not easily reached. The custodian was not always cooperative and the girls found the whole thing embarrassing. Finally, in desperation and exasperation, the principal had all the doors removed. With this act, among others, the older girls felt discriminated against and they became unruly and defiant. They were even successful in arousing some parents who started circulating a petition for the removal of the principal. A consultant was invited to work on the situation. After a few days of quiet and unobtrusive observation, the consultant began interviews and consultation with the older girls. For them, the removal of the doors in the lavatory symbolized the discrimination they felt in the school. They "felt too old to be treated like babies." They "needed their privacy." They were punished for something for which they were not to blame. "The little kids didn't care."

Space does not permit the full story of grievances held by the students nor a description of the process of consultation. It is sufficient to report the end result of the interviews and conferences. Doors were returned to a number of the toilet booths in the girls' lavatories. Locks were raised, out of easy reach of the younger children. The consultation process had required the acceptance of an expression of feelings and points of view. Out of this process, integrity in relationships between teachers and students and among the students themselves was regained.

TEACHER RESPONSIVENESS, SOME DETERRENTS

Teachers desire to be creative in their response to children and youth. The limitless character of individual differences demands creativity, if we are to aid in the constructive development of individuals.

Interactions in the classroom are multiple. They are rapid. The art of responding within the meaning of each child is one most of us have yet to learn. Unless *we* can learn to do so, can children learn to relate themselves increasingly to wider aspects of the world? Can we help them build confidence in themselves and involve themselves in constructive activity that also meets their own needs for self-actualization or self-realization? Can we maintain a human and situational environment that is sufficiently safe and yet challenging so that children build fewer defenses and, therefore, remain more open to their "encounters" with the world?

The meaning within which the child is responding develops from the manner in which he views the situation. The child may see in the situation a threat to himself; he may find it so ambiguous that he cannot make an intelligible response; he may view it as a situation in which he can demonstrate what he knows or test his prowess. It may further or frustrate his most cherished purpose. It may excite his curiosity; it may waken old fears.

Children often respond to elements in the situation that adults do not anticipate.[14] For example, five hundred fifth and sixth grade children were invited to read a description of a classroom scene and then to respond to the question "What do you think the teacher was doing?" In the situation described, a teacher was helping a class draw a human figure. She asked a girl named Rhoda to pose as a happy person and then to pose as an unhappy person. The teacher discussed the latter pose at some length, mentioning the downward slope of the mouth, the stance, and so forth. More than one out of five children identified with Rhoda in responding. Most common remarks were:

"I wouldn't want to get in front."
"I couldn't get in front like that."
"It was unfair for the teacher to make Rhoda ugly."
"No one should look ugly like Rhoda."

The reward or cost of being in a situation is known only to the child himself.

Teachers face another difficulty in their inability to see all that goes on among a classroom group of twenty to forty students. All too frequently the act that comes to the attention of the teacher is the culmination of a sequence of actions and reactions. The total sequence is not observed. To illustrate: An observer was in a primary classroom where the teacher was reading with a small group while the other children in the room were working with quiet materials at their tables. The observer noticed a small boy intent on making a picture of a boat at sea. The smoke from the funnel, the clouds and birds in the sky, the wake of the ship were drawn with a concentration and satisfaction that was a delight to witness. The boy completed his picture, put his crayons carefully back in the box, then got up and went to a cabinet to get a large pencil with which to write his name. The box of pencils was on the top shelf. He reached into the box and turned to walk quickly back to his seat without noticing that in picking up his pencil he had pulled the box forward, where it teetered on the edge a second before it fell to the floor with a clatter. Several children immediately called out that Duane had spilled the pencils. Meanwhile, Duane was busy writing his name on his picture, oblivious to

14 Arthur Carin, "Children's Perception of Selected Teaching Acts," Unpublished Doctoral Dissertation (University of Utah, 1959).

the situation. The teacher said, "You spilled the pencils, Duane. Go pick them up." Duane denied the spilling of the pencils. The teacher insisted that he pick them up. Duane crushed his picture into a ball, put it in his desk, and then went to pick up the pencils. What alternatives might the teacher have taken?

"Duane, will you help John pick up the pencils for us?"

"Accidents do happen. Will you pick them up this time, Duane?"

"Who has finished his work and has time to pick up the pencils?"

"Sometimes there are accidents. Wouldn't you like to choose someone to help you pick up the pencils, Duane?"

The integrity of the relationship is maintained with the absence of the accusation of spilling the box of pencils. An accusation tends to carry with it an assignment of intentionality. Since intentionality is seen as under the control of the individual, the accusation is received by the individual as an evaluation of himself as a person.

As teachers we work hard to inculcate the accepted virtues of telling the truth, acknowledging blame, leaving other people's property alone, keeping one's word, following the rules, being a good sport, and so forth. Perhaps the search for the best ways of teaching values is not over. Perhaps a more creative responsiveness to each particular situation will be more successful in helping children internalize necessary controls and handle their conflicts with authority.

The identified deterrents to creative responsiveness on the part of teachers have been those that are inherent in the complexity of the teacher-learner situation—the multiple interactions, the difficulty of perceiving all that happens, and the differences in perceptions of children. Another area of deterrents to the most creative response to the meaning of children lies in the prejudices and biases of each of us. The teacher is a product of his national and subgroup culture. As such he is subject to the errors of thinking, feeling, and action embedded in the culture. However, in his role of teacher of children, he is the guardian of democratic values. Foremost among these values is respect for the individual. This means that the teacher must act without personal prejudice in relation to all races, religions, ethnic and socioeconomic groups. Fairness in the treatment of children, regardless of the "power" position or lack of "power" position held in the community by the parents, is basic to the maintenance of integrity in classroom relations. The top prizes of a school, such as the lead in the school play, the designation of valedictorian and salutatorian, the appointment of office helpers and ushers for assemblies, all call for a teacher who has genuine respect for human beings, with a commitment to democratic values. A teacher prejudiced for or against a child or group loses objectivity and, therefore, becomes unfair in assigning blame and granting favors.

A visitor in an elementary building happened to see a lively blond boy get a drink from the fountain and then, with a mischievous grin, place a stick in the fountain handle so it could not be turned. Later the principal came by, saw the stick, and said to the visitor, "You know, our Mexican children don't know how to take care of anything."

Some children have problems so severe that they have a penchant for getting into trouble. Their skills are weak, their impulsiveness strong, and their sense of discrimination underdeveloped. Teachers throughout a building soon come to know them and, unless they work at a high professional level of objectivity, often assign blame to these unfortunate children without sufficient evidence. Whenever this is done, the quality of integrity in the relationship is lost.

In addition to the general cultural prejudices and statusmindedness, teachers as people have personal beliefs and prejudices that may prevent them from responding to children with genuine professional objectivity and understanding. To illustrate:

A group of sixth graders were in a principal's office to discuss an episode of their ill treatment of another child. Finally the spokesman of the group said, "You know Jane isn't much good anyway. At least the teacher doesn't think so." The principal had earlier learned from the teacher herself of her disapproval of this girl who was more mature than the others. Jane had attended some evening junior high school parties and had been known to experiment with the use of lipstick. How unfortunate that the children became sufficiently aware of the teacher's disapproval that they felt free to torment the girl. Before the end of the year, Jane secured a transfer to another school within the city. The integrity in teacher-child and child-group relations had been completely destroyed with serious results. Evidence gathered at a later time indicated that it took some years for the girl to get over her extreme feelings about her relations with this teacher and class.

A kindergarten teacher learned what was happening to her classroom when she received an answer to a question posed to all the mothers in her scheduled interview with them. She asked, "What children has your child talked about at home?" Through this question she hoped to gain some insight regarding the manner in which the children were relating to one another. The answer given without fail by every mother, no matter what additional information she had given, was "—— says the worst child in the room is Dale." Some mothers elaborated with, "Teacher gets after him all the time." "Teacher likes Ronald better than Dale." "Teacher won't let Dale play with the tools." "Teacher makes Dale sit beside her." "We don't like Dale." "We won't let Dale play in the playhouse."

With such evidence, this thoughtful teacher gathered more data on her own, only to discover supplementary proof of her own reactions and her ways of responding to this irritating child who was so unpleasant to have in the group. Then she began to work creatively to respond differently to him. She allowed him to come earlier and use the tools and workbench until a given time. (The privilege had been taken away from him because he endangered others.) She consulted him about some of the things he wished to do and made it possible for him to do some of them. In the process she discovered that he had difficulty hearing. Now she took extra pains to talk more directly to him in regard to plans and agreements that involved the entire group. She called the group's attention to his socially constructive and responsible acts. She helped other children include him in dramatic play. The major change, however, was her increased discrimination in the use of her own corrections of his behavior. He did not change overnight, but he did improve. His smile became more frequent. His attention became more active. Perhaps more important, the end-of-year interviews with mothers showed that the children had lost their image of him as the worst boy in the room. The quality of integrity in relationships had developed instead of deteriorating.

The foregoing episodes illustrate the process of legitimatizing that the teacher as the power figure often discharges, albeit unconsciously. There is no end to the variety of things about which we can make a show of disapproval, thus legitimatizing exclusion and even scapegoating. Of course, it is not often that a single episode legitimatizes any action. It is done, instead, with a continuous and consistent manner of responding and reacting.

When too big a fuss is made over a mistake, the penalty becomes too great and children become afraid to try unless they are very sure of themselves. When making a mistake is viewed as a legitimate accompaniment of learning, children may dare more. In the same manner, the asking of questions, the bringing in of outside material, the questioning of a solution, the expression of personal feelings are all made legitimate or not by the response of the teacher.

As one observes in schools, he becomes aware of differences in relationships between teachers and children. In one school, he observes accusations of children, the quick and rude manner in which children are asked to get out of the halls, to hang up their coats, to get their drinks. The indiscriminate responses cannot but mean loss of integrity in some of the relationships.

In another school, children are not accused; there is a positive response to the child who enters the hall with a prized possession that must be placed safely in the desk or locker. Children are hurried and "shushed" less often. Some children are even permitted to use the telephones and to elect to stay in the classroom to complete work started earlier. This kind of discriminating response helps to maintain integrity in the several levels of relations that are involved.

In Summary

The American teacher holds as the objective of the school that *all* children be given an opportunity to develop to their full potential. This implies that conditions which foster the development of creativity be present in our schools, since all children possess creativity.

This discussion has attempted to identify the dynamics of the teacher-child and child-child relationships that promote individual development, including creativity. The concept of integrity, defined as a "state or quality of being complete, individual, or unbroken; entirety; an unimpaired state," has been used as the primary ingredient in classroom relations. The maintenance of "wholeness," of confidence, of self-acceptance in the individual, makes it possible for him to relate himself to the world in an open manner. He is freer to take in more from his environment and to risk the giving of more in terms of ideas, solutions to problems, artistic products, inventions, and so forth. He can become concerned and involved with people, objects, and situations. It is with personal commitment that he gives of himself enough to be creative.

The teacher has unlimited opportunity for creativity in his response to children. If the teacher is able to respond within the meaning of the child, he may be able to further the child's purpose, enlarge his perception of elements in the situation, or open new possibilities to him.

It is the teacher who is largely responsible for the integrity of relationship that keeps the reward of being in a situation (reading, chemistry, etc.) greater than the cost to the child, thus making it possible for the child to want to re-enter the situation. It is only under these conditions that the child can continue to use the school as nurture for his own growth.

It is the teacher who accepts and actively looks for alternatives, thus making way for the new ideas, the new interpretation, the new way of doing things.

It is the teacher who is responsible for the kind of classroom organization and management out of which mutuality develops. Mutuality gives support that leads to confidence and to feelings of personal adequacy.

It is the teacher's search for the meaning of the situation to each child that leads to the development of his own creativity in teaching.

ABOUT THE AUTHOR ... Jeannette Veatch has taught children in Michigan schools, and has taught teachers at New York University, Goucher College in Maryland, the University of Illinois, and The Pennsylvania State University. Teaching in labor education centers of the University of Wisconsin, the University of Michigan, and the International Ladies Garment Workers Union gave her experience in a unique type of adult education. Working as Director of the Program Development Division of the Girl Scouts of the United States of America gave her further experience in non-school-centered education. This rich background she has brought to her writing.

Many teachers, influenced by Miss Veatch's teaching, lecturing, and writing, are finding ways to break through stereotyped ways of teaching reading. One of her recent publications in this field is Individualizing Your Reading Program *(G. P. Putnam's Sons, Inc., New York, 1959).*

NOTE: *For information about the co-author of this chapter, Alice Miel, see Chapter 8 of this volume.*

5 DEVELOPMENT OF CONTENT

"One teacher was an inspiration," writes an observer after a visit to an elementary school. "He enlivened a dreary recitation—a paragraph on the subject of catching a fish—by nimbly running to and fro with a stick to which he had tied a string and a hooked pin, hauling in an imaginary fish. He was the turning point, the spark which lighted the glow of hope in my heart."

That such a simple attempt at bringing meaning to the printed page should be considered inspiring may seem puzzling until the teacher is located in a rural school in a country underdeveloped economically and underprivileged educationally. The actor-teacher was unusual among his fellows. He exemplifies what the more creative teacher has always done in every age and in every part of the world—sought for connections between what each learner already knows and what the teacher would teach.

Explaining the new in terms of the familiar is one step in developing content, and meaningful explanation will continue to be an important part of the teaching function. But the teacher's responsibility does not end there. Information should be of a sort that aids in the discovery and organization of further information.[1]

[1] See Jerome S. Bruner, *The Process of Education* (Cambridge: Harvard University Press, 1960), Chapter 2, for a discussion of the importance of teaching structure (how things are related).

Yet, even though it is significant and related to other useful ideas, information is not enough. An enormous quantity of new knowledge is made available with each passing day. Through mass media of communication, adults and children alike are flooded with a stream of ideas. To be equipped for life in modern times, an individual must gain increasing control over certain processes. In other words, he needs skills for keeping his information up to date and for putting information to use in solving personal and social problems. And skillful use of up-to-date information is still not enough. Unless an individual cares about the consequences to himself and others as he reaches and acts upon conclusions, he is not educated adequately to live in a crowded and troubled world. Finally, an individual must actively struggle for flexibility of approach to people, situations, and objects if he is to remain open to new experience.

A good curriculum *contains* the possibilities of all of those kinds of learning. Curriculum *content*, then, is of four sorts, each highly important for today and tomorrow. The first is in the form of information itself—facts, generalizations, and theories that are understood by the individual and seen in relationship. The second is a set of skills—for securing information from varied sources, for organizing, interpreting, and evaluating information, and for putting information to work in solving problems. The third is in the realm of feelings—good feelings toward self and others, values to guide in the interpretation and use of information, and appreciation of integrity, beauty, and order. The fourth is a repertoire of approaches to be used as appropriate—analytic, experimental, intuitive, imaginative, and creative modes of experience.[2]

CREATIVITY IN DEVELOPMENT OF CONTENT

Content is being developed if an individual's learning is being extended in any of the four dimensions named. Unfortunately, teachers sometimes concern themselves mainly with informational content. They become overzealous about feeding in a great deal of subject matter that they believe important, not realizing that this is an almost outmoded function in view of the amount of information already pouring in upon their students from the world

2 For an elaboration of this idea see Alice Miel, "A View of Curriculum Content," *Educational Leadership*, 13:337–340 (March, 1956).

outside. Worse still, they teach in ways that close doors instead of opening them, that tend to incapacitate individuals for independent, avid searches for knowledge.

Schachtel has described with frightening clarity the process by which curiosity is stilled in the young:

> It is safe to assume that early childhood is the period of human life which is richest in experience. Everything is new to the newborn child. His gradual grasp of his environment and of the world around him are discoveries which, in experiential scope and quality, go far beyond any discovery that the most adventurous and daring explorer will ever make in his adult life. No Columbus, no Marco Polo has ever seen stranger and more fascinating and thoroughly absorbing sights than the child that learns to perceive, to taste, to smell, to touch, to hear and see, and to use his body, his senses, and his mind. No wonder that the child shows an insatiable curiosity. He has the whole world to discover. Education and learning, while on the one hand furthering this process of discovery, on the other hand gradually brake and finally stop it completely. There are relatively few adults who are fortunate enough to have retained something of the child's curiosity, his capacity for questioning and for wondering. The average adult "knows all the answers," which is exactly why he will never know even a single answer. He has ceased to wonder, to discover. He knows his way around, and it is indeed a way around and around the same conventional pattern, in which everything is familiar and nothing cause for wonder. It is this adult who answers the child's questions and, in answering fails to answer them but instead acquaints the child with the conventional patterns of his civilization, which effectively close up the asking mouth and shut the wondering eye. Franz Kafka once formulated this aspect of education by saying that "probably all education is but two things, first, parrying of the ignorant children's impetuous assault on the truth and, second, gentle, imperceptible, step-by-step initiation of the humiliated children into the lie." [3]

Creative development of content has as its purpose the building of an intelligence that is continuously being informed and that is committed to the higher human values. The process of shutting off

[3] Ernest G. Schachtel, *Metamorphosis* (New York: Basic Books, Inc., 1959), pp. 292–293.

inquiry, as described by Schachtel, need not occur if four kinds of content are developed concurrently. Teachers do not sacrifice but, rather, guarantee a large fund of useful and meaningful information through development of other dimensions of content.

Creativity in the development of content, the aspect of design in teaching selected for emphasis in this chapter, may well consist of solving, day after day, in situation after situation, in the case of one young person after another, the delicate problem of helping an individual to learn from experience in such a way as to make it more, not less, possible to be open to new experience and to new learning.

Four-year-old Donna picks up a rhythm instrument, a triangle, and taps it with a metal bar. Her face lights up and she exclaims, "I've made a scientific discovery. When I hit this I feel it in my fingers." She runs to the teacher and repeats, "I've made a scientific discovery. When I hit this I feel it in my fingers."

The teacher may pay little heed except to utter an absent-minded "Yes." The teacher may respond with enthusiasm that en-courages but does not teach: "Isn't that nice!" Or the teacher may respond, as she actually did in the episode as observed, in a way that takes no more time but which gives the child something on which to move ahead, something to add to her feeling of competence. The teacher says, very simply: "Yes, you feel the vibrations." Donna then walks about the room telling others, "I feel vibrations when I hit this. I've made a scientific discovery." [4]

The story of the teacher's response to Donna is an illustration of a basic way in which development of content proceeds. Life in a classroom is made up of a series of episodes, some brief, some prolonged. These episodes may or may not be related to a large-scale study under way in class. They may not be at all closely interrelated, in the sense of flowing logically from one to the other, but if they are to contribute to the education of human beings they should be seen as opportunities to develop content according to a plan of which the teacher is ever aware. In other words, a teacher can develop content creatively only if he has in mind an image of

4 This anecdote and many of the others in the early part of this chapter were collected by Audrey Dickhart in an unpublished study of accuracy of information being gained by young children today through firsthand experience, television, and other avenues of learning. For this reason most of the examples come from elementary schools. However, they illustrate processes that go on in secondary schools also.

the kinds of content generally worth developing in our kind of world and if he can select for development specific content important and appropriate for particular individuals.

Whether the sequence of events in the development of content is of longer or shorter duration and whether the sequence has been initiated by teacher or pupil, the creativity of the teacher is called upon at the point of dealing with the "data placed in the situation" by the learner.[5] The response of the teacher to the data may be immediate or deferred. It may be verbal or nonverbal. The response may consist of planning a full-scale study or of revising plans for such a study. It may consist of creating a situation in which curiosity will be aroused or one in which a young person is confronted with a new set of choices. The teacher may create a special opportunity for following up on a lead from a learner or he may wait for an opportune moment.

The more creative teacher knows that new meanings must rest in each individual's present meanings and so he builds on firsthand experience. He makes of his classroom a laboratory in which individuals make discoveries—headquarters from which young people go forth for new experience and information and to which they return to process and order and use their findings. He knows how to help children and youth move beyond concrete experience to abstractions from such firsthand contacts. But more than that, he knows how to help these same individuals reverse the process and apply abstractions meaningfully to new concrete situations, keeping themselves open to new data meanwhile.

Every day in every classroom there are more opportunities for development of content than can ever be utilized. The creativity of the teacher is put to the test in deciding which leads to follow, when and how. The remainder of this chapter is devoted to illustrations of opportunities for development of content. Some were grasped by teachers and exploited creatively. Others were overlooked, at least for the time being, or were misused. Included with each example are comments about factors that may have been influential in the teacher's handling of the situation and, in many cases, proposals for more creative development of content. In turn, examples are given of opportunities for developing informational

[5] See Marie M. Hughes and Associates, *Development of the Means for the Assessment of the Quality of Teaching in Elementary Schools* (U.S. Office of Education Cooperative Research, Project 353, 1959), p. 69.

content, skill content, feeling content, and content in the form of approaches to experience.

OPPORTUNITIES FOR DEVELOPING INFORMATIONAL CONTENT

The simplest opportunity for new informational learning is casual but deliberate vocabulary development. It takes only a few moments to fix attention upon a new word and the results may range all the way from more complete understanding for some pupils to the first awareness of the word for others.

An example comes from a second grade. The children were preparing to go to the art room when Nancy remarked, "I love to go to the art room. I think it is a privilege." Betsy, overhearing this remark asked, "What's that?" Several children offered opinions, all of which involved the idea of a reward for being good. The teacher then checked back with Nancy, "Is this what you meant?" "Well, not exactly," said Nancy, "I mean that it is a chance that some children don't have. We are lucky to get to go to the art room." The teacher usefully reinforced this explanation: "We are lucky—*privilege* means we are given something special—a special favor."

The teacher of young children has many opportunities to help them sort out a great deal of half-understood information. A child in a kindergarten looks at the globe that the teacher is using in talking about the ocean. The child points to Africa and says, "Say, there is Texas." The teacher replies, "No, that's Africa." "Well," says the child, "Texas is big like that. It looks like Texas. On TV it showed Texas with a big patch like that."

Another child walks into a kindergarten one morning carrying a vial of mercury. The teacher asks, "What do you have there?" When the child replies, "Oh, you know, it's a planet," the teacher says, "It's mercury, isn't it?" "Yes," the child rejoins, "a planet."

The teacher in such cases will take several things into consideration in deciding what use, if any, to make of the cues the children have given him about the state of their understandings. He may weigh possible damage in letting inaccurate ideas go unchallenged too long against possible damage in challenging on the spot every statement made by a child. He may judge that a correct concept cannot be ensured at the present no matter what efforts he makes, or he may decide to start the child along the road to later, fuller understanding. In the case of the second child, a teacher might stop with a simple, matter-of-fact statement such as, "We use the same word for two things—for this material you have brought and for one of the planets you see in the sky at night." With the first child, a teacher may try taking him a little further, such as making a comparison between the maps of Texas and Africa in a way that does not make the child feel uncomfortable about not knowing the difference and in a way that does not suggest that the child will be expected later to pass a test on the information.

Children often need help in classifying information according to accurate and well-understood categories. An example from a first grade classroom shows the kind of task a teacher often faces:

> TEACHER: "You remember we were talking about food that will help us to be big and strong. What vegetables do you think are best for us?"
> SALLY: "Is rice a vegetable? I like rice."
> JOAN: "Rice pudding is good."
> TEACHER: "Let's talk about vegetables today. Do you know any yellow vegetables?" (*Perhaps the teacher does not know whether or not rice is a vegetable. If and when she starts investigating, she may discover that the problem she has set for the children, deciding what is a vegetable, is not as simple as she supposes.*)
> JOAN: "Carrots are yellow but they are rabbit food."
> MAVIS: "Some people eat them—I like them."
> TEACHER: "Do you know any others that are yellow?"
> GORDON: "Apples are yellow and good for you, too."
> SALLY: "Yes, apples."
> BILLY: "And pears and peaches and a lot of stuff."
> TEACHER: "Tomorrow we will have to find out more about vegetables. Apples and pears are fruit."

Another conversation, this time between a teacher and third grade children who have been studying electricity, illustrates the continuing problem that children have in sorting out information and attaching proper labels to it:

> TEACHER: "Today we will talk about the way electricity gets into our homes. Can you tell me how electricity is wired into your house?" (*Sometime, perhaps, it will occur to the teacher to invite children to tell US, not just ME.*)

Don: "It comes in under the ground."

Teacher: "No."

Ann: "It comes on telephone poles."

Teacher: "No, not on telephone poles."

Cindy: "On wires on telephone poles."

Teacher: "No, the wires are on poles but not telephone poles. The wires come from the electric plant. The wires are on poles made just for electricity."

Pete: "They are covered, though."

Teacher: "Yes, what is that called—the covering?"

Don: "It's—oh, what is that—we learned it yesterday."

June: "It is rubber."

Teacher: "But what is the name of the covering? Weren't you listening yesterday?"

Ellen: "Is it consolation?"

Teacher: "No, it is called insulation. Don't you remember? Now let's see who knows how electricity gets into our homes."

Cindy: "On telephone poles."

Teacher: "No, not on telephone poles—they are for telephone wires. See if you can remember next time."

The two illustrations have much in common. Children are being expected to guess the answers the teacher wants, but they are not being helped to guess intelligently. Bases for making distinctions are not being *developed*. No one can expect children to *remember* something they never really *knew* in the first place. How does one distinguish a vegetable from a fruit? What do father and mother say about it? The science consultant? What books will help?

In what ways would a telephone pole look different from a pole carrying electric wires? Are wires ever underground? How many opportunities can be found to use the word insulation in concrete situations?

No teacher can creatively help an individual or group to develop a meaning for something unless he takes pains to discover the thought processes being used and plans his teaching accordingly. A memorized response may not be understood at all. An example of this comes from a visitor of a first grade that had been studying about rocks according to suggestions of a science consultant:

Teacher: "How can you tell whether a rock is soft or hard?"

ESTHER: "If you scratch it with your fingernail, it is soft."
TEACHER: "Good, you are remembering what we learned."
ESTHER (*turning to June and whispering*): "It can't be soft though, 'cause if you would hit someone with it, it wouldn't feel soft."

The teacher does not hear this remark. The observer does, however, and also notices a child who is printing a sign to describe a rock she is going to display. The sign reads: "This is a soft rock and a hard rock." The observer decides to find out what the child is thinking:

OBSERVER: "This is an interesting sign. Is the rock soft *and* hard?"
JANICE: "Yes, it is soft and hard."
OBSERVER: "I wonder which part is soft and which is hard."
JANICE: "It is both *soft* and *hard*."
OBSERVER: "Will you tell me more about it?"
JANICE: "Well, you can scratch it with your fingernail, but pick it up and you will know it is hard."
OBSERVER (*picking up rock*): "Oh, it is heavy, isn't it?"
JANICE: "That's what I mean—it is soft and when you lift it it is hard."

Two teaching problems are highlighted in such conversations. The first is to discover the source of apparent confusion or, better, to ascertain the child's logic to obtain a clue to the kind of information needed and how and when to supply it. The other problem has to do with the purpose of the whole exercise. Does the teacher have a larger plan of which understanding these properties of rocks is a part? Will children be aided in their learning if they know something of this over-all plan?

In a junior high school Miss Gregory, a seventh grade teacher, was expected to cover world geography in the broader setting of man in relation to his environment. The teacher decided to tackle this challenge in a way that was new for her and that she hoped would yield more valuable information for the students. Pulling down a world map she said, "Let's not use our textbooks right now. Can some of you show us where your parents were born?"

After much scrambling, searching, and pointing, it was developed that only one child had a parent born outside the United States.

"Now, where were your grandparents—all four of them—born?"

Some knew and some didn't. Those who knew pointed out the locations on the map. Many grandparents were also born in the United States but some were not. The period closed with the assignment made, to get information not from a book but from their families:

"See what you can find out about your families. How far back can you go? Where do they all come from? Dig into your past. Bring anything that you think we would all like to see that would show something about how your ancestors lived."

From that beginning, the class launched into their allotted study of world geography but in a new and unusual way. Even though confined to one fifty-minute period a day, there was investigation, information-gathering, and exploration from the start. For the time being, the teacher quite rightly ignored the textbook, which had been written to suit children all across the nation.

Working on graph paper with which they were familiar, the pupils began charting their family trees. An expendable world map, pins, and colored yarns were used to show locations of various ancestors.

From the family tree the students proceeded to find out, list, and organize several types of information, such as:

1. What kinds of jobs are represented? What ones are missing?
2. What nationalities are represented? What ones are missing?
3. What races are represented of the world's stocks? What ones are not?
4. What continents are represented? From where is there no representation?
5. What interesting stories could our ancestors tell if they were here?
   a. Did they have a hard trip to America?
   b. What was the country like at the time they arrived?
   c. How did they get the idea for coming?
   d. Were they connected with a war somewhere, sometime?
   e. What happened to them when they got here?

As the weeks rolled by and the class dug deeper and deeper into their past, a realization grew in one student's mind.

"Hey," he said, "We started at our own house and just *look* how we got around the world!" There was much agreement and another spoke:

"You know, I hadn't thought much about it, but we are terribly alike. We have no North American Indians as ancestors, no Negroes or *anyone* from Africa. No one comes from China or Japan or from a Spanish-speaking country. We think of South America as closer than Europe—yet practically all of our ancestors came from Europe."

Miss Gregory had hoped for such conclusions when she suggested that the students note what was missing as well as what was represented among their ancestors. With such information before them, the teacher picked up the thread, stating in words what she sensed was the wish of the class, "Should we study the people and places that are not represented in your ancestry?" The students adopted this proposal and turned to their textbooks, which contained information they now needed.

With the area of search widened, the children wrote to embassies of Latin-American, African, and Oriental countries and to agencies of the United Nations. Very much as detectives follow clue upon clue, so did those seventh graders search for information. They continually worked to crystallize and test the conclusions already made. Finally, near the end of the term, they made a trip to a nearby Indian reservation.

The trip and a summary during their final class concluded the study, which ended with all the students knowing a great deal more about their own origins, the geographical setting whence their ancestors came, and the historical and economic reasons for their coming. The world had been studied far more intensively than if only the textbook had been used. The teacher believed that attitudes toward minority groups became more enlightened—and yet nobody ever told anybody *what* to think. Exceedingly important to the teacher, also, was the improvement of students' attitudes toward learning in general and social studies in particular.

If a magnifying glass had been brought to focus on separate episodes in the chain of events that made up the study in Miss Gregory's classroom, as was done in the brief anecdotes presented earlier in this section, there is no doubt that failure to capitalize on promising opportunities to develop content would have become visible. Creative use of other opportunities would likely have shown up as well. The longer, more superficial description of classroom operations fails to capture important details, it is true. However, such illustrations are useful for showing both continuity and interrelatedness in content development.

In the foregoing examples, as children were observed in the process of acquiring information, inferences could be made as to whether or not the teacher was utilizing the same opportunities to develop skill in searching for information. In the present section are further illustrations relating to development of skill content.

Some of the faster-learning children in a fourth grade had been reading the fifth grade book in a basal reading series. On the day of observation they were working in a workbook that accompanied the reader. A visitor asked two of the group whether they knew how to use the synonyms they were entering in the blanks on one page:

> Lucy: "Oh, we don't have to do that unless they are in the book."
>
> Joel: "You see, we are the ones who can read better, so we get to go into harder work all the time. This is a fifth grade book and we will be ready for another one soon."
>
> Lucy: "So, if we can do the work in the book, we get to go on—you just have to know the work in the book."

The teacher might have been shocked to know that this was the view of the learning process which these children were acquiring. Probably he did not intend to teach this attitude nor to limit the children's study skills to such a low level of development. Nevertheless, this attitude and this limited kind of competence were the content being developed with these children.

To a sixth grade the teacher says, "Our next study will be about Mexico. Let's think about what we want to learn about our neighbor, Mexico." The teacher writes on the board as the children make suggestions: geography, government, food and clothing, products, natural resources and history, education, cities and sites.

"These are the same ideas we gave for the study of China," the teacher comments.

Paul replies, "You know why, we always have tests on these same things." The others nod in agreement and the study begins.

For children to list as guides to their search merely the questions they think adults want answered does not promise much real learning of the skills for making a genuine inquiry. Perhaps the teacher will think about Paul's reply and try to find ways to build respect for the process of question-raising as a rigorous and demanding one.

An example from a third grade shows children having a better opportunity to learn skills of inquiry. The teacher decided to launch a study of the local community by taking a walk with the children in the area of the school. Plans made with the children included looking for the post office, the drug store, homes of the pupils, and some of the surface features of the area, such as hills. Some pupils planned to keep track of directions as they saw a good opportunity to use the compasses they had received for Christmas.

When they returned to the classroom, the children with compasses decided that they wanted to make a map showing the places they had been. While the teacher had hoped for this suggestion and was prepared to make it herself, she did not at the time foresee how far she would go in helping children develop skills in deriving information from maps. By planning intelligent steps, the teacher was able to take these children a long way in map study.

Many of the other children joined in the map-making activity. When they had finished, the teacher collected the maps and put them away for future reference.

The following day the teacher brought in a map of their journey which she had made to scale. The children helped put in the places they thought were important enough to be represented. Their suggestions as to ways of representing those places resulted in an interesting system of symbols, a word which the teacher used and made certain the children understood in that context.

The teacher's next step was to obtain maps of the entire city from the transit company. The class was delighted with these. When they saw the scale of miles and the symbols used, they were even more thrilled. They traced their walk on those maps too. The smaller scale of this map was immediately noticeable. "Our walk is very short on this map," one child quickly concluded. The class began locating places on the map that meant something to them: the zoo, the business district, the state capitol building, and their parents' places of employment. Each child was able to tell the direction he lived from those places.

When a field tour was arranged shortly afterward, each child took his map and followed the route very closely.

At the end of the second week, the teacher employed many games and devices to introduce the pupils to the use of grid lines. The children showed increasing skill in using the grid system to locate towns, rivers, cities, and vacation spots on the map of their state. They checked the distances, one way and round trip, from their own city. Among other things, they discovered why fir trees were found in greater abundance in the north and why more people lived in the southern half of the state. They made outline maps to illustrate such things as population centers, vacation spots, and historic sites.

The teacher thought that, since they had gone that far, she might touch lightly on the map of the United States to show the children their location in relation to the rest of the nation. But the children had other ideas. The teacher felt that she had a comet by the tail as her children pursued their location out into their nation and their world. The study ended with the pupils considering, among other things, their relation to the rest of the solar system. The teacher declared that she had no idea at the outset that she would go so far beyond the local community and so far beyond herself.

This account illustrates well the interrelatedness of content. While these children were developing skills for learning through maps, they were also developing analytic approaches to knowledge as they sought to reason out why certain facts about their state would be true. The story does not tell what use was made of the early, crude maps that the teacher saved. Perhaps they were brought out toward the close of the study for children to employ in assessing their own growth in skill and understanding.

OPPORTUNITIES FOR DEVELOPING FEELING CONTENT

Teachers have many opportunities to develop educated feelings and values. Some arise out of familiar subject matter discussed in classrooms year after year. But even these perennial topics turn up new twists in thinking because a unique individual expresses an idea in his own way.

A second grade teacher had told the Thanksgiving story in the time-honored way and the children were talking about Squanto, the Pilgrims, and such matters when a Negro child announced, "My aunt says that the white men stole the land from the Indians."

Totally unprepared for this the teacher lamely said, "Aren't you glad the white men did settle in America?" The child answered, "No."

The teacher was so startled that she did nothing at the time but she did much thinking and asked all of her friends for help, for she believed that the child was entitled to a truthful and nonsentimental answer.

A third grade teacher ran into several value problems in connection with the Father of Our Country:

> TEACHER: "Yesterday we learned that George Washington was an honest man. What do we mean when we say *honest?*"
>
> BETTY: "That he told the truth when he cut down the cherry tree."
>
> GRANT: "That he never told a lie, not even once."
>
> TEACHER: "Yes, but what do we mean when we say a person is *honest?*"
>
> JUDY: "Someone who is honest is always good."
>
> TOM: "To be honest means that you can prove you were right—like when you take a lie-machine test."
>
> GRANT: "That's not a lie-machine test—it's something like lie-deflection."
>
> TEACHER: "You mean a lie-detector. But what does it mean to be honest?"
>
> BETTY: "That if you smash up something, you will go tell on yourself, like Washington did."
>
> HELEN: "I think it means that you believe in God."
>
> KITTY: "Yes, and if you tell a lie, you are going to let the devil get you."
>
> TEACHER: "What is it we do when we are honest?"
>
> GRANT: "We tell the truth, that's what."
>
> TED: "Washington must have been the best man in the world if he never told even one little tiny lie."
>
> JUDY: "It is a sin to lie."
>
> TOM: "Sometimes you get in more trouble if you tell the truth—so it is better to lie—sometimes it is."
>
> TEACHER: "Is it ever better to lie? Washington didn't think so!"
>
> LARRY: "Sometimes it takes a lot of nerve to tell the truth—and you might not even know the truth. What then?"
>
> LINDA: "Sometimes you get spanked when you tell the truth."
>
> TEACHER: "But it is better to tell the truth, isn't it?"

LINDA: "I suppose so."

TOM: "What I wonder is how people knew Washington always told the truth. They didn't have those lie—you know—machines then."

BETTY: "The books say he never told a lie."

TEACHER: "Do we know what it means to be honest?"

JUDY: "Yes, you can tell the truth because then you are good."

The teacher next had the children repeat different pieces of information about Washington.

Later, perhaps, the teacher would find ways to help the children deal with some of the puzzling problems they raised. How difficult it is to know what the truth is and to know when to tell it, especially if spanking is to be one's reward! One hopes that the teacher will value and encourage Tom's logical way of thinking, that he will help Betty to learn that books can't always be believed, that he will help Judy to achieve something more than her present pat formulas as guides to conduct. The teacher might well consider the danger that he may be teaching children to support an argument by appeals to the authority of personal prestige when he makes statements like "Washington didn't think so."

Perhaps the teacher needed more time to think how to help the children analyze some of the problems they had raised. Perhaps another day they would return to the subject and on that occasion the teacher might be less of an oracle and more of an encourager of speculation and counterspeculation by young philosophers. Three aims he might have in this further development of content: (1) to show that no one has any easy answers to value questions, (2) to show that each individual has to resolve such questions by making considered judgments based on application of values to present circumstances, and (3) to help children value analytic approaches to problems.

Stories read and discussed by children often involve feelings and values. Second grade children have read a story about building a house and the teacher remarks, "The picture here shows the man putting in the telephone. Do most houses have telephones?" A lively discussion follows:

PATTY: "Every house should have a telephone."

JILL: "Every house does have a telephone. Who ever heard of one that didn't?"

ARNIE: "Even my maid has a telephone."

ERNIE: "Telephones are put in every house."

TEACHER: "Where might one find a house without a telephone?"

PATTY: "That's impossible."

TEACHER: "No, houses in rural areas don't have telephones sometimes."

ANN: "I know someone who doesn't have a phone because she doesn't have enough money."

PATTY: "Everyone has enough money for a telephone."

TEACHER: "Who puts in the plumbing?"

In turning to plumbing, the teacher may be buying time to think how to deal with the misconceptions the children have shown about how other people live. If it is important to teach about plumbing, the teacher still can return on another occasion to develop content that might help to educate for caring about others.

When a child reveals a fundamental misconception that likely is shared by many adults, the teacher may well take heed. For example, after a fifth grade child had read aloud the story, *The Man Who Didn't Wash His Dishes*, the teacher asked for suggestions of what the man might do to solve his problem. Suggestions ranged from setting the dishes outside to be washed by the rain to getting a wife. Finally, Jack spoke up: "Of course, if the man had been smart, he would have had them insured. Then he could break them all and the insurance company would buy new ones for him." The teacher probably had not planned to get into matters of ethics and economics as a result of a period of sharing favorite stories, yet it is difficult to imagine any content more worth developing with Jack at the earliest opportunity than facts on who pays for insurance losses and the responsibility of individuals in such matters.

Many studies can be used to develop better feelings and values if the teacher seeks to include this dimension in students' experiences at school. A beginning teacher describes her approach to a study of "The Home," which was required in her first grade. The children in her class were from a low economic group and were deprived in their homes of many of the physical and psychological comforts which she had taken for granted. Therefore, she decided not to pursue topics like "What do people who live in deserts use for homes?" Instead, the children explored various types of homes they themselves came from—trailers, apartment houses, apartments shared with other families, homes of their own, and an orphanage. Since these were city children, they were interested in the teacher's description of the country home where she grew up, with seven acres and no near neighbors. They discussed the advantages and disadvantages of various home locations.

The children were particularly interested in hearing about Nelda and Teddy and their home in the orphanage. Since these children had the best of care, though they were unhappy to be away from their families, they were proud to tell the others about their life. The children were fascinated with the idea of living with so many other children, eating in one big dining room, and having to "visit" one's own brothers and sisters in another part of the building.

When the class paid a visit to the orphanage, they began to sense that life in a large group of children meant always obeying rules, always following a schedule, never being left to one's own devices. But they realized also that Nelda and Teddy were loved and cared for just as they were.

How much more significant was the content developed with these children than if they had spent all of their time on informational items like names and functions of rooms in a house and homes in other lands. To come to understand that Nelda and Teddy might get tired of obeying rules and doing what the teacher said and to see justice in special treatment for them would be to take a big step in feeling for others. Truly the teacher had created opportunities for developing content in response to data placed in the situation by the children.

Children continue to give teachers cues that they may be ready for a new learning. The response to these cues may be watchful waiting for an opportunity to help the individual take on the needed learning. An example furnished by a fifth grade teacher illustrates such a response:

> As we discussed how we could set up a classroom library, Jim said he wouldn't bring any books in because they might be torn or stolen. And anyway, he continued, they were given to him for his own use, not for others to read. This brought sharp criticism from several members of the group, but Jim remained adamant.
>
> Several weeks later, after our library was running successfully, I noticed that Jim was reading freely from the books others had brought in. I asked him what he thought of the

wide selection that was available when so many shared their books. He said it was a great idea and mentioned that he had several books which others might like. I didn't press him at this point, and a few days later he brought in four books to add to our library.

It takes self-control on a teacher's part to wait until a child can have a chance to see for himself the value of a particular way of behaving. The temptation is to use little lectures to make a point. The teacher was particularly understanding when he did not express special satisfaction at Jim's "reform." It was important that Jim come to his own decision on the merits of the case rather than to conform merely to please someone else.

A teacher is charged by society to perpetuate the higher values of that society. The teacher, then, must stand for something and should show in every way he can that he is really committed to such values himself. When it comes to teaching, other than by example, however, opportunities to see consequences of behavior in real situations are superior to verbal approaches to value development.

Children continue to need help in deciding what is just and fair as they learn more about what man has done to man over the centuries. A sixth grade teacher writes of the penetrating question raised by one of his students after they returned from an assembly program put on by a Navajo Indian lecturer and dancer. The question put by Justin was: "Does the good always win?"

The teacher was caught off guard and stammered, "Well, uh, no, I don't think we could say that," meanwhile wondering what the boy meant.

"No, I don't think so either," said Justin, "because look what we did to the Indians. They were here first and we took their land." It is to the teacher's credit that he immediately gave time for discussion of Justin's point and, further, encouraged the children to search for answers to some questions which they formulated together: How many Indians do we have now? Where are they? How could we have driven off the Indians if there were more of them than there were white men in the early days?

The teacher felt that as a result of their study the children had expanded their meanings for "good" and "bad." He realized that they had no final answers but he had grasped an opportunity to give them experience in using information in weighing value questions.

A sixth grade teacher carried out a carefully planned campaign to influence the feelings of his class about themselves and other people. He had noted that some children played the role of clown or expressed themselves through behavior that was not conducive to progress as a group. He also noted children who felt inferior scholastically and who seemed to have resigned themselves to this status. As he dealt with different pupils, the teacher tried to show that he understood reasons for various behaviors and he clarified these reasons for the individual. Then he embarked on what he described as "a program of psychology instruction" in the hope that better self-understanding would enable the children to contribute more to the class and consequently to feel more self-worth. The teacher writes, "My method most often has been to pick up an action before it has cooled off too much, giving an example of a similar piece of behavior and possible reasons for it, without pointing out any individuals in question."

When a new student, a shy and academically retarded girl from Florida, joined the group, the teacher noted what he believed were the fruits of his "psychology" teaching: "I began to observe that the other children were becoming concerned about Edna, who was virtually a lost soul. Some would ask me for permission to help her with some phase of the class work and in this way more than one acquaintance was established. Soon, there were girls waiting to accompany Edna home after dismissal. Of course there were incidents on the negative side of the ledger, but they did not outnumber the more pleasant experiences."

The teacher watched for opportunities to increase Edna's good feelings about herself. During a study of "Scouting" a boy was discoursing on methods used to treat snake bites. Here the teacher moved in. As he describes it:

> I threw a log on the fire by asking if there were any poisonous snakes in New Jersey and, if so, how they could be distinguished from non-poisonous snakes. Edna's hand shot up but I made sure to recognize the hands of other children; I wanted her to feel her hand up over her head for as long a time as possible, especially since this was her first attempt to be recognized. I had made it a practice to go to Edna's desk to discuss matters with her rather than to expose her to the necessity of speaking to me across the room. But now she wanted to speak and I finally recognized her hand.

What a sensitive teacher. He wanted the girl to *feel* her hand up for a long time! The rest of the story is less important. Edna did know a great deal about snakes and she was able to hold the attention of her classmates. When the children began to ask many questions, the teacher took one more step which showed much insight. He stated that there was no more time for questions but that individuals could consult Edna outside of class. Thus was Edna given a continuing role as their "snake expert," a status which should have contributed to good feelings about herself.

Even an inherently factual study like following the construction of a new school building can be made to yield human values. A sixth grade teacher conducting such a study helped her pupils to gain awareness and respect for those who work under difficult conditions—in the cold, with noisy machines, where clothes and hands become very dirty, in small spaces, or where there is heavy lifting or hauling.

Sometimes firsthand experience is not possible for bringing meaning to a study. In that case a verbal comparison with something familiar may help. A high school history teacher, in 1956, began his class one day by stating that he wasn't going to talk about American history but preferred to discuss the recent revolt in Hungary. He went on to point out how all-powerful the Russian state was and how unmercifully it had treated the Hungarian rebels.

He asked the students to imagine that they were living in Hungary under the Russian yoke and to assume that one day they were approached by a group of Hungarians urging them to join publicly in a revolt against the State. This group was interested in publishing a list of rebel supporters who would be willing to fight against the Communist might in order to establish a free Hungary. The teacher then asked his class if, knowing what the consequences were for openly defying the State, any of them would be willing to sign such a statement of defiance against the Communist regime.

After some discussion, it was discovered that, while most of the class would be willing to fight in an "underground" movement, none would be willing to risk death or imprisonment by openly challenging the government.

At that point the teacher said that he was going to tell them about a group of rebels who did just what they, the class members, were afraid to do. He pointed out that the oppressive government was not that of Communist Russia, but was just as strong and would repay traitorous opposition with similar punishment. Their chances of succeeding in their struggle for freedom were just as slim as those of the Hungarian rebels of the present day. He concluded by saying that the government they fought was the British Empire and the public listing of their names was on this document—the Declaration of Independence! He unrolled the document in question and showed the class the names of the courageous rebels against authority who were brave enough to take on the most powerful government of the time and were brave enough to risk the consequences.

The class felt like cheering. These familiar names took on a whole new dimension. As one student aptly phrased it, "Man! There was nothin' chicken about those guys!" Testimony, the reporter thought, to effective teaching.

Some may question that the parallels drawn by the teacher were as close as he declared. In fact, it is to be hoped that the teacher went on to encourage his students to challenge such parallels and to help them seek reliable authority for agreement or disagreement. On another occasion, the teacher might have the students discover their own modern examples of historical events and thus gain more independence in thinking about human affairs.

A twelfth grade class studying American literature came upon the poem "Thanatopsis" by William Cullen Bryant. The teacher, aware of the fact that high school seniors usually need to work out their feelings about death, said:

"Bryant was about your age when he wrote this poem. This is his philosophy about death. Many of you probably have quite different thoughts on the subject. I wonder what they are? I wonder how different religions look at this matter?"

It developed that the three major Western faiths were well represented in the class, even though some students were entirely without ideas on the topic. Answering the question "What is my own belief?" aroused intense interest, which led to further reading. Gunther's *Death Be Not Proud* [6] was brought in. Norman Corwin's classic recording of "The Lonesome Train" was played. Saroyan's *Human Comedy* [7] was read and discussed.

The teacher noticed that, while the students were never morbid,

[6] New York: Harper & Brothers, 1949.
[7] New York: Harcourt, Brace and Company, 1943.

many confessed to a fear of death. Several found that writing out their feelings about this fear was an unexpectedly satisfying experience. Thus, by beginning with one piece of literature and fostering free expression of feelings about this and other reading, the teacher helped the students to make connections between their own concerns and feelings as recorded by others.

OPPORTUNITIES FOR DEVELOPING FLEXIBILITY OF APPROACH

Teachers, at all times and unavoidably, are helping young people become either more flexible or more inflexible in their approaches to experience. Teachers influence learners by the ways they themselves operate and by the behavior they close off or tolerate or encourage. It is not easy to find examples of teachers deliberately setting out to develop in learners the ability to vary their approaches to life situations, now dealing analytically with a problem, now making intuitive leaps, now being freely imaginative.[8] Attempts to cultivate one approach or the other may be seen in the illustrations that follow.

A first grade teacher decided to give her children some experience in observing and generalizing with respect to likeness and difference. She had the children bring in musical instruments, whistles, and records. The children were asked to create sounds on these instruments. When asked which sounds were alike and which were different, the children verbalized, "My whistle is louder." "My instrument makes a better sound." "A whistle makes a different sound from a flute." "You can't expect the same sounds from different whistles and musical instruments." The teacher asked the children when out of school to listen to the sounds of automobiles, trains, and any birds they might see, and to tell the class about them the next day. The next day these reports came in, "I have two automobiles, and the engine on one sounds different from the engine on the other." "My brother's car is souped up and makes a lot more noise than my father's car." "Some birds can sing and some birds can't sing."

On direct questioning as to what they made of all this, the

8 Jerome S. Bruner in *The Process of Education* (Cambridge: Harvard University Press, 1960), Chapter 4, discusses intuitive and analytic thinking as complementary processes. He recognizes the difficulty of cultivating intuitive thinking and suggests that research be done on the problem.

general expression was that "Different things make different sounds." "You can't expect the same sound from a bird as a train." "Whistles that are alike can sound the same way."

The teacher went on to help the class see that children might weigh the same and yet one might be taller than the other or have hair of a different color. From this they drew such conclusions as, "A short boy can weigh as much as a tall boy" and "Your color has nothing to do with what you weigh and how big you are."

As a next step, the teacher placed on the bulletin board without comment a series of pictures of animals and birds of different colors. After discussion of these the teacher asked, "Is it only animals and birds that have different colors?" Replies to this were, "Automobiles have different colors," "Houses have different colors," "Clothes have different colors." The teacher finally asked directly whether people have different colors and drew these responses: "We are all white," "Some people are chocolate," "Japs are different."

The teacher knew that it would be a long jump for the children to make from the color of automobiles to the color of people and she realized that such exercises were not going to remake attitudes in any dramatic way. She was being as creative as she knew how in helping her class to do analytic thinking and she had plans for further experiences designed to foster a rational approach. Who knows what might be accomplished if more teachers set out intentionally to develop such content with children?

Even a standard study such as the westward movement can be used to develop comparative thinking. A sixth grade teacher, knowing that his children liked TV westerns, decided to personalize as much as possible a required study of the United States following the Revolutionary War. He proposed to the class that each student elect to join one of three imaginary wagon trains leaving from Boston, Philadelphia, and lower Virginia. Thus, they could follow the northern, middle, and southern routes across the country. Once the teacher had suggested the basic idea, the children joined in the planning. They decided that each group would study the physical features, the climatic conditions, and the natural resources as they went through each state. They would then try to project their ideas from their beginning date in the early eighteen hundreds to the present, in imagining what would grow, what industries would develop, and the like. Scouts would "ride off" and in turn come back to report findings.

One detail of the study will serve as an example of experience with an analytic approach to a question that arose. Through using maps obtained from the Army Engineer Corps, the northern group found that one of the rivers they needed to cross was too deep to ford at their date of crossing. This led the class to investigate why the same river could be forded today. Their research showed that since the eighteen hundreds great stands of timber had been removed from the areas up river and since then soil erosion had filled the river bottom with muck.

Teachers can help students value imaginative thinking by welcoming evidences of such an approach when they occur. A third grade teacher was preparing for a study of weather and suggested that the children go to the window on a clear, bright day to observe the clouds. He undoubtedly expected rather factual answers to his leading question, "What is a cloud?" Notice the answers that came and how they were received:

> JAN: "A fleecy pillow stuffed with air."
> PAUL: "It is just hanging there—all milky white."
> LOU ANN: "It's a tree, or a bird, or a puff of cream."
> RICHARD: "That is all make-believe. A cloud is part of the atmosphere."
> TONY: "There are different kinds of clouds. What kind do you mean?"
> RICHARD: "I'm not sure of the names."
> ADAM: "It's like a great, nice easy chair."
> LILY: "It's a puff of air all joined together."
> GEORGE: "Sometimes it is all scary and black, and big like a bad dream."

The teacher then closed the discussion: "Tomorrow we will learn how clouds are formed." He had allowed the fanciful and poetic responses to flow freely. He could wait until another day to develop scientific explanations, although Richard had given him an opening to turn to a factual approach had he chosen to take it.

The teacher might have helped the children to be more aware of the difference in approach within the comments made on that day and might have been more explicit as to the values of each. Perhaps, when he returns to the topic on another day, he will point up the distinction between fact and fancy and will make clear that both have a place in human affairs.

Three illustrations will show how young people sometimes are hampered in development of rational approaches.

In a third grade the children are asked, "What do you think of when you think of the earth?" The answers include volcanoes and land and water, rocks and sand and animals, plants and mountains and plateaus. An observer turns to a child and says, "Do we think of people too?" "No," was the child's reply, "because this is going to be a study of science—you know, the earth and what it is made of."

It seems that these children are compartmentalizing their thinking in a needless way and that such rigidity can only be a barrier to either imaginative or rational thinking.

The children in a second grade have taken a walk to observe fall colors. The next day they are talking about the experience:

> TEACHER: "What makes the leaves fall? Remember we talked about this yesterday?
> DICK: "Their energy runs out—that's what makes them fall."
> NOLA: "Energy means to run and play."
> MARIA: "How can leaves have energy?"
> DICK: "They do because when it runs out they begin to fall."
> TEACHER: "The leaves make most of the food for the tree— food makes energy."

The teacher may have meant to close the door on the subject of energy, assuming he had "taught" its meaning. He may, on the other hand, have signed off temporarily to give himself time to think of ways of developing more meaning. Most deplorable is the circular kind of reasoning that Dick is exhibiting. It is hoped that the teacher will find ways to help the boy both to understand fully the process he describes so glibly and to state his explanation more precisely.

A fifth grade teacher opens a discussion by reminding the children that yesterday they learned that their bodies are like machines. "What happens when an important part of a machine breaks down?" she asks. Peter, the first child to respond says, "They have to be repaired or the machine stops." This seems to have suggested the teacher's next question, "What would happen if your heart stopped working?" It is impossible to know whether or not the teacher meant to invite the kind of response Peter gave next but a study of the interaction that follows raises some interesting questions:

> PETER: "Don't say we'd all die because now they can take out hearts and massage them—and you are all set again."
>
> TEACHER: "No, they don't take out hearts—they can massage them sometimes, but not all people live even then."
>
> ELLEN: "But it can be done now because science has advanced."
>
> TEACHER: "Let's put up here on the blackboard all the things we need to keep our bodies in good working condition." (*One of these was, "Get plenty of fresh air and exercise."*) "All of you should get lots of fresh air and exercise. You should have at least two or three hours each day in the out-of-doors."
>
> TED: "Yes, that's what you keep saying and the books say. But if it is so important, what I'd like to know is why we have so much homework that you don't have a chance to get out after school."
>
> SEVERAL: "Yes, why?"
>
> TEACHER: "You don't have that much."
>
> TED: "Enough to keep us inside most of the time."
>
> TEACHER: "What kind of exercise do you like best of all?
>
> TED: "Well, it isn't homework exercise."
>
> TEACHER: "Homework isn't exercise, is it?"
>
> ELLEN: "To most of us it is—writing exercises and things like that."
>
> TEACHER: "Is watching TV an exercise?"
>
> TED: "No, but it is something we don't have to do and it does make more sense than what we do in homework anyway."
>
> TEACHER: "We are going to move on to the next thing our bodies need."
>
> TED (*under his breath*): "That's just what I mean."

Several pieces of data have been placed before this teacher. Even if Peter and Ellen are right on how far heart surgery has advanced, do they have, in general, too optimistic a view of the marvels man can accomplish? Are not many of the children in the class ready for information and concepts far beyond the simple health rules in the "book" and in the teacher's mind and thus may they be developing a distaste for "learning"? What basis does the teacher have for his arbitrary statement on the amount of time these children should spend outside each day? Would the children develop a better process of thinking as well as a better attitude toward the health "rule" if they went to these authoritative sources themselves? What makes this teacher and others refer to active recreation as exercise? Do the children really understand the function of exercise? Could they be helped to see a relationship between two apparently different uses of the same word (physical exercises and writing exercises)? Do the children have a right to an honest answer when they point out what they see as adult inconsistencies? Do they have a right to homework that makes sense to them? Lastly, this teacher had an opportunity to help children make order out of undigested information they already had but he chose instead to "move on to the next thing" on the list to be learned.

BARRIERS TO CREATIVITY IN DEVELOPMENT OF CONTENT

Many of the barriers to creativity in grasping opportunities for developing content have been implied in the comments on the preceding examples. Stereotyped thinking is a frequent barrier—the belief that only certain subject matter is worthy of school time, for example. Insensitivity to cues that show lack of understanding or need for help on a certain value or skill is another major barrier. Often, however, a teacher stops short only because he does not know what to do with an opportunity at the time.

One barrier that has not been illustrated so well is lack of judgment in selecting subject matter to place before a group in the first place. When a teacher plans to introduce new informational content, he should have a sound basis for deciding what concepts it is important to present to children of the age he is teaching. Further, he needs to have such full knowledge of his class that he can judge what materials will be within their range and what may be a waste of their time, if not actually a source of misconceptions. A first grade teacher had been attempting to help her pupils to learn about the earth and why the seasons change. While she was showing a film strip illustrating the earth in four positions around the sun, this conversation took place:

TEACHER: "See how the earth changes position?"

BOB: "If the earth is round, how come water can stay on it?"

TEACHER: "Gravity keeps it on—this is hard for you to understand."

JOE: "What is gravity?"

TEACHER: "You will understand that when you are older."

JOE: "Why do you have to be older?"

TEACHER: "Look at the film strip now."

TONI: "What makes the earth turn?"

STEVE: "The earth is like a balloon—air coming out of it makes the earth turn around."

TEACHER: "We will talk about that later. See the earth in four different places here?" (*Points to the positions shown in the film.*)

JOE (*turning to Bob*): "I didn't know we had four earthses, did you?"

JOE (*whispering*): "I wonder which one we are on now?"

The teacher finishes the "lesson" by talking about the change of seasons in relation to the earth's position.

Teachers may misjudge their pupils and not anticipate how difficult certain concepts may be. Teachers who are more creative will observe and listen as carefully as they can for evidence of understanding or the lack of it and will gather clues to help in correcting misconceptions. They will be especially shrewd in sensing when to drop a topic that has proved to be ill timed. To keep children confused over too long a period, especially if they are made to feel that the matter is clear and simple and that they really do understand, is to make it difficult for the individual to maintain his capacity for knowing when he understands and when he does not and to be able to declare publicly that something is not clear.

This principle was clearly being violated by a first grade teacher who had her children copying the following sentence from the chalkboard: "The plant in the terrarium is watered by condensation." Not one child who was questioned could explain what condensation meant. One perhaps had a glimmering of understanding: "It's like putting ice water in a warm glass." Another was getting practice in thinking he understood something he clearly did not: "I'm not sure, but the teacher says it is when the water in the air evaporates, so that is what it must be."

Another barrier to development of meaningful content is to

teach for testing. When a second grade teacher asked, "Who were the Pilgrims?" she drew many disappointing answers:

> TOMMY: "They were like Davie Crockett and Daniel Boone."
>
> AUDREY: "They lived in olden times when they had to use a churn to make butter."
>
> BARBARA: "They worked to make a good country—like George Washington."
>
> TEACHER: "Are you thinking about our trip to the village museum? Let's think about Pilgrims."
>
> ANDY: "They fought a war with the Indians."
>
> TEACHER: "No, you are confused."
>
> EDWIN: "Pilgrims came here long ago and helped to make our country great—they helped Daniel Boone and things like that."
>
> TEACHER: "We are going to have to learn about Pilgrims. I thought we were ready to have our test but we will have to go over the material once more."

It is one thing to help children build a gradual picture of the story of their country as stories and pictures raise questions. It is another to try to develop accurate chronologies of events at ages when the remote and the near past are difficult to distinguish. To teach material such as had confused the minds of these second grade children in order that they may pass a test on it does not seem a promising route to a vigorous, self-propelled search for knowledge.

One last barrier may be another individual with power to prevent the teacher from using his own best judgment in selecting opportunities for development of content. A "room" mother came to say goodbye to her son's fifth grade class. Her four-year-old daughter, Alice, had developed leukemia and would have to be hospitalized until her death, since there was no known cure for the disease. The mother wanted the children to know why she could not help them any longer.

In addition to wanting to do something for the little girl, the children had many questions to which they desired answers: "What is leukemia?" "Why can't they cure it?" "Does Alice know she is going to die?" "How does it feel to be in a hospital for so long?" "Does leukemia hurt?" "Are doctors and nurses nice?" "It must cost a lot of money to stay in the hospital so long—how much?" "Is Alice by herself all day?" "Are there a lot of people in hospitals?"

The teacher realized that the children had real fear of doctors and nurses and hospitals. Also they took a deep interest in the small girl and wanted to make puppets and put on a show for her and other patients. The teacher could see value for the children in hospital visits, talks with doctors, puppet shows put on for patients who were children like themselves. However, when he asked the principal for permission to undertake such a project, he was refused. He could not be allowed, it appeared, to take time away from a study of the westward movement.

Conclusion

Children and youth want to know so many things: Do people have to get married to have children? Is Jimmy adopted? Why do some people live in trailers? What is a Jew? What is the difference between Catholics and Protestants? How come we don't have a king? Why is the United Nations building in the United States? Why are we afraid of other countries? How come Puerto Ricans speak Spanish? Who will own the moon? What makes an American? The barriers to development of content do not seem to rest in the pupils, who offer many opportunities to their teachers.

Whether a child presents his teacher with a piece of rock that will "pick up iron and steel like a magnet" or with a question he would like answered ("I heard a man on TV say that scientists need academic freedom—what does this mean?") or with evidence that he lacks sensitivity ("Everyone has enough money for a telephone"), the teacher must decide what to do with this offering. If the young student is ignored or put off each time he shows that he needs or wants information, he will not be likely to continue communicating his needs and wants.

The illustrations presented in this chapter suggest that creativity in teaching begins at the very point where many teachers stop and close the door to further inquiry. This is not to say that the teacher must pick up every lead. In fact, to do so in many cases would be to attempt to correct misconceptions or develop a change in attitude through mere verbalizing. Some opportunities can be grasped at the moment; some must be postponed or never followed up at all. Usually the data placed in the situation by a child can be received in such a way as to leave the door open for future attention. If the teacher at least stops to probe a little for a clue to the child's meaning, he will be helped in planning what to do next. Sometimes the child may be invited to give the matter further thought, to talk it over with someone else, or to go to another source of information, with assurance that new data on the subject will be welcomed by the teacher and that time will be provided for receiving it.

Creativity in the development of content lies in making deliberate, well-based decisions on what to let pass and what to follow through, and on how to follow through, including finding time to do so. Frequently, it seems, a teacher must give up some intended path in content development in order to respond to unexpected data placed in the situation by a pupil. Creativity in teaching should result in such flexibility in planning that there is room for new ideas, room for more than the ideas a teacher *needs* to deliver.

For a teacher to show relatively more creativity in the development of content, there seem to be three requirements. First, it is essential that the teacher have in mind a more or less clear image of content worthy of development, a framework within which to operate. What are the important areas of human experience to which young people should be introduced? Over what processes should they be gaining increasing control? What meanings should they be developing for their living with others? The teacher needs a sense of direction, a way of judging when decisions he has made are "good."

Second, a teacher must understand the structure of the content with which he may be expected to help another individual deal. He must see the interrelatedness of knowledge, the interdependence of means and ends, the mutual support of analysis, intuition, and imagination.

Third, he must have convictions with respect to the importance of multidimensional content which cause him to find the time and the ways to provide the experience necessary for satisfactory individual progress at any point.

The method that appears to be common to those developing con-

tent creatively is dependence on the discovery motive in learning—
reliance on the individual's need to explore, to express what has
been found through exploring, and to gain the needed cultural skills
or tools to help the exploration and expression become more satisfying and fruitful.[9]

[9] The writers are indebted to Dwayne Huebner of Teachers College, Columbia University, for this concluding formulation.

ABOUT THE AUTHOR ... *Prudence Bostwick, contributing a chapter on one aspect of design in teaching, has gathered ideas from many sources but she has drawn especially on her own broad and varied experiences. She was long a member of the Denver, Colorado, public school system, which gave her the opportunity to be among the teachers experimenting with a high school core program as part of the Eight Year Study. She was a constructive leader in the "progressive education" movement and later contributed her imaginative leadership to the Association for Supervision and Curriculum Development. She has been Coordinator of Curriculum for the Division of Education of the San Fernando Valley State College at Northridge, California, where she is a professor of education.*

Always enthusiastic about trying new ideas and helping children and adults to try them, Miss Bostwick has been particularly active in projects to improve intergroup relations. She has contributed widely to professional yearbooks and periodicals. An essay most pertinent to her chapter in this volume is "Schools for Growing," written with Isabel W. Dible (Childhood Education, *April, 1958*).

6 INVENTIVENESS WITH TIME, SPACE, AND MATERIALS

Developing a stimulating environment for learning is one of the primary responsibilities of a teacher. He must accept the past experiences which young people bring to the learning situation, and then provide the material, events, and circumstances to which they may relate. He can provide the sensory appeal that gives quality to learning and can open up the many different avenues through which knowledge is gained and behavior changed. The teacher can have available for each young person resources for mind and spirit, for eyes and hands with which he can express his own uniqueness and through which he can come to know the uniqueness of others.

As a teacher plans for learning opportunities that will make possible for children and youth experiences of heightened vitality, he seizes upon his own resources as a person—his feelings, his imagination, his power of thought—and he seizes upon the environmental resources of time, space, and materials. Just as the artist selects line, color, form, and texture and arranges them in the interest of use and beauty, so a teacher must select and arrange the physical environment of space, time, and materials, to call forth maximum responsiveness of learners.

It is not difficult to spot a classroom where a more creative teacher is at work. Although inventiveness with resources is more difficult when the funds with which a teacher must work are limited, it is amazing what a teacher who puts his mind to it can discover in the fields, prairies, deserts, and woods of rural America, and even in the vacant lots and dumps of the city and what he can find by way of free and inexpensive materials.[1] No matter what the monetary limitations under which teacher and children must work, their creative spirit with even modest encouragement will continue to seek ways to bring color and life into the classroom. There are shells from the beach, dried grasses and reeds with which to make baskets, wood for construction, crayfish from the pond, the cocoon of the Cecropia moth, frogs' eggs in season, and jars of finger paint made of water thickened with cornstarch and bright with pure vegetable coloring.

When sufficient funds are available from tax dollars, the resources assembled through teacher ingenuity are liberally supplemented. The classroom usually is rich in books, maps, globes, posters, hangings, possibly a color reproduction of the work of a master painter—all arranged with an eye to relationships and with a good measure of restraint. There are electric outlets, a screen, a tape recorder, a phonograph, a television set, dark curtains; and ready for the teacher's use from the school library or other central repository are recordings, films, and film strips. Storage areas and work rooms are ample.

If the room is an elementary classroom, there are centers of interest, tables with chairs invitingly drawn up where books with individual titles are arranged, where science materials tempt the curious, where art materials stand ready for use by a group of children who are to record an experience, whether in water color, crayons, colored paper, or clay. It is obvious that here is an atmosphere in which children are invited to express their ideas, an atmosphere created by a teacher who is himself awake in every pore of his being, and whose pleasure it is to share with children the wonder and delight that he has never lost.

[1] See (1) Association for Childhood Education, *Children Can Make It! Experiences in the World of Materials,* Reprint Service, Bulletin No. 28, 1954, and *Uses for Waste Materials,* Bulletin No. 41, 1949; (2) Field Enterprise Educational Corporation, *Sources of Free and Inexpensive Educational Materials,* Merchandise Mart Plaza, Chicago 54, 1958; and (3) Frances W. Keene, *Fun Around the World,* Pelham, New York: The Seashore Press, 1955.

Except for shops and laboratories, the classrooms of the secondary schools usually are much less bright and cheerful than are those of the elementary school. That the older students tend to deal more with abstractions and symbols than do younger children is no reason to defend the sepia atmosphere of so many secondary school buildings. The words which Paul Diederich wrote more than twenty years ago helped to usher in a new point of view about a learning environment that today should be even more generally realized by high schools and colleges in this country:

> Pupils should be unwilling to live and work in the usual drab and impersonal classroom . . . which often has nothing in it which pupils have made—nothing which represents their own ideas and feelings. They should set about immediately to liven it up with objects of their own manufacture which have color, humor, spontaneity, and charm. Their dread of putting any marks on the walls and the austerity and aloofness of anything they think proper to mount there should be overcome. A mural does not have to be guaranteed perfect in advance in order to be fit decoration for a classroom, and it does not have to be regarded as permanent or unalterable. Anything which the occupants of the room do not like can and should be painted out and replaced by something better. No school should be regarded as doing its duty by the arts in which any classroom is dead. The walls should ring with the color and form in which the occupants of the room have recorded their joy in living.[2]

It is obvious that if children and older boys and girls are to be free to express their joy in living, they must live in an atmosphere in which they are free to explore media, to toy with words and ideas, and to communicate without fear the forms and figures and events that reveal how the world looks to them.

INVENTIVENESS IN THE USE OF TIME

In time-conscious America, life has become a series of experiences separated into measurable sections. Seconds, minutes, hours, and days and nights are allocated to a variety of duties and responsi-

2 Paul Diederich, "Common Function of the Arts in General Education." Included in *Materials Prepared by Participants in the Arts Group of the Progressive Education Association Summer Workshop,* Sarah Lawrence College, Bronxville, 1937, p. 12.

bilities. With tremendous vigor, life is lived in a number of dimensions : earning a living or going to school, seeking recreation, doing homework, caring for one's self and for one's house and family, participating in community affairs. In schools, especially, there is tremendous emphasis upon schedules, promptness, and bell-ringing ; an activity is stopped, not because it has been finished, but because a new activity must begin. Schedules provide for balance in the program and the assurance that every aspect of the curriculum has its fair share of time, but great danger comes from scheduling in accordance with long-standing patterns built in the days of atomistic theories of learning. Twelve or more different subjects may be taught to elementary school children in compartments of time, each unrelated to the other. This is a serious threat to the wholeness of experience and seldom provides a child with the opportunity to explore or to manipulate ideas. The fifteen- to twenty-minute period of the elementary school becomes the forty-three-and-a-half minute period of the secondary school and the fifty-minute period of the college.

There is a sense of well-being, of efficiency, in an industrial plant or school that is run on a regular and predictable time design. Almost everyone believes that the discipline of promptness and the fairness of equal distribution of time are guarantees of accomplishment. They are the enabling force of the assembly line and genius of mass production. They make possible the rise of living standards ; but are they conducive to creativity in teaching?

It is generally conceded that creativity comes out of uncommitted time, unstructured time, free from imposition outside the individual.[3] Playing with ideas or things, considering new combinations of the old, or sensing new relationships seems to flourish best in an atmosphere of leisure and relaxation. A person deeply involved in problems to be solved or questions to be answered who has no concern for immediate pressures may suddenly seize upon a new idea. An incubation period for ideas must be provided. Biographies and autobiographies of creative thinkers include accounts of these times of apparent quietness, of free and drifting ideas, out of which may suddenly emerge clues for the solution of a problem or a whole new approach to a situation that seemed to

3 See Karl W. Deutsch, "Creativity in a Scientific Civilization," in *Changing Attitudes in a Changing World* (New York: Bank Street College of Education Publications, 1958).

have come to a dead end. This inner searching seeks out new relationships; its loneliness is an essential element of its being.

The Orient, where there is greater respect for the meditative life than there is in the Western world, recognizes that an individual contemplating is "in a little house of his own." He must not be interrupted nor even asked what he is doing. Intrusion upon this life of the mind and spirit is considered an affront, not only to the individual and the respect due him, but also to the mores of the culture. The right to privacy even in a crowd, the right to time to think, to create, must somehow be granted in larger measure to the people of the Western world and especially to teachers, whose profession is an art.

Teachers and administrators have not been blind to the effect of time pressures on their own creativity and have sought for new ways of organizing the school year, the school day, and activities within the day. In some schools larger blocks of time than usual have been provided, in which teacher and students (of whatever age) can concern themselves with a problem or broad topic and plan for activities that make possible a multidimensional approach to learning. In this way some teachers avoid the shallow and unrewarding experiences that come from hurried covering of subject matter on a verbal level—without relating the content to its use in living. As knowledge of the physical, economic, and social world accumulates, the pressure on the schools to teach more and more content and skills is overwhelming. The problem can be solved only by a more intelligent approach to the whole field of curriculum and teaching. *It may well be that if concern for creativity in teaching becomes paramount, the school will be a place where each person will be able to learn at his own rate and stay long enough with a problem to solve it or long enough with an interest to deepen it and make it a part of himself.*

Conserving Time Through Emphasizing Meaning

One of the most important ideas coming again to the fore in curriculum development is that time can best be conserved for use in the learning process by emphasis upon meaning as an indispensable accompaniment of skill development. The hours that have been spent in drill have been lamented in modern educational theory primarily because drill has been entered upon with too little understanding of its method or purpose. When children see relationship between practice and power over ideas, intelligence is at work to speed up the acquisition of skills.

Another area of concern is concept development. Here again is recognition of the need for clarification of purposes in learning and the need to gain knowledge and understanding through a variety of experiences in which three vital aspects are present in varying degrees: the practical to insure reality, the intellectual to provide meaning, and the emotional to give unity to the whole.[4]

In addition to taking time for a variety of experiences that achieve their meaning through relationships to the larger goal, teachers must see time as a dimension in the creative process. Of all the resources needed for creative thinking and acting, the one most difficult to manipulate is time. It has a way of slipping away from us, of passing most rapidly when we want to think through an experience in a leisurely way. Creativity in teaching means somehow managing time so that boys and girls can work at their own speed and frequently without interruption when the mood is on to finish something. This much attention to individual differences is almost impossible to provide in a schedule built on bells.

Manipulating Time in the Elementary School

A self-contained classroom in the elementary school may become through the creativity of the teacher an environment where children have time and freedom to explore, to manipulate materials, to achieve that wonderful sense of "awareness toward the inside to bring it out and awareness toward the outside to bring it in." [5]

Even within a self-contained classroom care must be taken to organize the school day in such a way that provision is made for interrelationships in learning. One way to insure time for thinking, planning, and exploring is a unit method of teaching, in which interests may be pursued and problems solved without regard to subject boundaries. The nature of a unit itself demands new arrangements in time. For example, instead of a formalized succession of periods of fifteen to twenty minutes each devoted to spelling, penmanship, reading, geography, and art, teacher and children plan together for study of a large problem area through which

---

[4] "Emotional" is used here as John Dewey uses it, not to refer to *an* emotion like anger, love, or hate, but rather to a generalized feeling that suffuses the whole of a vital experience. See p. 41 in *Art as Experience* (New York: Minton, Balch and Co., 1934).

[5] Ross Mooney, "Research as Creative Inquiry," unpublished study, p. 118.

knowledge, skills, interests, and appreciation all may develop. Whatever drill is necessary to establish skills or habits becomes a meaningful part of the work of the unit.

In such teaching there is time for exploration of ideas, browsing in the library to find appropriate resources, going on field trips to find material not otherwise available, reading, writing, speaking, dramatizing, painting, summarizing and evaluating, and planning again for the next step and the next unit. Time is saved through integration of experiences achieved through focusing or organizing ideas and through consciously planned relationships in learning. Here is time flowing like a river, in which a sequence of experiences moves toward a recognized goal. Here are children involved in an ongoing process and teachers creating an environment in which children can respond in a variety of ways to a conscious purpose.[6]

To move in this way, however, a teaching unit must be carefully planned with a beginning, a middle, and a foreseeable end, but planned with flexibility to permit side explorations, and even complete redirection of the unit when these are fruitful, and ready acceptance of new ideas when they are appropriate. The genius of any unit lies in being spontaneous enough to give the imagination of teachers and children free play and yet provide a discipline that will give design and meaning to the whole.

A favorite resource unit among teachers of second grade children in one school system is entitled "Our Five Senses." [7] Its primary purpose is to help teachers to design, for and with the children, learning experiences that will increase their sensitivity to the sights, sounds, smells, tastes, and textures of their immediate environment and that will help them to express their heightened awareness in a variety of ways. An introduction to the unit sets the tone and identifies the purposes for which it was created.

> Are children in the second grade beginning to take things for granted or are they continuing to wonder and to question? Have they lost the natural curiosity of little children? Have the newness and the excitement of the world worn off a bit, or are the interest and curiosity still there, ready to be stimulated and satisfied?

[6] For a detailed discussion of units and unit building in elementary schools see Lavone A. Hanna, Gladys L. Potter, and Neva Hagaman, *Unit Teaching in the Elementary School* (New York: Rinehart and Company, 1957).

[7] See *Social Studies Guide, Kindergarten Through Grade Twelve,* Denver, Colorado, Public Schools, 1954.

Appreciation, understanding, and awareness of the world about us come largely through sensory impressions. Too often we do very little directly to develop, stimulate, and refine these five senses through which our lives may become rich and colorful. Artists, poets, and novelists fill their works with sights, sounds, odors, and tastes that stimulate sensory impressions which enhance our understanding and appreciation. . . .

Through this unit we may make a very simple approach to the scientific method and the development of a few concepts in natural science. . . . As presented here, the terms simply suggest that we will help children to observe and to want to find out. From there we go on to understanding, interpretation, personal response and in many cases to creative imagination.[8]

As teacher and children develop their own special way of carrying out the unit, they find enjoyment of the world around them, in the good smell of rain on hot pavements, the feel of wool and silk, the sight of wind bending prairie grasses, the taste of apples, the sound of bells. Children draw upon songs, poetry, stories, and their own imaginations to help them to relish these moments of sensation and to make it possible for them to carry their experiences out of their own immediate world into a wider world where they share their wonder and delight with people who have experienced similar sensations and found them good.

It is the very essence of this unit that the teacher's responsiveness to the children's adventuring be of a high order. Nothing must be rushed through. A child must have time to consider thoughtfully the purposes he has in exploring his world of sensation. The teacher must help him to believe in his own urges as a creative person, to "open his mind outwardly to the play of the environment on his senses," to develop a "heightened awareness, a capacity to see more, hear more, and sense more than is usual for him." [9] A child must also have time, not only to concentrate on the sounds that come from bells of varying sizes and materials—the tinkling of sleigh bells and the great boom of a Japanese gong—but also to be caught up in his own feelings as he listens. This is the beginning

8 *Ibid.,* p. 3C.
9 Ross Mooney, *A Preliminary Listing of Indices of Creative Behavior* (Columbus, Ohio: Bureau of Educational Research, The Ohio State University, September 24, 1953).

of discovery and evaluation, the opening up of an experience that may be communicated to another. The variety of activities in this world of the five senses and the multitude of resources easily at hand must be enjoyed to the full and understood in meanings appropriate to the second grader. "Take time," writes the author of the unit, "for the children to enjoy, talk about and sniff the odors they find in their stories and songs." [10]

As children share their pleasure in "a bowl of flowers on the library table, branches tapping on the window, a favorite record, a gentle stroking of a rabbit that is guest for the day, the fragrance of hot gingerbread floating up from the lunchroom," they step up their awareness of the world around them.[11] Enjoyment of colors, textures, sounds and odors grows with each day's experiencing. Children may start a "five senses" center that grows through the weeks. If the sense of leisure and experience in depth are provided for, the children will read poems that bring pictures to the mind's eye, prepare dioramas of their most important discoveries, write stories and paint pictures to record their feelings, and find in music, either in songs or recordings, response to their own moods of joy, defeat, elation, quietness, anger, and loneliness. They will respond in new ways to the touch of rain and wind on their faces and to the feel of vibrating drums or violins.

In increasing the sensitivity of children to the world of their five senses, a creative teacher may help them to increase their ability to enter imaginatively into the feelings of other living beings. One second grader in summing up his response to the unit said, "I'm more careful now when I pick up my rabbit; I try to make my hands feel soft to him." [12]

Two comments may be made on the unit just described. The first is that a teacher need not organize such experiences as a unit of work in order for children to enjoy the benefits of so many different ways of discovering the wonder of things. The second is that the unit format does not in itself guarantee time for leisurely exploring of whatever is the chosen focus. Units may be "covered" as compulsively as chapters in a textbook. The lesson to be learned from the unit on the five senses is the value for children of time to savor.

[10] *Social Studies Guide, Kindergarten Through Grade Twelve,* Denver, Colorado, Public Schools, 1954, p. 21C.
[11] *Ibid.,* p. 3C.
[12] *Ibid.,* p. 28C.

Manipulating Time in the Secondary School

Manipulation of time at the secondary school level is a much more difficult task than at the elementary. The self-contained classroom gives way in junior and senior high schools to special classrooms where students go to meet teachers in various subject fields. Although seventh and eighth grades may in some localities be under the management of one teacher for the whole day, the secondary school pattern is definitely geared to the teacher specialist. The advantage of this arrangement is in its provision of teachers who are extensively trained in one or two areas of the curriculum; the disadvantage is in the necessity of cutting the day into six or seven "periods" and limiting students to a scheduled number of minutes with any one teacher or any one activity.

The result is a tight schedule and one that is difficult to change. A few voices are raised, however, with questions as to whether we must always be subject to this time pattern. Would it not be better to use one-half or one-third of the day under one teacher to design a curriculum to provide for interrelationships in learning? Would it not be wise in the interests of guidance and closer relationships between teacher and students if a teacher could meet fewer students over a longer period of time? Would it not be better to divide the schedule in such a way that general education, including the basic requirements of the secondary school, be given a consecutive time in the school day so that students might take field trips, make interviews, prepare materials, and solve problems that demand concerted effort without having to take time out of the more specialized areas of the curriculum?

Could we not learn from the foreign language training directed by the Armed Forces in World War II? It was found that the most successful approach to languages was one in which a whole experience was focused on the problem at hand. If we wish to develop a nation of people who can actually use a foreign language, do we not need to make possible periods of time when the effort of the student is focused upon the language, its people, and its culture? To take French, Spanish, German, or Russian one "hour" a day for four years often results in ability to read but in almost no feeling of being "at home" in the language. To be immersed in it, to live it, breathe it, and speak it in order to communicate at all— this would be an exciting and rewarding use of time and would give, to one who experiences it deeply and wholly, power over another language and an understanding of another culture. If we would not give an extended period of time during the regular school year, could we not use vacation time for such a concentrated interest as a foreign language?

It is true that at the secondary level, especially senior high school, and at the college level, there is a lessening for most students of the time devoted to experiences in the arts. Already, with a new emphasis on mathematics and science in the junior high school, time for academic studies is encroaching seriously on time for the arts. Perhaps the answer is a twelve- or eleven-month school program with summer camping, summer schools in arts and languages, and summer travel supplementing and giving new vigor to the educational experiences of young people.

It is not necessary, however, to wait for such drastic changes before inventing new ways of using time. For almost twenty years schools in various parts of the country have been designing new schedules to make possible larger blocks of time within which teachers and students may work together on problems or topics of interest and importance. The story of the core curriculum in the secondary school is a familiar one. It began with the fusion of subject matter (usually language arts and social studies) in a two-hour period to provide for relationships in learning. After a number of years of experimentation, it has developed into a curriculum area that has as its chief concern consideration of the personal, social, and economic problems that boys and girls face in common as they grow up in our society. As the members of the class work for the solution or resolution of these problems, they move, under the guidance of the teacher, from immediate and sometimes narrow interests to concerns for the wider world of the community and nation. The core draws upon whatever subject fields are necessary for examination and understanding of the situations involved and for guidance in projection of solutions. Language arts and social studies provide most of the resource material, but there is also extensive use of materials from science and the fine arts. Mathematics is drawn upon primarily for interpreting data of social significance as in graphs and statistics and in recording and interpreting data that students themselves have gathered.

The core comprises that part of the curriculum which is regarded as general education in the secondary school and which is required of all. Often it is scheduled for one-half of the school day in the seventh grade and one-third of the school day from the eighth through the twelfth grades. The rest of the school day is divided into periods of the usual length of forty to fifty minutes and provides for physical education and the special or elective program. Outside the core are courses in science, mathematics, foreign languages, and the arts: music, homemaking, industrial arts, and fine arts.[13] The core as thus described is designed to help students identify and, if possible, resolve their common problems and concerns; the remainder of the school day is designed to meet their special interests and needs, vocational and avocational.

It can be seen that one of the great responsibilities of teachers in a school where the core program flourishes is guidance of students in selection of problems to be studied in the core and in selection of courses outside that will help them in their vocational plans and in meeting their personal needs. Generally speaking, it is the core teacher who carries this guidance responsibility and whose relationship with a student may extend over more than a year's time.

The great issue in core programs today is whether most of the problems for study should be identified and organized in some kind of sequence in learning, with placement of problems at various grade levels and with resource units built in advance, or whether the problems to be studied should be selected by teachers and students from those that are identified at the time as having the greatest significance for any given group. The advantage of the predetermined structure lies in its guarantee of adequate resources, its planned sequence, and the use of problem areas that have been tested for opportunities for growth in skills and intellectual power. The advantage of the unstructured core lies in its greater spontaneity, its chance for intellectual adventure, its greater appeal to students because of its closeness to their special interests and needs.

One possible resolution might be to have part of the time of the core given over to problem areas already tested as significant in the lives of young people and have part of the time free for the study of timely problems unique to the class concerned. Or a

13 For a detailed and illustrated account of the time design of a school day in which a core curriculum of this type functions see Lucile L. Lurry and Elsie J. Alberty's *Developing a High School Core Program* (New York: The Macmillan Company, 1957), Chapter 2.

number of cores, not just one, might be developed to provide variety in purpose and flexibility in scheduling. However these differences are resolved, it is important for those interested in core curriculum to continue to work for a program that is centered in problem solving, that relates closely to the needs and interests of the students concerned and to the demands of a democratic society, that cuts across subject matter lines to use whatever material is appropriate to its work, and that uses a unit method of teaching. It is by such persistence that time schedules of the past may be challenged, old habits questioned and broken where necessary, and new curriculums planned. There must be a continual reaching out for new combinations of facts and processes and ideas that will go far beyond the gaining of information and skills and extend to their final application and use in the control of life situations.

Inventiveness in the use of time is in no way limited to teachers in the core program. Teachers in the social studies, language arts, mathematics, science, and the fine and practical arts search within the limitations of the single period, five days a week, for more satisfactory ways of using time. As in the elementary school the need is for finding ways to provide for increased meanings and more purpose and relationships in learning. Much time is wasted in forced motivation, especially in the extensive use of verbalization.[14] Time must be taken for planning and exploring so that many different avenues may be opened for learning. As pressures increase for more content in the courses of the secondary school, teachers must find ways of evaluating content more carefully so that there is no repetition of subject matter that is not carefully planned and there is no material that does not have a real bearing on the purpose at hand.

Secondary school programs and materials are being geared more and more toward a unit method of teaching. Where highly creative teachers are at work, students learn by consideration of problems or topics that are developed by means of organizing ideas or themes. A chronological order or a sequence based on geographical distance from neighborhood to universe is no longer by itself an

14 L. Kathryn Dice, in her article "Unmet Needs of High School Students" in *Educational Leadership,* December, 1958, pp. 169–175, reports a study of the aptitudes and abilities of 433 high school seniors and the extent to which the high school program failed to meet the personal and vocational needs of most of them.

adequate organizing scheme in the social studies, for example. In its stead we have the kind of unit planning that takes into account the age and interests of the students, gears learning to development, and provides for a balance in activities and abundant resources. In the selection of units for the seventh, eighth, and ninth grades of the English program of one metropolitan school system—to take another example—care has been taken to include as organizing themes such areas of interest as friendship, adventures with animals, hobbies, stories through poetry, a new look at heroes and heroines, world understanding, laughing out loud, living with ourselves and our families, suspense and thrills, American folklore, hall of fame (lives of people who have helped mankind), and teen-age responsibilities in a democracy.[15] Resource units have been prepared at each grade level, kindergarten through grade twelve, by classroom teachers, supervisors, and librarians in cooperation with university consultants. They include a general introduction that sets the tone, special aims and language aims, suggestions for launching the unit, lists of activities, a sample lesson, suggestions for evaluation, and bibliographies for students and for teachers. At the end of the volume are charts that indicate direction of growth in processes and skills in language for pupils from kindergarten through grade twelve. From such a guide as this a teacher may find help to plan with his students for work that is significant to them and through which they can become aware of their own purposes and direction in growing.[16]

Summary

Arnold Bennett once wrote a book on how to live on twenty-four hours a day—a book that is both the inspiration and despair of his readers. One of the impressions that remains long years after its reading is that a man can, with imagination and energy, determine how he will spend the moments of his life. So it must be with a teacher, whose power to design the uses of time is important not

15 Denver Public Schools, *A Program in English, A Guide for Teaching the Language Arts,* Denver, Colorado, 1953, pp. 200–202.

16 For a similar approach to unit teaching in the language arts see Seattle Public Schools, *Unit Plans for the Language Arts, A Planned Sequence from Grades Seven Through Twelve* (Seattle: 1954). Among units especially concerned with fostering creativity in teaching are "Appreciation Through the Five Senses," p. 56; "The Individual and Self-Realization," p. 76; and "Approach to Maturity," p. 86.

only to him but to the hundreds of children and young people who come under his influence. Some time must be given over to practice and housekeeping; but more of it must be spent on adventures and activities that give zest to living and provide insights into purposes and values that must be discovered, tested, and improved. More time must be made available for serious thinking and planning and for exploring below the surface of human experience. More of it must be made available for toying with ideas, trying out new ways of manipulating materials of all kinds. Students must develop a greater command of what is already known so that the future may be explored with greater strength and power.

Perhaps what we need most is to be less conscious of time and more conscious of purpose. We must reduce our fears of the pressure of time and spend it in "abundant experiences, deeply sensed, dwelt upon, manipulated and rearranged" in the interest of the creative life.[17]

INVENTIVENESS IN THE USE OF SPACE

The concept of space is being reconstructed. Not only are we exploring space beyond the earth, the moon, and the planets, but we are reaching out to discover how far beyond the edges of our Milky Way other galaxies are rushing to their unimagined goals. We are looking inward at space dimensions in our intellectual and emotional life and speaking of "depth psychology" and of psychological distance between groups and individuals. We are concerned with sociometric studies and are intrigued by Moreno's analysis of the accepting and rejecting forces of personality and by his term "emotional expansiveness" to describe the capacity of a person to reach out toward others, a characteristic that appears to vary in marked degree from individual to individual.[18] We consider with Kurt Lewin the outer and inner spaces of personality portrayed in concentric rings, with the hard core at the center symbolizing the inviolate self and the outermost rings symbolizing those areas where, through shared experience, we may be able to

17 Ross Mooney, *A Preliminary Listing of Indices of Creative Behavior* (Columbus, Ohio: Bureau of Educational Research, The Ohio State University, September 24, 1953).

18 J. L. Moreno, *Who Shall Survive?* Monograph Series No. 58 (Washington: Nervous and Mental Disease Publishing Company, 1934).

relate ourselves to others with varying degrees of depth and intimacy.[19] Combs and Snygg use the concept of "phenomenal field" or "life space" to describe the private world of each individual, his world of objects, people, and processes with which he transacts and which is unique to him.[20] Of all the foregoing concepts, the one most appealing to a teacher is life space. This is a personal field to which the school can contribute, where a teacher with imaginative and careful planning can extend the life space of the children or young persons who come to him, help them to increase their awareness of their environment, and open up to them new areas in which to explore.

Manipulating Space in the Elementary School

The elementary school, with the best environment for creative learning, includes abundant resources for thinking, feeling, and acting. Here an effort is made to arrange rooms and furnishings functionally for a variety of activities—for individual and group reading, for painting, for listening to a story, for seeing films or film strips, for drawing a map or designing a mural. There is space for books, freely accessible to children; there is a science table where aquariums, terrariums, and a kit for science experiments awaken curiosity. Plants are growing on the window ledges. A display of children's work is on the bulletin board, which reaches all the way across the rear of the room. Tables and chairs are free for movement anywhere in the room, and the room is large enough to permit their arrangement in small or large groups to encourage cooperative thinking and planning. Individual desks and tables are set off by themselves for children who wish to be alone with their work. There is storage space for art materials, for display and science materials, and for extra books. A sink with running water is built at a height convenient for the children who will use the classroom. The room is obviously a laboratory for living, with endless possibilities for new structure and meaning.

The teacher has designed an upright container with partitions to hold posters and pictures that can be kept in one of the large

19 Kurt Lewin, *Resolving Social Conflicts* (New York: Harper & Brothers, 1948).
20 Arthur W. Combs and Donald Snygg, *Individual Behavior* (New York: Harper Brothers, 1959). The authors say, "The perceptual field has also been called the personal field, the private world, the behavioral field, the individual's life space and the phenomenal field." p. 20.

storage cupboards. Because he has a place to put things when he is not using them, he and the children can change displays frequently to illustrate the topics they are exploring. Variety and usefulness are served by the teacher's recognition of the truth learned from the art of Japan: one beautiful thing is all we need to know at a time.

In the files at one end of the room are the manila folders where children's work is kept for evaluative purposes. One drawer serves as a vertical file for photographs and small pamphlets for use in various units.

Although the room is rich in resources it never has a feeling of "too much." Only materials appropriate to the work at hand are given space in the classroom. This is not a museum where materials are kept, but a workroom where materials are used and where there is always space for a new project. Creativeness is expressed not only in what is selected for keeping but in what is selected for discard. Learning as it goes on in the classroom must always be fresh and new, since each year the children themselves are new to their grade level and their experiences are uniquely theirs.

In addition to using space flexibly in the classroom, a teacher who is concerned with the quality of children's experiences will want to utilize every possible opportunity for expansion of those experiences outside classroom walls into the school library, into laboratories or workshops, and into halls, patios, and courts. Where school librarians are assigned full time to the elementary school, children can go to the library alone or in small committees to find materials. If a library has a library classroom easily accessible or plenty of space at library tables, a whole class may go hunting for information. Workshops or art laboratories add useful dimensions to the opportunities of individuals or groups who are working on projects that need more complicated resources and more extended space than can be afforded in the regular classroom. Hallways, covered outdoor spaces, and playgrounds add useful space for living and working.

In addition to the library and workshops, the teacher often uses the space beyond the school as a primary resource in teaching. Because field trips are not in the daily routine, they lend themselves especially well to the fresh perspectives that are so much needed for lively, authentic learning. Whether the journey is around the block, to the park, into the city, or into the country, it begins auspiciously with a sense of adventure, strong and vital. To shape the adventure to the purposes for which it is intended is the job of the teacher-pupil cooperative planning. In this process the teacher's own responsiveness to the anticipation that children feel is a key factor. He welcomes their ideas, he encourages their imaginative projection of themselves into the new environment of people, machines, processes, plants, animals, or stars—whatever is sought in the experience—and he helps them to relate their plans to the reality of the situation and the purposes that the trip is to serve. Together they formulate the questions they will seek to answer through direct experience: What plants live in the stagnant water by the bridge? What plans does the city council have under way for helping in the control of smog? How does man use tools to move the earth? What work goes on at the city water plant to purify drinking water? Together pupils and teacher work out the specific information they will need to make the excursion worthwhile, wherever they may go, whatever they seek.

Taking a field trip brings about a new configuration in the special relationships of teacher and children. They see themselves against a new backdrop, the world outside the classroom in which each person has a somewhat different relationship to the other. There is nothing of the average or ordinary in a good field trip; especially is this true if school buses can be used for transportation. The rapid change of scene, the closeness of the group, the sense of adventure—always at the very surface of the experience—tend to provide the increased vitality needed for creativity. In this heightened feeling that permeates the whole, a teacher comes to see students with fresh perception of the meanings of their laughter, their tears, and their zest for life.

As teachers become more inventive in their use of the physical environment of classroom and community, they see with new appreciation the resources of the unique "life space" that each young person brings with him to school. There is a promising first grade unit called "Other Places," [21] which is designed to encourage children to share with each other what they are learning about the world that is theirs through travel either in person or by television.

21 *The Social Studies Guide, Kindergarten Through Grade Twelve,* Denver, Colorado, Public Schools, 1954. "Other Places," a unit for Grade One, pp. 50b–57b.

"Other Places" may be as near home as the little park ten blocks away or as far as Grandmother's house in Ohio or the volcano on the island of Hawaii that roars and smokes on television. The purposes of the unit are four: "to help children become conscious of the world beyond the range of vision, to gain some idea of time and distance, to remember things observed along the way of any journeying, to share experiences so that others may enjoy them too." [22] Maps and globes are used to help children begin to understand distance and direction and to see that maps, like words, have stories to tell. The teacher reads Margaret Wise Brown's *My World* (Harper, 1949) to lead children to see "that a child's world grows as he becomes older and as he notices and remembers." [23] In many other ways the teacher helps children to relate through extended and deepened meanings their experiences in home, family, and community to the experiences that the school provides. In this way he helps a child to begin to see his "life space" all of a piece and furthers the process of integration that is so essential for the maturing personality.

Manipulating Space in Secondary Schools and Colleges

Possibilities for the extension of the space environment for learning have been seen by teachers in elementary schools. However, the more inflexible time schedule of the secondary school and college has tended to limit any full development of the field trip program during regular sessions. Where core programs exist, teachers and students have made extensive use of excursions into the community and, where teachers are responsive to the behavior of their students, the experience has proved as revealing and helpful as in the case of elementary teachers. Perhaps it is even more revealing since the more formal organization of classes and classrooms tends to limit the insights that teachers have into the personalities of their students.

Space and time problems and the sheer numbers of human beings involved tend to reduce for teachers in secondary schools and colleges opportunities for knowing students as individuals. In both of these institutions, however, art and science laboratories, libraries, shops, and gymnasiums often partake of the flexibility and in-

22 *Ibid.*, p. 50b.
23 *Loc. cit.*

formality of the best elementary school classrooms. Problem solving, working with a variety of materials, close relationship between things and ideas—all characterize those areas where students and teachers work closely together in designing and carrying out learning experiences. It is in the academic classrooms of secondary school and college that space becomes largely a matter of containing the largest number of chairs or desks that the fire ordinance allows. Space is not generally provided for setting up centers of interest; for working with materials; for grouping students into planning, working, and evaluating groups; for making it possible for individuals to work alone; for storing materials, for filing records, and for setting up exhibits.

A few concessions have been made to changing theories of learning; among them are equipment for audio-visual materials and movable furniture. It is a sad commentary on the persistence of old habits that in almost every academic room of high school and college these movable chairs and desks are set in the same unchanging rows that characterized the seating of an earlier day. Static rows of desks, the teacher still talking in front of the room, the podium in place—all these keep the brave new world nailed down tight. The *tabula rasa* theory of the mind still persists; the learner who would be dynamic and purposeful still sits and listens.

Not only are the academic classrooms of high schools and college limited primarily to verbal learning, but there are not even enough classrooms to house each teacher in a place he can call his own. The utilization of space is so arranged that some teachers must move every period of the day and every teacher must share with other teachers the room in which he meets his classes. The result is often the gradual dispelling of any ideas a teacher may have had about creating a rich environment for learning in the room in which he teaches. Bulletin board space must be shared; frequently displays are poorly arranged or the space may not be used at all. No one is responsible for the room. The result is barrenness, disorder, or both.

This state of affairs does not exist in every room, of course. Some creative teachers persist in their purposes until the places where they go are bright with color and full of interest. Some rooms are made inviting with the work of students; some are hung with tapestries borrowed from the resource collection of the art department; in some a handsome color print is changed each week to provide interest and new learning. Junior high school teachers especially, as a more dynamic philosophy pervades the curriculum, begin to show concern with the classroom environment. However, teachers in typical academic classrooms need a vision of how the physical environment can be modified to stimulate learning, to supplement and give new meaning to ideas.

An enterprising teacher of the social studies, in thinking of the low state of his student's knowledge of physical geography, hit suddenly upon the idea of using the ceiling of his room for a display of a polar map of the world. He had it made on a gigantic scale with clear, readable labels, mounted it on Compoboard, and fastened it in place. He gave a test to his class prior to the installation and one at the end of the semester and found that there had been real growth in knowledge of places. He believed that the ready availability of the map and a fine, long pointer to use in teaching were factors in the increase in knowledge; but he speculated that the often roving eye of the beholder also contributed to the excellent results.

Some inventive teachers, in both high school and college, have used the extensive field trip as an integral part of study and learning. The members of the graduating class of the Ohio State University Laboratory School take a week's trek each year to a large city to gather data that will help them to study problems of industrialization and urbanization in the United States. Other schools, often from long distances, send students to observe the work of the government in Washington, D.C. In summer workshops or laboratories at the college level, extended field trips have been utilized as part of the regular work. For years this has been the pattern in biological and anthropological research for small groups and individuals. More recently whole classes in the social sciences and education have used field experiences to add concreteness, immediacy, emotional tone, and reality to the learning process.

A number of years ago the author had the experience of leading a group of students in a field seminar, sponsored jointly by the University of Denver and the Open Road, Inc., of New York City, in a study of the problems of cultural and social integration and isolation of certain minority groups in the Southwest. Two weeks on campus made possible preparatory studies and evaluation where resources of the University were available. Three weeks in the field added study, observations, and interviews on location, where experiences could take on the meanings that only direct contact with the people and the environment of the Southwest could evoke. In the memories of those who experienced them these five weeks still live with a vividness and meaning that come rarely.

The Southwest seminar was one of several which the Open Road, Inc., sponsored with colleges and universities. Noteworthy are the studies of mill towns of New England and the South carried on at Antioch College at Yellow Springs, Ohio, and of Colorado communities carried on at the Colorado State College of Education in Greeley. World War II brought these adventurous seminars to an end. What is needed now is another such leader as John Rothschild of the Open Road, Inc., to project these imaginative undertakings, to interest foundations in their support, and to intrigue the imagination of professors of education and the social sciences to the point where their energy will be expended in the cause of this kind of creative teaching and learning.

The idea, however, is not dead by any means. Each spring the San Fernando Valley State College in California, under the leadership of a professor of anthropology and a professor of education, sponsors a field trip into the country of the Hopi Indians. Here through direct observation and limited participation, students learn the nature of "the Hopi Way." From conversation with Hopi artists, and with political and religious leaders, students see in new light the problems identified in books and lectures. Traveling seminars for experience abroad are sponsored by other colleges. The challenge lies in extending greatly the opportunities now available to relate what one learns on the verbal level to what one does and to what one becomes.

Summary

Inventiveness in the use of space begins, like all inventiveness, with an idea. In teaching, it begins with the recognition of the fact that each person has a "life space" of his own that he alone can extend. A teacher works with life space, his own and that of the children who come to him. The extension of that life space is brought about by the growing power of the individual to interact with new ideas, things, processes, and people, and to assimilate them into his own becoming.

Use of physical space is one key to the process. Elbow room for experimentation and freedom for thinking away from the impinging crowd must be provided for individual young people, who in moments of intense interest may need to keep on with an experiment or a project regardless of the time and place. They need to be "in a little house," thinking, with no one to ask them what they are doing. A creative teacher needs to be concerned about this—both for children and for himself. Is it asking too much of the world that a teacher should also be given a room of his own in which to engage in the quiet intensity of thought?

There must be enough space in the schoolroom itself for a wide variety of activities and for furniture that moves to make possible work and play groups of various sizes and purposes. There must be space for storage of materials and for keeping important information on file: records of children's work and cumulative reports on their weaknesses and strengths and their special qualities as people.

As learning becomes more and more verbal—as we substitute intellectual processes for activity—we must not lose sight of the importance of direct experience in making possible a curriculum where thinking is supported, stimulated, and enhanced by feeling and doing. Laboratories are still needed.

Inventiveness with space beyond the walls of the school calls for imagination and fortitude. The field trip calls for planning that will make it an integral part of the whole learning process so that what is seen, touched, smelled, or heard enters deeply into the consciousness of the receiver. In this way experiences are built that may undergo reconstruction in mind and heart and emerge remade in a new image.

INVENTIVENESS WITH MATERIALS

If there is one thing more than any other that helps to create a liberating and stimulating atmosphere for growing, it is the learning materials that teachers make available to their students. Materials may be seen, heard, examined, rejected, accepted, used, dispensed with, recovered, re-created, and seen anew. Materials may be made up entirely of symbols—letters, figures, musical notes —or they may be of the flesh and blood of living things as are the two goats that may be staying in a small shed in a corner of a kindergarten playground. One can never be completely surprised at the form that materials take: one may hear a rooster crowing from the fenced-off enclosure near the door of a first-grade room; or see against a hill at the south end of some campus, near the physics laboratory, the outline of a cyclotron, or watch a college library rising where before there was only a vacant lot. The art in the management of materials is to have them at the right place, at the right time, in proper condition and amount, and appropriate to the need of the moment: the right book for the little boy in the front row, the fresh egg for the experiment in osmosis, the new film on transportation that introduces the jet plane, enough copies of the "Mysterious Cat" for the fourth-grade choral reading, an extra bag of apples for the children who might have forgotten to bring theirs, the newest reports of satellite launchings for the seven o'clock evening class.

There are some schools where the problem is a dearth of materials; but more often the problem with materials arises from a willingness to accept the obvious, the humdrum, the dull, the usual. Teachers sometimes fail to distinguish between material that is useful for drill or looking up information and material that introduces new values and ideals, stimulates new feelings, and provides the precise and substantive knowledge that is needed at the "input stage" of creative thinking and doing. ". . . even creativity requires a sense of criticism and precision." [24]

Utilizing Humble Things Creatively

Often it is in the use of nearby, humble things that a teacher can encourage in his students the power of observation and appreciation. Few materials introduced into a class for just these purposes have as delightful results as the apple. This was one of the resources used in a senior high school English unit which, like the unit for second graders, encouraged, on a more adult level, exploration of the world of the five senses. Smell, taste, sound, sight,

[24] The author is indebted to Karl W. Deutsch for the idea and wording of the close of this paragraph. Note the following: "Creativity requires relaxation at the combinatorial stage just as it requires precision and substantive knowledge at the input stage. And again even creativity requires a sense of criticism and precision." From "Creativity in a Scientific Civilization," in *Changing Attitudes in a Changing World* (New York: Bank Street College of Education Publications, 1958), p. 35.

touch—these were the proper subjects of study. To start off the adventure with anticipation, each student brought to class an apple of his choice: Jonathan, Spitzenburg, Northern Spy, Delicious, McIntosh. As he studied his apple, he turned it slowly in the light, sniffed it, felt it, and finally devoured it. In this process, he recorded the words and phrases through which he might communicate to others the sensations and thoughts that crowded in on him. A class list composed of contributions from individual students began to look like this:

Sight	Sound	Taste	Touch	Smell
red	swish	refreshing	waxy	aromatic
rosy	crunch	juicy	smooth	fragrant
autumn scarlet	crack	cool	rounded	tangy
ivory flesh		moist	tapering	
flecked		mealy		
shining		tart		
striped				

Aware that much of the aesthetic satisfaction of language is found in imagery, the members of the class tried their hand at the field of association:

> red berries against white snow
> autumn haze in the valleys
> red sumac
> Halloween
> winter fires

With words and ideas on paper and on the chalkboard, the class was now ready for writing. Each student wrote no more than a page to record in whatever way he wished the thoughts that had come to him during the feast of apples. The rarity of the experience, the emphasis upon the unique and the personal, the informality of the relationships engendered between teacher and students, the common search for meanings and words to express them, the appreciation of each one's final "masterpiece" as it was shared in the group—all led to transactions of the kind that permits everyone to be himself and to write freely of himself and his feelings. No one was limited to a single topic. As a result, there were papers about the taste of Jello, Thanksgiving turkey, toothpaste, and Chinese tea as well as apples. Here are two:

AN APPLE

There in the bowl it lay, surrounded by bright oranges and the pale yellow of bananas. I took it from the bowl. It was a beautiful thing with its bright red streaked with yellow, where the apple tapered to five distinct points. For a moment I pondered; should I eat it? After all there were many apples in the world. But to me this apple symbolized all apples. Then my hunger overcame me and I took a bite. Such a crisp lusciousness as I sank my teeth into this ruddy fruit. Again and again I sank my teeth and each time I relished that renewed flavor. I looked at the apple; it was no longer a smooth waxy fruit. I had a feeling of sorrow for having destroyed its beauty.

—Norman

JELLO

With his napkin tucked under his chin, a spoon clutched in one chubby hand, Henry was waiting for dessert. Soon it came, a quivering mass of lime Jello topped with a cap of foamy whipped cream. A tiny gurgle of delight escaped him; then he began with the whipped cream. Like air-spun floss it was, or a melting snowflake; but this was only an introduction to what lay beneath. He popped a glassy-green spoonful into his mouth; he had a cool slippery sensation as the tangy mouthful went down. Then he scooped out another transparent bit and let it slowly dissolve on his tongue, the puckery sweetness slipping down his throat. There was but one, firm, shiny morsel left, and Henry was loathe to eat it, not wishing to end this delectable experience. Soon, however, the plate was bare, not one savory lime drop left.

—Jeanne

As the students continued their exploration of the world of the five senses, they listened to music, smelled perfumes and camphor, blindfolded themselves and tried to guess things by touch, and sought for words to communicate something of the beauty and meaning of a pot of red tulips in the spring. A few samples of the writing that emerged, after first drafts and later revisions closer to the heart's desire, give some indication of the results:

YELLOW ORCHIDS

Have you ever seen a whole mountain side of yellow orchids gleaming in the sun? The lady slipper orchid is a small, dainty yellow and purple flower, shaped like a tiny slipper above pale green stem and leaves. The particular group that I saw was in a valley at the foot of Long's Peak, that could be reached only by a two day pack trip over a rough mountain trail. Entirely surrounded by high, snow-capped mountains, it is entered only once or twice a year. The morning after our pack train had arrived I decided to go exploring. While climbing over a small ridge, I came to a normally shady hillside where a great mass of yellow orchids nodded and glowed in the rays of the morning sun. This sight lasted about five minutes, and then as the sun rose higher, the hillside became shadier and where a few minutes before a golden mass had gleamed, there now showed a few yellow flashes to mark the spot where I had seen one of the most beautiful sights of my life.

—*Gerald*

SOUND

What I love to hear is a new bird song that I have never heard before. It stimulates me to action so fast that I nearly break my neck trying to see the bird, which, of course, is a very bad way to hunt for a little warbler or any other bird.

When I hear the scream of an eagle or the cry of a sparrow hawk, I am set back into reverie, thinking about the thrill the age-old falconer had when his falcon swooped for game. I love it!

—*Norton*

THE CITY

Have you ever heard the city,
Really heard the city
Breathe and laugh and talk and cry?
Listen, and you will hear the city breathe,
A throbbing, rumbling breath
Of far-off traffic:
Horns, whistles, bells,
Screaming brakes, screeching trams,
Thundering trains, zooming planes,
Humming busses, lumbering trucks.

PRUDENCE BOSTWICK

Listen, and you will hear
The city's voice,
The multiple voices of people,
Laughing, crying, singing,
Raised in anger, wild in excitement,
Hushed in grief;
Little ones, crying, calling,
Young ones laughing, jesting,
Women softly chatting,
Men arguing mightily,
Old folks sadly remembering.

Listen, and you will hear a dog barking,
A cat calling,
A piano tinkling,
A toy whistle,
The wail of a saxophone,
Pulsing drums,
A sleepy bird,
The evening breeze.

Listen and you will hear the city,
Rhythmic, faltering, monotonous, exotic.

—Marian

CONTRAST

If you sense an offending odor when you reach the third floor, you realize the chemists of East High are at work. As the repulsive stench of rotten eggs floats by you, you are assured that hydrogen sulfide is being used. Butric acid is in its glory if nasty, malodorous fumes reach your nostrils. If, on the other hand, a pleasant smell comes by, you realize that you are lingering about the cooking rooms. The air is filled with the scent of spice and the tangy fragrance of molasses. For, instead of mixing sulfuric acid with sodium hydroxide, the homemakers are completing a recipe for gingerbread.

—Judith

The class followed up their adventure in writing out of their own immediate experiences by hunting through books of poetry in the library for ways in which artist authors had caught in imaginative language the emotional impact of seeing, hearing, tasting, touching. With an appreciation unusual for high school juniors they selected such lines as these:

"The clustered apples burnt like flame."

"As they bowed beneath the burden
  Of the white fruit of the moon."

"Bournless slopes of sea room."

"Grey clouds sagging like webs."

"Snow in its white and awful indifference."

A special favorite was Amy Lowell's "A Decade":

When you came, you were like red wine and honey,
And the taste of you burnt my mouth with its sweetness.
Now you are like morning bread,
Smooth and pleasant.
I hardly taste you at all, for I know your savor;
But I am completely nourished.[25]

In this way through the use of the simplest materials and a fresh approach to learning, a group of high school students grew in powers of observation, in skill in expressing their reactions and feelings, and in appreciation of imaginative writing of lyric poets.

Utilizing Literature Creatively

The work of Taba and her associates in the Study of Inter-group Education in Cooperating Schools sponsored by the American Council on Education has brought into clear focus the use of materials for building understandings and insights concerning people who are different from ourselves. Here the emphasis is not so much upon the aesthetic experience that literature provides as an art form, as upon its power to stimulate the imagination, to grasp vicariously the feelings and problems of others. Out of this need to use literature for instrumental as well as aesthetic purposes has come a new way of organizing the book report. Closely akin to the concept of the focusing idea, the plan calls for students to read books around important themes such as differences in race, in age, in social class, in sex, or in national origin. Students who have read

25 Amy Lowell, "A Decade." Published in Louis Untermeyer, *Modern American Poetry* (New York: Harcourt, Brace and Company, Inc., 1936), p. 195.

titles dealing with a particular theme then form a panel to present to the class their various interpretations of what they have read. They clarify meanings and relate findings to the broader theme of problems in human relations and their possible resolution.

To make it possible for teachers to organize their classes in this way, important resource materials are available.[26] Not only are titles given according to themes in human relations, but books are classified according to grade level and reading difficulty all the way from elementary grades through junior and senior high school. Books for very mature readers are so indicated.

One does not have to face problems of intergroup relations to come to understand with poignance the feelings of other people. Dr. Helen Lodge of the faculty of the San Fernando Valley State College works with student teachers to help them to use literature to awaken the imagination of the young people with whom they work. She points out how high school students can be stirred by hearing a reading from A. B. Guthrie's *The Way West* of the moment when the family home is sold and the man, the woman, and the boy are leaving it for the journey along the trail to the far West. As they turn from the old familiar house, the mother leaves with sorrowing heart the safety of the familiar, the place where she had given birth to her child and where she had spent her youth, the garden she had planted, the trees she had loved. She wonders whether she will be able to build it all again. The father is glad that at last he can get out from under; he is a free man, life ahead will be different, maybe even good. The boy looks forward to the future; he is all anticipation and hope. At this point the class is asked to project the events of the future. Will they make the journey to Oregon? Will they die along the way? Will they be separated? Will life begin anew and will the mother build her life again?

In addition to projection of ideas through reading, there are now available resources for class discussion in the form of films that show moments of high tension and climax, the resolution of which is left to the audience. Such a film is an excerpt from *The Informer* in which the issue of man's loyalty is met head on. Another is an excerpt from *Alice Adams*, in which her pretenses are

26 See Hilda Taba and others, *Literature for Human Understanding* (Washington, D.C.: American Council on Education, 1948), and Margaret Heaton, *Reading Ladders for Human Relations* (same publisher, 1955).

mercilessly shown. These are resources for senior high school teachers to use in helping students to clarify areas of conflict in values and to grasp the nature of the ethical problems involved in decision making, whether the stakes are high or low.[27]

Recordings are another resource close to the reality level of experience. Music, the human voice, songs of birds, calls of wild animals—these are available for giving new quality to experience. In a series called *Ways of Mankind* anthropological and sociological studies are dramatized with extraordinary effect to demonstrate the cultural life of a people; for example, "Desert Soliloquy" tells the ways of the Hopi, and "Greek Meets Greek" presents the contrasting Athenian and Spartan philosophies of life.[28] Edward R. Murrow's *I Can Hear It Now* captures the past in such a way as to make it the living present. An extraordinary collection of records for use in teaching is called "Folkways Records." [29] In this collection are to be found authentic folk music and folk tales from a wide variety of countries; literature of the United States and the world, read by the authors themselves or compiled and discussed by readers in their respective fields; descriptions of folkways, which provide cultural data on many areas of the world; and a science series that reconstructs happenings through sound, from turtle mating calls to jets.

Appearing in recent years are books that provide material teachers can use in helping children to grasp some of the deeper meanings of experience. Especially successful in this respect are the Young Scott Books.[30] Take, for example, the "Point of View" book by Dr. Irma E. Webber entitled *It Looks Like This*. Four little mice look at a cow, a donkey, and a pig from four different points of view: above, in front, at the side, and at the back. "One thing," writes the author, "can look many different ways—as many different ways as there are ways to look at it."

Instead of ignoring death, or frightening children with the ideas of death, the little book *The Dead Bird* (1958) by Margaret Wise Brown deals with the sorrow the children feel at the sight of

---

27 See catalog of Teaching Film Custodians for the series in Human Relations from which these excerpts are drawn.
28 Produced in two volumes by the National Association of Educational Broadcasters with the Ford Foundation.
29 Folkways Records and Service Corporation, 117 West 46th Street, New York 36, New York.
30 William R. Scott, Inc., 8 West 13th Street, New York 11, New York.

a dead bird, with the pathos of the end of its flying and the tragic sense of "no more." It tells of the sadness of the children as they bury the body. Yet the book reveals the healing that life brings: "And every day until they forgot they went and sang to their little dead bird and put fresh flowers on his grave."

Miriam Schlein's *When Will the World Be Mine? The Story of a Snowshoe Rabbit* (1953) shows the resources that the rabbit's mother and his native environment provide in order that he may grow to independence. Margaret Wise Brown's *Young Kangaroo* (1955) reveals how in the life of a very young thing there can be adventure, but how the animal also needs the sheltering care of its mother that it may grow in safety.

A teacher who wants to provide children with resources that have color, interest, and warmth must rejoice in Remy Charlip's *Where Is Everybody? An Easy Book To Read* (1957) where with simple words and beautiful illustrations children are introduced to sky, sun, bird, hills, and river; to fish, woods, road, and deer; to man, boy, house, boat, and clouds with rain. Each passes before the eye of the reader and finally all are lost in the grey twilight as the night comes on.

The most important use of such books is at the "input stage" for extending and deepening the personal experiences that children have. In addition, some books like *Is This You?* (1958) by Ruth Krauss and Crockett Johnson help a child to become more conscious of his own identity and to enjoy the humor of the absurd and incongruous.

Utilizing Graphic and Plastic Materials Creatively

Materials that are primarily associated with the graphic and plastic arts—clay, paint, wood, paper, paste, glue, crayons, to name a few—have the wonderful quality of being available to teachers for all kinds of purposes. They may be made accessible to children for purposes of exploration and manipulation or, when familiarity with the materials is achieved and skills are maturing, for purposes of expressing an idea in some relatively finished form. It is at the time of exploration that teachers can provide a variety of materials and create the atmosphere of friendliness and helpfulness in which pupils may become increasingly well acquainted with the possibilities of art media. Within the limits of courtesy and safety there should be freedom for both discovery and expression. In describing her work with a sixth-grade class a teacher writes:

> My group included little eleven-year-old boys and fast maturing twelve-year-old girls.
>
> Exploring hands were continuously busy with clay, woodcarving and modeling, puppet making, knitting and creative stitchery for both boys and girls. And these activities seemed to meet an almost compulsive need for manipulation and self-expression. I hope that worthwhile learnings took place. There was some indication that creative attitudes began to jell. At one time Michael wrote, "At first I didn't understand your way of art. You are the most different teacher I've ever had." (This bit foiled me!) At the end of the year after our visit to next year's junior high, the same boy wrote, "I don't think I am going to like the woodworking class. Everyone has to make the same thing. First you have to make a stool and then next a shelf. You can't make what you want to in your own way. You have to make it the way they tell you to."

A research study to evaluate children's growth through art experiences bears out the importance of stimulating materials "that are ample enough to permit wide exploration and necessary mistakes, that arouse curiosity and encourage investigation, that are suitable for a particular stage of maturity, that present a variety of possibilities and choices." [31] How one teacher encouraged her children to try out new art experiences in the kindergarten is additional evidence of what an inventive teacher can do:

> During the first few weeks in kindergarten, some children find security only in the familiar blocks and sand box. Others go to one of the art centers but tend to return to the same center again and again. As they get acquainted with me and the other children, their confidence grows and they seem more eager to try something new. Sometimes I say to children, "Some of you seem to have a favorite place. If you always work at the same center, you'll learn how to do only one thing. There are lots of things that are fun to learn to do. If you try them, we'll help you learn how to do them." Before the work period begins, we look at things and

---

31 Edith M. Henry, "Evaluation of Children's Growth Through Art Experiences," *Journal of the National Art Education Association*, May, 1953.

handle them. We dramatize what we may want to paint. Each child is encouraged to choose what he wishes to make and to do it in his own way. Now we seldom hear "I can't." [32]

Extending Experiences Creatively

In addition to the development of an environment in the classroom that is abundantly provided with materials appropriate to the work at hand, there is growing discrimination and creativity in the use of the resources of the community itself.

An intensive use of the community outside the school to change the misconceptions of children through direct experience is described by a third grade teacher. This teacher discovered during a unit on clothing, including a study of cotton, wool, and the like, that the children in her class had no idea of how wool was sheared and thought that it came off sheep that were "all woolly and white." She wanted the children to see sheep shearing; but the farms were too far away from the city to permit the children to travel (bus difficulties). Undaunted, the teacher talked with a farmer in the area about the possibility of bringing the shearing process to the school. He said he would do it. After careful planning with the administration and with the children, the final decisions were made. In the teacher's words:

> We decided that the best place for the sheep would be outside our room, which was in an annex building and right by the playground. We spent hours in discussing the nature and temperament of sheep; the way we would have to act; the safety measures to be taken around the machinery of the shearer; and the things that we were going to look for when watching the sheep and the shearer.
>
> We had many delays in the shearing due to weather conditions, but this led to more learnings since we found out that sheep had to be dry for days before the shearing. Finally the day arrived and with it the farmer, his shearer (an elderly Mexican) and six sheep. We watched as all the sheep were sheared; we took in all that we could. The children asked questions during the shearing and afterwards when the farmer came into the classroom. Here they learned about the raising of sheep and their care.

[32] *Ibid.*, p. 7.

From actually seeing the dirty sheep, the children learned how necessary the cleaning process is. They saw how the shearer insured safety, how he got as large a piece of wool as possible at a time, and how he worked as fast as possible. They saw the wool rolled into a big bundle and tied with string; they lifted it and saw how light it was when it was weighed; through the actual handling of the wool they saw the lanolin and got it all over their hands. Until they saw the actual shearing, they did not believe that it did not hurt the sheep.

They spent the next day in writing stories telling what they had learned and in writing letters to the farmer to thank him for his time and kindness.

When direct experience is not possible, the use of vicarious experience, imaginatively selected and developed, can provide for wide stretching of "life space." We have already considered briefly the power of symbolic language to do this. An account by another teacher introduces the idea of combining the use of books and writing with a "real life" adventure:

While glancing through an educational journal, I noticed an advertisement which said, "Adopt-a-Ship Plan." The ad explained that fifth and sixth graders could by corresponding with the captain and officers adopt a ship that would be traveling around the world. I asked the children whether they would be interested in the activity and they were thrilled about the idea.

My class was assigned a cargo ship that was sailing to most of the countries we had planned to study about. The children decided that our objectives in studying foreign countries should not be limited to learning about the history and geography of these nations. They wanted to come away with a greater understanding of the people, their ideas and traditions. With the help of the teacher, they made a list of the things they wanted to know about each country. Their correspondence with the men of the ship centered about these objectives.

The reports that came from the ship included accounts of the voyage, descriptions of a typical day at sea, details of countries, ports and cargoes, and descriptions of foreign economies. Frequently maps, gifts, and trinkets obtained by the captain were sent to the class. The children kept track of the ship's progress by drawing pictures of the ship and its course on a large bulletin board. This required some study in basic navigation. The information obtained through correspondence was used by the children in their committee reports. Of course, other source materials were used: encyclopedias, textbooks, newspapers, magazines, recordings, films, film strips, and field trips. The entire year's work was conducted through committee reports and class discussions.

At the end of the year, the class gave an original play before the entire school and many parents. The children pretended that they were the crew of the ship they had adopted. They visited foreign ports, loaded and unloaded cargo, and portrayed life on a merchant vessel. They told something about each country in which the ship docked.

The experience seemed to have a tremendous impact upon the children. They were excited about social studies throughout the year. Their handwriting and writing ability increased greatly. For many it was the first time that they really had a reason to write well and legibly. Their letters were leaving the classroom and they were eagerly awaiting answers.

Summary

Experiences occur in the ongoing process of living in school, but whether they are instrumental in changing behavior and in illuminating and giving quality to learning depends on their fullness and vividness. Much of this is made possible through the resources that the teacher provides. They may be abundant or few, costly, free, or inexpensive (there is a teacher who supplies many of her schoolroom materials with trading stamps), but they must all have in common the power to help young persons satisfy their curiosity about the world in which they live, provide them with enough variety to permit their growth in different abilities and capacities, and encourage their reaching out for knowledge and understanding. Whether the materials are books or frogs' eggs, films or a recording of a Hopi Indian chant, sheep for shearing or a cargo ship bound for Singapore—all must help to keep open the way to adventure and to intense living.

Conclusion

Great programs in living are made only by men who stand back and look over their universe as an artist retreats to look over his canvas. And from that point they know where the high lights are to be placed. There is nothing precious about it all; it is not the idleness of the indolent. It is a profound and rugged challenge to those who are tempted to wear out their strength in futility.[33]

Creativity in teaching manifests itself in the kind of inter-relationship that grows between teacher and child as the teacher shares with the child in his experiencing. The feelings engendered in this relationship determine the atmosphere that nourishes the spirit of inquiry and that supports the willingness of teacher and child to undergo the struggle for thought and discovery. Creativity in teaching manifests itself also in the nature of the learning opportunities that the teacher provides, in their freshness and newness, in their flexibility and variety, and in the depth and breadth of their meanings. Only from such opportunities can a child find the experiences through which he may achieve that "interpenetration of the self and the world of objects and events" [34] which makes for his growth as a person.

In providing learning opportunities, the teacher must work not only with the human beings around him, but also with resources of time, space, and materials. These are ready for his hand. How he uses them is the test of his own creativity as a teacher. It is the privilege of teachers so to design learning opportunities that the dimensions of a learner's world will be broadening, keeping him alert to the inexhaustible nature of experience.

[33] Eliot Dole Hutchinson, "The Period of Frustration in Creative Endeavor," in *A Study of Interpersonal Relations,* ed. Patrick Mullahy (New York: Hermitage Press, Inc., 1949), p. 419.

[34] John Dewey, *Art as Experience* (New York: Minton, Balch and Co., 1954), p. 19.

PRUDENCE BOSTWICK

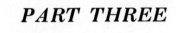

PART THREE

PART THREE

PART THREE

RESPONSIBLE PARTICIPATION
IN FOSTERING CREATIVITY
IN THE PROFESSION

Believing as we do that all persons who are qualified to teach have the potentiality of becoming more creative in their work, we now turn our attention to ways of increasing the creativity of the profession as a whole. To be sure, the creativity of future teachers has been either nourished or stifled in homes, schools, and communities as those young people were growing up. Even so, we are convinced that as they enter upon collegiate preparation for teaching and as they go out into positions in the schools, persons who are to teach can encounter surrounding conditions and have experiences that will counteract the deadening forces and enhance the enlivening ones they may have met. We believe the creative urge is so basic and strong in human beings that hardened crusts walling it in can be softened and creativity thus released if teachers of teachers and those responsible for the conditions under which they work on the job will act upon what is known and seek to discover more about human experiencing. It is important that the two groups, preservice and inservice teacher educators, join hands with teachers themselves in accepting the responsibility for fostering creativity in teaching and that all seek to maintain continuity in their shared efforts.

For teachers to use their own judgment creatively as they implement curriculum decisions made alone or with others has become more crucial with each passing year. Shoemaker has stated well the nature of the modern educator's task:

> The totality of accumulated and accumulating culture is immediately and simultaneously available through modern channels of communication—radio, motion picture, television, and picture press. It is, however, essentially unsorted and unstructured for the child, for instance, who watches the television screen for an average of twenty-six hours a week. And the teacher is called to formulate the rationale within which he creates opportunities for young people to find their way through the formlessness to shape new definitions of value and new dimensions of self-understanding.

> As Lyman Bryson showed us several years ago in *The Drive Toward Reason,* changes in systems of communication are at first agents of change in culture, then their index. With the sweeping changes in modern communication, there comes correlative change in the function of the school and the professional roles of the teachers. Where once their major function lay in transmission of the accumulated content of the culture, they now add comparably specific concern for teaching (1) the evaluation of the language of information and value, (2) the organization and structuring of current information and values within the cultural heritage, (3) the methods and habits of comparing the is and the ought to be that lead to innovation.

> For the transmission of information we have developed great skill, buttressed with vast accumulations of laboratory and classroom experimentation in learning and comparisons of method—enough to warrant the fairly general belief that education is, in major aspects, a science. By comparison, we have done almost nothing to increase our understanding of individual evaluation, individual patterning, individual commitment, from formulations of new ways to see in the areas of science, history, politics, religion, and the arts. We need to turn our attention to this aspect of education also. When we do, we may find ourselves involved in the essentially

artistic problems of design in teaching, with responsible participation coming from administrators, supervisors, and college teachers. To "education is a science" we may add, "education is an art form resembling in broad outlines the moving form of film, whose succession of montages the audience relates to one another in the transactions of characters in social context." Within this emerging definition, creative teaching may come to represent the strategic rapprochement of arts and sciences.[1]

Modern inventions have furnished not only mass media of communication feeding information to the young outside the school but also new devices for packaging and conveying information to children and youth in school. It is claimed that these devices can be employed to save time for both teachers and learners. Here is another challenge to the creativity of the profession. Can these devices be used to increase both the efficiency and quality of learning in the case of material capable and worthy of being programmed for a "machine"? If this can be done and if time is thus released, can teachers learn to use that time creatively?

In this part of the book we move away from the classroom, first to look at opportunities at the college level for teachers-to-be to develop some of the convictions, enthusiasms, and competencies prerequisite to creativity in teaching, next to examine the type of administration and supervision that will welcome and support the neophyte or any other teacher who wants to teach creatively, and third to consider how teachers may undertake to enhance their own creativity in teaching.

In Chapter 7, Margaret Lindsey discusses conditions in curriculum, teaching, and guidance at the college level which should make it more likely that young people entering teaching will look upon it as a creative field and know how to implement this concept.

Alice Miel presents in Chapter 8 conditions nourishing and rewarding creativity in teachers on the job and she suggests ways administrators and supervisors may fulfill their responsibilities in this connection.

In a final chapter, which looks back over the ideas developed in the entire book, Mary Harbage lets us listen in on a few teachers who are trying to help themselves to be more creative by examin-

[1] Francis Shoemaker, memorandum, October, 1960.

ing their teaching, by planning deliberately to be more adventure-some, and by supporting one another in the process.

Thomas Sprecher has named as elements of creativity "ideas, work habits, and opportunity." [2] Preservice teacher educators, inservice administrators and supervisors, and teachers in preparation or on the job all can help to build the ideas needed to teach more creatively, can develop in themselves the habits of hard work required for creating, and can collaborate to give opportunity to all who want to exercise their right and capacity as human beings to be creative through the medium of their profession.

[2] See *The Third University of Utah Research Conference on the Identification of Scientific Talent,* ed. Calvin Taylor (Salt Lake City: University of Utah Press, 1959), p. 31.

7 PRESERVICE PREPARATION FOR CREATIVITY IN TEACHING

Some of the ways teachers may creatively design learning opportunities that promote pupils' achievement of the best that is in them have been suggested in earlier chapters of this book. Not all teachers experience the joy, the inspiration, and the satisfaction that come to those who teach creatively and see their pupils respond with progress toward self-realization. Yet, even the teachers who fail to put creativity into their teaching have some of the same potentiality for creativity that other human beings have.

Many factors have a bearing on the ways and the degree to which an individual uses his full creative capacity. While some of these influential factors are located in the home, family, religious life, neighborhood, and community, and in the general characteristics of the times, it is clear that school experiences play a sizable role in determining abilities and attitudes one brings to his everyday activities. For prospective teachers, college experiences are added to other influences on the developing person and become substantial determiners of their behavior as members of the teaching profession. Hence, it would be productive to explore the

183

particular kinds of experiences holding promise for helping college students to become the creative teachers of the future.

To make such an exploration is the central purpose of this chapter. No attempt is made to examine the whole of teacher preparation or even all of the parts that may have a direct bearing upon the amount and kind of creativity employed by graduates of teacher education programs. Instead, attention is focused on a few important qualities that seem to be present in creative teachers, and on examples of experiences in preservice preparation that may contribute to development of such qualities. Illustrations, taken from various parts of different programs and not making up the whole of any one program, are used to communicate more adequately the meaning of ideas in practice.

QUALITIES THAT MAKE FOR CREATIVITY IN TEACHING

Examination of purposes to be served is a necessary first step in any consideration of what learning experiences are of worth. While general statements of purposes in teacher education may provide direction on a broad scale, they must be examined in more detail before they can be utilized in determining specific kinds of opportunities that ought to be available to future teachers. Assuming a primary goal of preparing teachers to work creatively and to help their pupils to do the same, one must then ask what characterizes such a teacher. If the stuff of which creativity is made can be analyzed for its elements, these may then provide a basis for exploring the kinds of experiences that might assist prospective teachers in learning to use creative approaches to their work in the classroom, school, and community.

What, then, does characterize the creative teacher? Various formulations in answer to this question are found in the general literature on creativity and in earlier chapters of this book. Here the intention is to describe the one who teaches creatively so that direction may emerge for those concerned with preservice preparation of teachers. For this purpose, one who teaches creatively is described as:

—having a primary image (model) that guides his thinking and
    acting

—accepting himself positively, accurately, and realistically and utilizing his full potential

—being aware of and sensitive and responsive to people, ideas, and events

—having a sense of security in uncertainty, a tolerance for ambiguity

—being a learner

The meaning of each of these qualities, and the kinds of experiences in preservice preparation that might help teachers-to-be in building such qualities, is the subject of the following sections.

THE PRIMARY IMAGE

The image an artist has of how he wants to communicate a message through his particular medium suggests to him forms, colors, rhythms, and relationships. In the same way the teacher's image of "good" teachers and "good" teaching guides his thoughts, feelings, and actions in performing various roles. Like the artist, the teacher must first have a general conception of goal, then choose from among the available means those that promise to help him to achieve the goal, and then employ those means with understanding and skill. The whole of the image that guides a teacher is made up of many parts, ranging all the way from basic beliefs about man and the nature of his existence to convictions about how the teacher should relate to each learner in his classroom. This image, on which much of the teacher's behavior is predicated, is the product of gradual development from early childhood through years of experience.

No contribution to education is more important than that of helping the teacher-to-be to develop an image of the greatness of his task and how he might succeed in the task. This aspect of preservice teacher education is the responsibility of all who come into contact with the future teacher, including parents and other citizens, and especially elementary and secondary school teachers and guidance counselors. Even so, special responsibility rests with preservice teacher educators.

Examples Set by College Teachers

The prospective teacher's image of teachers and teaching is influenced by the behavior, attitudes, and qualities of college personnel participating in the preservice program. College students, for the most part young idealists, are continuously examining the overt and covert attitudes and feelings of their teachers. For the student who plans to be a teacher, such examination is likely to take on more than passing significance because this student is trying to visualize himself in the professional role he is observing. Frequently, the aggregate of observations of teachers during college years is not a picture of creative teaching. It is entirely possible, however, for college teachers to contribute in many ways to the student's development of a challenging, inspirational, and at the same time practical vision of the task of teaching.

Consider Bill, for example, who, as a freshman, was taking a course in contemporary civilization.

> With the instructor, the class planned to take a field trip to the state capital to visit branches of the state government. Bill, along with three others, chose to explore the operations of the Department of Public Instruction. His instructor confessed to knowing little about this branch and stated that he had not usually included the institution of education in his course. But he was aware of and respected Bill's interest and encouraged him to follow through. As it turned out, when groups reported following the field trip, Bill's group discovered that many other students were interested in education. The instructor agreed with them that problems and issues of education as public policy ought to be examined as part of the course in the future.

Prospective teachers in this general education class were drawing conclusions about teachers and teaching as they observed the reactions and behavior of their college instructor. True, most of the students were not conscious of the subtle way in which experiences in this class were formulating in them an image of teaching. (Perhaps one of the responsibilities of teacher educators is deliberately to raise such observations to a conscious level with prospective teachers.) The following thoughts may have occurred to Bill and others in his class:

> This teacher respects me and my interests.
> He isn't afraid to say he doesn't know or that he hadn't considered something before.
> Not everybody has to do the same thing or have the same interests.

I got more out of this because I went right to the Department and talked to people.

Sometimes teachers can learn from students.

Shirley had a different opportunity to learn from a college instructor. The sophomore class of which she was a member was assembled in the teachers' lounge in a rural consolidated school. They had been visiting the school that morning and had just eaten in the lunchroom with the children. Shirley listened to the comments of her classmates:

"I'd like to be just like Miss Meredith. She sure has control over those kids."

"I disagree with you. I'd like to be like Mr. Smith. That class was really excited about what was going on. You could hardly tell the teacher was there, and yet you know he was responsible for the independent way everybody was working."

"I don't think he should have let that boy in the back of the room keep tossing his pencil to the floor."

"Yes, but did you hear what the boy said? He was trying to test an idea he just found in a new book. I heard him tell Mr. Smith."

"O.K. But children can be told those things and don't have to play around to find out."

As Shirley listened, she was inclined to favor the way Mr. Smith seemed to work. But she kept her eye on the college instructor, waiting to see what he might say. She was surprised that he did not cut in on the discussion and at least raise some questions. Finally, she heard the college teacher remark:

"We do have different ideas, don't we? What we need to do now is to explore why we feel the different ways we do and whether we can get any help through reading and other sources on some of the observations we have made. Let's each try to put down on paper what we saw a teacher do that we thought was what we would have done under the circumstances. Tomorrow we can use this material as a basis for our discussion."

Inside Shirley's mind, thoughts such as these might have been found:

"This is a nice lounge. I wonder if all schools have these? . . . Children in this school seem to be so happy and enjoy what they're doing—all except in that one class. That teacher just didn't like life; she seemed so disgruntled. I don't want to be like her . . . I think Mr. Smith is right. Children ought to have a chance to discover things in their own ways, at least some of the time. I don't think telling is going to do much good, judging from my own experience . . . Why did Professor Blackstone wait so long? Guess he wanted to hear what we said first so he could see what we were thinking. How could he sit there and listen so carefully to some of our awful comments? He seems to think everybody has a right to his opinions—but of course, he's going to make us support them . . . I can see myself and what I'd be like in Miss Meredith's room."

Whether or not she is aware of it, Shirley is beginning to develop ideas about what she wants to be like as a teacher. The college instructor who took the group on this field trip appears to understand what might be going on inside the minds of Shirley and her classmates. He is deliberately trying to demonstrate in practice his own convictions about teaching. He knows he is an example these students analyze, and he wants them to see him as a teacher who respects them and their ideas, who encourages each one to express himself, even though he may stand alone, and who holds high standards of scholarship in his requirement that they be informed and support their ideas with substantial reasoning.

Although Florence was having a very different experience, she, too, was building an image of teachers and teaching.

In a class on the modern novel, the instructor had suggested that each student select a novel and try to understand one particular character in it. Specific questions were to be answered: How do you feel about this character? What makes him do the things he does? What kinds of decisions does he seem to make consistently, and why?

Florence selected a novel in which the primary figure was a high school boy. While she could not accept all his behavior, she learned to love him as she studied him. When she wrote her report on the novel, she went beyond the assignment and talked about how she wished she could have been a teacher where he went to school and what she would have done to help this boy with some of his problems.

MARGARET LINDSEY

The instructor was pleased with the report. Furthermore, he commented that because Florence had so much insight into that boy she would probably be a good, understanding teacher. Why didn't she think about teaching as a career? It was a wonderful profession and she would be good in it.

Did this college instructor know how influential he was in molding Florence's ideas about teachers and teaching? Years later, Florence referred to him as the teacher who caused her to want to teach. She said he was a brilliant scholar, he liked people, and he loved to teach.

It was Alice's cooperating teacher who was helping her to crystallize an image that had been developing over a period of time.

After a long, hard day, Alice and her cooperating teacher were sitting at a desk talking about what had happened. Alice wanted to know, "Why don't you make John knuckle down to business and get his work done?" And, "Don't you think it would be easier just to use the textbook and go right through it? You wouldn't have to work so hard that way."

In their long conversation, Alice heard the cooperating teacher say: "But, you see, John needs all the understanding and help I can give him. He just has not found himself. I've got to discover how to help him see the special places he can succeed so he learns to like himself better . . . Oh, yes, I get tired, but not as tired as though I did the same thing day after day. The excitement and satisfaction for me come from experimenting with ideas, always finding something I did not know before . . ."

And Alice said to herself as she walked toward the dorm, "That's it. That's just what you've got to be able to do— keep discovering."

While the above episodes are only illustrative of the hundreds of similar experiences students might have in their college preparation, they do suggest how the college teacher influences the primary image the student is developing of what teachers are like, how they feel, and why they do what they do. Even from the limited experiences reported in these episodes, the young prospective teacher can be seen as acquiring (a) beginning concepts of what schools are for, (b) some important characteristics of effective teaching, (c) insights into the importance of teachers' respect for people, (d) some fundamental ideas about what learning is and how children really learn, as well as how teachers can promote their learning, (e) beginning concepts of criteria for the selection and organization of experiences in schools, and (f) ideas about himself as a teacher. In these instances, students were generally formulating desirable concepts, and the chances were good that the images built in their minds would contribute to their becoming creative teachers. It must be noted, however, that it is equally possible for students to draw conclusions from their observations of college teachers that are detrimental to their development as creative teachers.

Other College Experiences

In addition to the observations college students make of their teachers, other experiences assist them in building the kind of image that will foster creativity in teaching. Significant among these are the experiences students have as a result of the general philosophy pervading selection and organization of content in courses, procedures employed by college teachers, ways in which the college curriculum is examined and modified, and administrative policies and practices.

The actual content with which a student is asked to deal may encourage his own expression of individuality or smother it. Content included in the program or in particular courses may be suggestive of the process of teaching creatively or of the process of conforming to stereotyped patterns in teaching. In the study of developmental psychology, for example, students can be led to try to put all children into arbitrary categories, or they can be helped to see children as individuals. Study of educational methodology may result in students' adopting detailed, specific techniques from books, or it may lead to general principles that can be applied in many situations, with due regard for the facts of the situation. Assignments made in connection with courses may be so sterile and inflexible as to stifle any real thinking on the part of individual students, or they may be flexible and challenging, calling upon each student to employ his best creative powers in their accomplishment. In college program planning and in college teaching, when deliberate attention is given to helping students to develop a vision of creative teaching, content is selected to capitalize on individual variation, to confront learners with problematic situations that necessitate examination of alternatives, to present students with issues not yet resolved, and to demonstrate that more than one plausible and valid answer to a question may be supported. However, even when content is carefully selected, students' opportunities to experience creative teaching depend greatly upon approaches used by teachers within their classes.

Procedures employed by college teachers influence each student markedly, particularly with respect to his growing image of himself as a person and as a future teacher. Procedures may be varied. They may encourage divergent thinking, demonstrate real respect for learners, provide for independent study, and utilize resources within students; or they may do just the opposite. Of special importance are procedures used in planning and evaluating learning on the part of college students. Planning may take account of students in a class and actually involve them, or it may be done without reference to students. Evaluation may contribute to a student's confidence, or it may in fact convince him that he is of little worth.

The manner in which a college faculty as a whole goes about the task of examining and modifying the teacher education program also contributes to a student's image of teaching. Is an educational program something that, once designed, is fixed forever? Is it something that is built on the basis of whim and opinion? Is it to be determined by a few people at the top, with others being told what to do, as well as when and how to do it? If "yes" is the answer to questions such as these, then unfortunately there is great chance that rigidity and authoritarianism are becoming part of the future teacher's total image.

Finally, administrative procedures and policies, the concept of the curriculum that appears to dominate practice, and the role of guidance in the college program also contribute to the vision the student is developing of himself and of teachers and teaching. Are college teachers respected for their individuality? Do they have academic freedom? Are they encouraged to be experimental? Is superior teaching, as well as research and writing, rewarded? Is the curriculum viewed as including out-of-course as well as in-course activities? Is guidance seen as a function of all teachers, and are specialized resources available and used effectively? Here again, it is certain that college students, as future teachers, are constantly integrating into their total conception of education, as answers to such questions, the answers they see in practice in their own college program.

The image with which the teacher begins his first year of teaching has been developed in part through experiences he had as a student in a preservice program. The way he goes to work on his teaching problems and his feelings concerning learners, teachers, and teaching will reflect this image. As he encounters resistance, discovers wide differences among his colleagues, and runs into questioning laymen, his vision of what is good teaching must be strong enough to withstand pressures toward conformity, to reject the easy way of doing what everybody else is doing. College teachers must so teach that their students build an image that places priority on freedom to create, on security in uncertainty, on tolerance for differences, and on compassion for, as well as understanding of, human beings.

UTILIZATION OF INDIVIDUAL POTENTIALITY

"Do you really think it is an idea worth exploring?" Ronald asked as he shared his plan with the cooperating teacher.

"I'll tell you how it is," said the classroom teacher, "I couldn't carry it out myself. Not that I don't think it is a good idea but just that I can't feel comfortable working with these pupils unless I know for sure what is going to happen."

"I'm not so sure I can do it either, but I'd like to try if you think I can do it."

"I think you can. We're quite different, you know. The children like us both but they respond to certain things in you and to other things in me. They will help you. Why don't we go ahead with your plan? I want to help, too. It's just that you've suggested something I never tried before and I don't feel too certain about it. But I want to help in seeing if it works. I think your idea is good."

Here was a cooperating teacher who was helping Ronald in an important exploration of himself and his potential as a creative teacher—not only providing freedom for him to test his ideas in practice, but actually encouraging his efforts to innovate; not only listening to his expression of a new way of doing something, but actually reacting with pleasure and respect for the idea; not only saying, in so many words, "Go ahead and try it," but actually offering to help, to join in the exploration, to learn from experience with the student. This veteran teacher was openly recognizing a weakness within himself and his teaching and at the same time revealing wholesome acceptance of himself as he was. This is the kind of situation that assists students in identifying their own potentialities and finding ways to use them creatively.

To understand the import of this particular situation for Ronald, one needs to know some of his earlier college experiences.

> When Ronald enrolled in the state college almost four years ago he was not a person who would have dared to make such a suggestion to one of his teachers. In fact, he really thought of himself as having little to offer. In high school, unfortunately, he had learned through bitter experience that it was better to do what he was told exactly as he was told to do it. Although he was usually successful, he felt uninspired; he spent a good deal of time thinking about what he would do when he had a chance. As a freshman in college, he found a teacher who took special interest in him, spent time with him talking about lots of things, especially the hobby that had persisted since his early adolescence. It all came about because Ronald made a suggestion in the composition class about a device he had invented to practice grammatical construction. The device, based on geometric form, was of interest to the teacher, who had never seen anything like it before. He asked Ronald to share it with the class, and the result was that Ronald was in demand by his peers for help with their problems in composition.

> But everything did not go well for Ronald. As a junior, in connection with a course in teaching social studies in the secondary school, he was required to engage in some participation in a nearby high school. He was serious about his observations and his chances to work with the pupils. He prepared meticulously. He expected the pupils to respond exactly as he had planned they would. When they did not, he immediately concluded that they were making fun of him and was about to decide that he was not good enough. Fortunately, working with Ronald and the classroom teacher was a college instructor who recognized the strength this young man had and perceived part of his teaching role to be helping Ronald to see those strengths for himself. Skilled

in playing this role as a college instructor, he planned with Ronald a sequence of specific experiences calling for use of special strengths.

The next semester, just before he began his student teaching, Ronald was called upon to represent his class at a state meeting of the Student National Education Association. When he got there, he discovered that he was expected to make a presentation in front of the assembled group. He approached the podium with fear and he did what he knew, and others knew, was an inadequate job. Several times after it was over, his adviser talked with him about his feelings concerning the failure at the state meeting. It was painful for Ronald, but together he and his adviser finally reached the decision that Ronald should seek experiences to appear before small groups as a means of building confidence. Meanwhile, he would continue to capitalize on his extraordinary skill in working intimately with pupils in a classroom.

Today Ronald is a first-rate teacher. He values himself for what he has to offer in helping high school youth deal with their problems. He knows his weaknesses, those about which he can do something and those he must accept as relatively nonremediable. On the first ones, he works constantly, seeking help wherever it is available; on the second ones, he does not dwell. Ronald is peculiarly sensitive to all kinds of feelings his pupils have about themselves and, because he has learned, with much assistance from others, how to handle constructively his own feelings about himself, he is able to help his pupils modify their self-concepts and hence be much more productive, creative persons.

Assisting future teachers in their self-understanding and acceptance is not likely to be done by any one member of the college community or by any one particular kind of experience. The case of Ronald illustrates how varied experiences contributed to his growing good feelings about himself and what he could do. All cases are like Ronald's, in that all call for individualized attention. Some prospective teachers need psychiatric treatment for special problems. All need to be surrounded by college personnel who care about them and their problems, who view it as important to help every student to see himself positively, but nonetheless realistically.

One's view of himself and of how others perceive him is developed out of many experiences that are not designed for this purpose at all. Teacher educators must set themselves a goal of helping each student with his growing picture of himself and keep that goal at a level of awareness in all of their contacts with students. College teachers who are still trying to convince themselves and others of their own worth are not well suited to accomplishing this goal.

College teachers who help students in the ways suggested here are vulnerable from several sides. Such teachers may be in excessive demand by students who discover them as a source of help on professional and personal problems. Also, such teachers may unwittingly be pulled into involvement with deeper, more complex problems than any nonspecialist should try to handle. These are possibilities of which the college teacher should be forewarned. But the danger of vulnerability is not a reason to avoid developing an inner serenity that equips one to assist students in understanding and accepting themselves.

RESPONSIVENESS TO PEOPLE, IDEAS, AND EVENTS

There are teachers who can see a harassed school principal take his anxiety out on the faculty at a meeting and still not respond with hostility toward him. There are those who can listen silently while a colleague relates a tale of misfortune and know just the right thing to say. There are those who can hear a telecast of rapidly developing Africa and be moved to deep thought on problems of colored and white people learning to live together harmoniously. And there are teachers whose primary rewards from teaching come as a result of observing children as they explore, discover, examine, and imagine, each in his own particular way. How do teachers get this way? Can anything be done in their preservice preparation to encourage development of this fine sensitivity and responsiveness to people, to ideas, to events?

Among the many kinds of experiences that may contribute to increasing sensitivity and responsiveness to people, ideas, and events are (1) analysis of direct experience with people of all ages, (2) intensive studies of individuals, (3) deliberate improvement of language skills, and (4) abundance of contact with nonverbal communication media. Within each of these areas of experience are potentials for modifying the way individuals perceive other human beings and respond to them, for developing open-mindedness toward ideas, and for increasing the range of response to events.

Analysis of Direct Experience

Direct experience, as a kind of learning opportunity, is now commonly provided in preservice teacher education programs. Often purposes for such experience, in the minds of both instructors and students, are limited in scope and depth. Too often students get inadequate guidance in planning and analyzing their direct contacts with people in school and community situations. Without any attempt to examine the nature of an adequate program of laboratory experiences, two illustrations are used here to exemplify how such experience might contribute to future teachers' sensitivity and response to human beings, particularly to those persons usually associated with the task of teaching. The first example comes from a course in social foundations of education where students were carrying on a community study.

> Students in this course selected a school community for detailed study, not only to gain insights into community structure but also to ascertain what impact the particular characteristics of the community should have upon the school program. With the instructor they organized their approach to the study, delegating certain aspects to small groups. Data were to be secured by interview and observation in selected locations and, of course, some were to be obtained from background reading of material related to the study.
>
> Ken, Walter, and Susan chose to concentrate their study on what youth in the community did with their time outside of school, how the community provided for this group, and eventually what the school should do in relation to their findings. They located three popular "hangouts" and began observing in those spots. Learning of a teen-age program at the local "Y," they included that center in their observations. By late April they began to hear of private clubs to which families belonged and which provided certain kinds of recreational opportunities for children and youth. They obtained permission to visit and observe these spots.
>
> Data accumulated fast and the three students began to discuss ideas they had gleaned from their study. The instructor

met with them on Wednesday afternoon to participate in their analysis of what they had seen and heard.

"I have to admit," said Ken, "that I almost resent the people out at the Baxter Club. They're smug, snobbish, and think they know it all."

"I know what you mean," answered Susan, "because I feel somewhat the same. But, to me, the kids that hang around that drug store and have nothing more worthwhile to do really get me. I can't stand people who are lazy and do nothing but hang around."

"Looks to me as if we like people like ourselves," said Walter. "Funny, I always thought I was pretty broadminded, but I confess to having the same feelings you've mentioned."

Here are students preparing to be teachers, who need real help in extending their range of acceptance of and response to varieties of people. Here is the "teaching moment" when the college instructor, himself sensitive and responsive to people, may step in and assist these students in understanding why they react as they do, in exploring causal factors of why different groups of young people behave as they do, what their real feelings and aspirations are, and in planning other experiences that will modify these students' views of people. That some college instructors do not provide such help partially explains the oft-repeated criticism of teachers that they tend to react favorably only to their own class of people.

The second illustration comes from an opportunity provided prospective teachers in connection with a block program in elementary education where one-half day per week for a semester was set aside for "participation" in an elementary school classroom. Althea, a student in this program, was discussing her experiences with the college instructor.

"There are three children in this room that interest me almost more than any others."

"What makes them so interesting to you?"

"One is Harry. Do you know him? He's the one who never has anything done on time, always has something inside his desk that he is fooling around with, never pays any attention to the other children, even in the gym."

"How do you feel about him?"

"Well, I think if I were Miss Adkins, I'd get behind him and push. Why should he be allowed to be so different? Most of the others get things done on time and pay attention to what's going on. I think he is a daydreamer."

"What does Miss Adkins seem to think about him?"

"She says he really has unusual interests and that one of these days he'll surprise us, that his pace is just different but that he actually is quite gifted."

"Who are the others who interest you especially?"

"Guess they appeal to me because they can always be counted on to come through with what is expected. You know, they always have the right answer, they've always done good work . . ."

Althea is at a high point of readiness for help in analyzing her responses to these children and the reasons behind them. If the college instructor provides skillful help, Althea will perhaps come to understand that Harry needs freedom to explore in ways that are congenial to him, and may eventually extend her sensitivity to other children resembling Harry. If she does not get such help at this point and later on, she may become a teacher whose response to children and adults is rigid.

As with all good teaching, so with the use of direct experience—it is not just provision of the opportunity, but it is careful guidance in analysis of the meaning of the experience that makes for high quality in learning. To employ laboratory experiences of various sorts for the purpose of helping a student to improve his relations with other people and his understanding of them calls for competent guidance by college instructors.

Intensive Studies of Individuals

Making an intensive study of an individual is a common experience provided in the professional sequence.[1] What is the real purpose of the experience and what meaning does it have for students? Many values may be derived from such a study. Intensive study of an individual is, in a real sense, a vehicle for the discovery of

[1] The study here referred to is the kind undergraduate students might be expected to make, not a case study in the clinical sense.

such basic facts as these: that behavior is caused, that a range of forces affects behavior, that each individual is unique, and so on. If the student making such a study is left to draw conclusions within the narrow limits of an individual case and is not helped to formulate generalizations that have meaning for understanding all human beings, the responsible college instructor has deprived the student of the most important value in making a case study. Understanding that people behave the way they do because of past experience is basic to a high level of awareness of individuals and constructive responses to them.

Deliberate Improvement of Language Skills

Some of the language arts skills play an important role in an individual's sensitivity and responsiveness generally, but very especially with regard to ideas. The sensitive person, for example, not only listens but hears and reacts to what is said in group situations. He not only understands what he reads but he thinks about it. Not only can he express his own ideas in writing but he is able to place himself in the position of his reader, and his awareness of his reader enters into his writing. For the teacher who desires to teach creatively and to have pupils realize their full potential as creative people, it is particularly important that he have an attitude of caring about getting the full meaning of what a child is trying to express. If a teacher really *wants* to understand ideas expressed either by colleagues or children, the likelihood is that he will develop the necessary skills to make this possible. Can future teachers be helped through their preservice experiences to build attitudes of caring and skills of understanding what people are trying to express through whatever medium is being employed?

Yes, they can be helped in a great many ways. For example, in the study of literature students can be assisted in searching out different interpretations of characters and events, seeking to uncover not only the obvious ideas but also the implied.

Direct attention to listening as a skill can be given in many different kinds of situations—in discussions where differences of opinion are being expressed; in planning situations, where individuals make proposals for study, action, or evaluation; in report situations, where peers are communicating the results of their efforts; in recitations; and in lectures. College instructors should take time in such situations as these to help students study how much they hear, the selectivity present in their hearing, and the prejudices playing a role in their listening. Tape recordings are an excellent medium for this purpose.

Both the art and skill of questioning can be improved through deliberate attention to them. Students can be helped to examine critically the kinds of questions that seem to assist people in expressing themselves more fully, as compared with the kinds that tend to cause people to "clam up." Such help can be provided in many ways—detailed analyses of films, studies of recordings of teaching-learning situations, and analyses of students' own feelings in response to questions in various kinds of situations, particularly their own college classes.

Powers of observation can be increased through careful guidance by college teachers. Perception of possible underlying feelings as well as what is openly expressed is vital to sensitivity and responsiveness to others. Direct experiences in recording observations, interpreting what was observed, and testing perceptions help students to become more aware of their powers of observation.

Much creative work remains to be done in the utilization of closed-circuit television and tape recordings for the purpose of assisting students in communication skills useful in responding to people and ideas. One of the important advantages of these mechanical instruments (assuming that Kinescopes or recordings on video tape are made) is that they permit repeated use of the same material for study.

The technique of role playing has much to offer when used well by college instructors. Through a sequence of (1) setting up a situation, (2) role playing it, (3) analyzing the dynamics of the observed role playing, (4) replaying the situation, and (5) analyzing it again, students can be helped to improve the scope and depth of their perceptions and their responses and to begin to build bases for generalizing.

Nonverbal Communication

Ideas conjured up in pupils' minds are communicated in ways other than through verbal symbols. As a matter of fact, ideas most important for teachers to understand and accept are often expressed through movement, through color and form, or through bodily posture and facial expression rather than through words, written or spoken. Prospective teachers need a great deal of experience in analyzing their own communication through such media as well as in interpreting what others (children, youth, and adults) are expressing by the same means.

If graduates of teacher education programs are to be creative teachers, sensitive and responsive to people, ideas, and events, direct attention will have to be given to the goal of understanding nonverbal communication. Even though young adults have already assimilated into their behavior a good many recurring patterns of responding to people, much still can be done in four or five years of preparation to modify patterns that appear to decrease teaching effectiveness.

SECURITY IN UNCERTAINTY

In specific teaching situations there are seldom single right answers to problems. This is true for many reasons. First of all, education is a young science, with new knowledge being discovered every day, knowledge that frequently implies new and better ways of dealing with teaching-learning conditions. Second, each setting in which teaching and learning take place is characterized by a complex configuration of factors unique to that situation. A procedure that is constructive in one situation may be destructive in another. Third, each teacher is a unique individual who must discover for himself his own best ways of utilizing available knowledge and developing his art of teaching. Because new knowledge is constantly being formulated, because each teaching situation calls for particular specific behaviors, and because each teacher is a person unlike every other—one who must discover his own ways of behaving—there is present in teaching a high degree of uncertainty. To be highly anxious about such uncertainty inhibits creativity in teaching.

Many teachers suffer from such anxiety. When teachers ask to be told exactly how to do various tasks related to their work, when they reveal resentment because their principals and other consultants deal in principles rather than in specific techniques, they may be expressing a fear of trying ideas out for themselves, a lack of faith in their own ability to discover the meaning of ideas in practice in their own classrooms. In some instances, at least, when teachers show resistance to newer concepts of method, their resistance is centered not in disagreement with the newer concepts, but rather in the insecurity they experience as they think of trying something new about which they cannot be sure. Feelings of having to know the answer in advance, of having to rely always on one's tried and true methods, and of fearing the unknown are deterrents to creativity in teaching.

Healthy security, a confidence in the self and the factors affecting one's welfare, is basic to productivity in all aspects of life and work. Much has been written in educational literature about the need to help people at all stages and in all phases of development to build self-confidence and feelings of security, with special reference to respect, acceptance, and success as contributing factors. Far less attention has been given to helping people to accept and use constructively feelings of insecurity. Yet a sizable amount of insecurity exists for teachers who work creatively in their classrooms. What kinds of experiences in a preservice teacher education program might help future teachers feel secure in the face of unknowns, in situations where the results cannot be precisely predicted, in the continuous exploring and discovering that is part of creative teaching?

Some of the concrete places where students might be helped are revealed in these questions often asked by students just prior to student teaching:

> What am I going to do if they (the children) ask me questions I can't answer? How can I possibly "keep up" with all the areas that are likely to be of interest to them?

> What if I try something and it doesn't work? How can I know that what I have tried is as productive as some other way might have been? How can I criticize the cooperating teacher's way when I don't know what might happen if I used my method?

> How can I be sure we will get the job done if I let the children help in deciding what we will do and how? I don't see how I can have everybody doing something different at times and still have control over the room. Don't I really have to know exactly what everybody is doing so I can teach what I should?

Among the insecurities expressed by students as they approach student teaching is fear that their knowledge will be inadequate to deal with questions that might come up in a classroom. The very request for help on this point reveals that somehow these students have arrived at unfortunate and, indeed, unsound conclusions about teaching and their roles as teachers, about knowledge and its development. In a dynamic situation, where every individual is using his creative potential, new ideas are being formulated, new relationships are being discovered, and new methodologies are in the making. The teacher in such a situation cannot know everything that may be discovered when learners are free to learn in their own best ways, cannot be informed in every area that individual pupils may need to explore. Actually, one of the things a teacher needs most to know is that he does not know and cannot know all that pupils are going to learn.

What has been said about "knowing the answers" informationally is true also of knowing procedures. Here, too, students often express considerable insecurity. They feel unsure of their right to examine procedures critically and of their ability to test an idea in practice. Expression of such insecurity by students going into student teaching permits the assumption that what they have learned from experience up to this point in their preparation is almost this: "The technology of teaching is a matrix of highly refined skills and the task of preparing to teach is completed with the acquisition of these skills." Of course, this is not a true generalization, for there is far more to teaching creatively than making application of a given set of specific skills.

Involving pupils in important decision making with regard to selection and organization of school experiences is another idea that prompts a good deal of insecurity on the part of beginning teachers and veteran teachers as well. To maintain complete control over content and activities in a classroom, these teachers seem to believe, makes it possible to plan in advance in such ways as to guard against any threat to their security. A teacher can be sure of his informational background, because he controls what information will be considered; he can be sure of his procedures, because he holds the reins tightly and does not permit a relaxation that might be picked up by anyone else. But to share the controls with learners themselves demands a completely different orientation for the teacher, a faith in learners and their individual and collective intelligence, a confidence in his own ability to use human resources well, a coveting of opportunity for others to experiment and to discover—in short, a degree of wholesome security in uncertainty.

Even a cursory look at some preservice teacher education programs reveals an interesting inconsistency in dealing with the need for security in uncertainty just cited. On the one hand future teachers are admonished to build habits of intellectual curiosity, to explore unceasingly for new ideas, to discover their own best ways of responding to various stimuli, to realize that new information is being created every day, and on the other hand they are graded solely on the degree to which they can reproduce someone else's (usually the instructor's or the textbook author's) organization of facts. On the one hand they are told that individuals are unique, that learners must be free to pursue their interests at points of readiness, that teaching is fostering and encouraging the full development of each pupil, and on the other hand they are herded into college classrooms, given the same assignments, asked to make responses that conform to what the instructor believes. In the process they experience very little welcoming recognition of their own potentialities. They are asked to believe that there are few situations in the classroom that can be handled rightly in only one way, that each teacher must build his own best ways of working with children, and at the same time they are put into teaching situations where they are expected to imitate, almost exclusively, patterns already established by an experienced teacher. If there is any validity at all (and there surely is a great deal) to the theory that we learn what we experience, then it is little wonder that some beginning teachers come from their preservice preparation with a high degree of security in doing things in the patterns established by instructors and an equally high degree of insecurity in trying their own wings.

To teach creatively at any level requires a quality of security in uncertainty. However, there is another side to this coin which must not be overlooked. The human being who has the necessary security to be comfortable and productive in unpredictable, uncertain situations is the individual who also has the security that comes from a strong foundation in the predictables, the certainties. Such a foundation for the teacher is composed of theoretical principles that have meaning to him because he has tested them in teaching situations, and a repertoire of practices that have proved to achieve desired ends. Furthermore, this foundation must include a range of knowledge and ability to use it appropriately. A firm foundation, providing the teacher with a launching platform as

MARGARET LINDSEY

well as with a foothold and the security that comes with possession of such a foundation, is as essential to creativity in teaching as is the self-confidence to feel secure in uncertainty.

In most teacher education programs, students have ample opportunity to develop the security that emanates from the kind of foundation just referred to. There is little indication, however, that college faculties make deliberate effort to assist students in building the necessary security in unpredictable, uncertain situations. Sometimes students actually learn the meaning of such security by contagion—that is, by their tendency to acquire values, attitudes, and principles of behavior they see in those whom they admire. Consider the following illustrations. The first comes from a class studying discussion as an effective teaching procedure.

A college teacher and class were studying ways of making discussion an effective teaching procedure. In the course of their deliberations, a student made a comment to which the instructor responded emotionally with nonacceptance. Then he proceeded to another point. A keen student, observing what had happened, called to the attention of the instructor that he had probably made the first student feel uncomfortable and closed off his future contributions.

In this instance, the instructor had several alternatives from which to select his response to the observant student. He might have disregarded his comment and gone on with the discussion; he might have become emotionally disturbed and felt threatened by the student; or he might have capitalized on the incident to demonstrate the importance of learning to employ a technique even though one felt very insecure in the tryout stage.

The instructor chose the third alternative, suggesting to the class that the skill of using all students' comments constructively was one he was trying to develop and that he found himself making blunders as he tried to improve. He revealed a real sense of security in his efforts, although he knew his discussion-leading skills were less well developed than his lecture skills.

Later the same day, several students came to the instructor and mentioned the incident. Their comments showed that they respected him for the way he went about trying to extend the range of his classroom procedures and for his self-confidence in the face of a problem. Some actually said they hoped they would be able to try out new things even though they couldn't feel comfortable in doing them.

The second illustration comes from a course designed especially for future teachers of core classes in junior high schools.

> Having taught the course several times, the instructor had built a sequence of topics that had meaning and logic to him. On the first day of class, he presented to the group an overview of the content they would be dealing with and the sequence in which topics would be considered. Contrary to what had happened in previous semesters when he did this with his first class, these students asked some questions, showing that they saw logic in starting from a different point. What they wanted to do was to observe some core classes as the very first step in order to have something concrete to which to tie their reading and discussion.

> Now the instructor had planned for such observation to occur at another point in the course and for other purposes. On his feet in front of the class, he later reported, he had to recognize that the students had a good point, that there were values in their approach. For a moment he felt so unsure of what would happen that he was inclined to insist on his planned approach. He shared his feelings with the group and together they decided to test the suggested new approach.

> Throughout the semester both students and instructor were consciously appraising the effectiveness of the preliminary observations. More than once the instructor openly shared his uncertainty, but always with a confidence that there were many ways to accomplish the same end and that it was good to try different ways.

The third episode used for illustration occurred in a women's residence hall.

> As was common practice, the elected residence council got together to establish regulations for conduct in the hall. Always before, the council had pretty much reaffirmed the rules and regulations that existed from previous years. But this year the council took the position that having specific time rules (for coming in at night especially) was insulting to young adults. If these students did not learn now to use some self-discipline and good judgment, when would they?

The proposal was that every student be free to establish her own regulations, using criteria (having to do with physical condition, parental attitudes, social mores, work, and other responsibilities) that the group would set up.

Although the director felt very uncertain about how such a scheme might work, she decided to give it a try. Her report of its effectiveness was so positive that the practice was extended to selected classes and other organizations on the campus. Here was another opportunity for students to observe that a person with responsibility for guiding young people could, with confidence, permit freedom of expression and action.

Prospective teachers' need for help in developing security in uncertainty is not fully met, however, by opportunity to observe others who have acquired this quality. Even where such observation is possible, to profit most from it students should be guided in their interpretations and particularly in conclusions they draw. In addition to this kind of help, provision should be made for more direct approaches similar to those suggested in earlier parts of this chapter.

PROSPECTIVE TEACHERS AS LEARNERS

Above everything else, a creative teacher views himself as a learner —learning with and from pupils, learning from his own testing of ideas in practice, learning with and from his peers, learning from confrontation with challenging problems in all phases of his work. Some of the kinds of experiences that contribute to helping future teachers gain a view of themselves as learners have been suggested in earlier sections of this chapter.

If college teachers are themselves creative people and if their teaching stimulates creativity on the part of their students, the concept of teachers as learners will be central in students' images of teachers and teaching. It has been suggested that direct attention should be given to helping each college student fully realize his unique potentiality. When this happens, a student cannot escape the fact that one of his most important capacities is that of continuing to learn. Responsiveness to people, ideas, and events is needed not only so that a teacher may understand those with whom he works but also that he may learn from the environment.

As indicated earlier also, to be comfortable in uncertain situations is a quality needed by a creative teacher, not only that he may free others to learn but also that he himself may be free to learn through exploration and discovery. Hence, previous discussion of the kinds of experiences in teacher preparation that contribute to helping future teachers in developing a guiding image of teaching and teachers, in accepting and utilizing their own potentiality, in being sensitive and responsive, and in having a sense of security in uncertainty is relevant in the present consideration of assisting students in building a view of themselves as learners.

Prospective teachers need much help in acquiring a commitment to continuous learning and they also need opportunity to become acquainted with a range of resources that have promise of contributing to their learning in the years ahead. Furthermore, they need to build skills in using available resources appropriately. Not all of the many ways in which a teacher capitalizes on opportunities to learn and their implications for preservice preparation can be explored here. Selection has been made of ways that have particular significance for the teacher who strives to teach creatively.

For such a teacher his own activities in his classroom present fertile opportunity for learning. This teacher also learns much from association with his colleagues in his school as well as in his profession generally. He utilizes professional literature to good advantage. How can the preservice program contribute to the cultivation of teachers who will continue to learn in ways that enhance their capacities for teaching creatively?

Learning by Teaching

Disposition toward an action research approach to teaching is an integral part of creative teaching, for to be creative as a teacher does not mean to act on whim and be satisfied with the results, whatever they may be. It means, rather, a releasing of the self to innovate, to discover, and to explore, but always with a concern for the results. Hence it is important for future teachers to build awareness of the need to examine results of their efforts and competence in making such examination. Few procedures are more productive in this regard than the application of action research to teaching. By this is meant (1) clearly defining the problem to be studied, (2) exploring a variety of approaches to deal with the problem, (3) selecting one approach to be tested, (4) defining the evidence needed to test the effectiveness of the approach, (5) planning how to secure the evidence, (6) collecting and interpreting the evidence, and (7) drawing conclusions on the basis of the evidence.

While teachers-to-be may acquire a positive attitude toward such an approach through observation of its use by their college instructors, they also need specific help in acquiring the skills essential to testing their own ideas in their practice. Student teaching offers rich opportunity for helping students to test ideas. If this opportunity is to be used, however, those who guide student teachers must make deliberate plans with each student, make sure that the environment facilitates unbiased study of teaching and learning, provide assistance in conducting a study, and help students in careful interpretation of findings. Moreover, for greatest benefit in their future work, students must be carefully guided in examining possible application of conclusions to other similar teaching situations.

It is not enough, however, to provide a student with generalized experiences in researching his own action. To learn from study of his teaching, the teacher is required to have control of complex skills of observation, of test construction, of interviewing, of interpretation of factual data as well as of analysis of information that cannot be factored easily. In a wide range of settings, the college program must provide a student with experience in specific skills and techniques applicable to a study of teaching. Although well-taught courses in educational research may contribute greatly to a student's acquisition of these skills, it is doubtful that such courses will do the whole job. As important as direct teaching in courses of this type is, the experiences a student has in participating in action research being carried on by a college instructor, particularly when these experiences include analysis of each step in the process, are probably more effective.

Learning from Associates

Some teachers learn from association with other professionals, and other teachers do not. Frequently failure to learn from others is caused by a kind of insecurity. Often fear that the self-image may be adversely affected makes an individual build protective barriers around himself so that he cannot take in ideas. In rare cases, a teacher's inability to learn from colleagues is due to his feeling of superiority. An important goal for teacher educators is to help students develop great capacity to learn from others and to decrease barriers to such learning.

Two illustrations may serve to suggest some of the kinds of experience in preparatory programs that would seem to contribute to accomplishment of this goal. The faculty of an education department in a college, together with the student advisory board (a group of students elected by the student body to represent them in deliberations with the faculty), planned a series of informal get-togethers that would provide opportunity for both socialization among students and faculty and discussion of important events related to education. Among the topics discussed during the year were these:

> *The Meaning of Giftedness in Children (as viewed by the scientist, the artist, the psychologist, and the humanist).*
> Here four specialists were brought in to make brief presentations. Discussion centered on what could be learned from their presentations that had implications for teaching in the elementary school.
>
> *Variation in Human Beings: A Report of a Research Conference.*
> A faculty member who had just attended a research conference on this topic made a report. Her own obvious learning from the conference was communicated to the students.
>
> *What Our Students Tell Us: Consideration of Data Collected in Recent Study.*
> A faculty-student committee had just completed a study of students' reactions to the quality of advising they received. The program consisted of a faculty panel reporting what they had learned from the study and open discussion of what action could be taken on important things that had been learned.

Other programs continued to emphasize the point that students should have experience in seeing their college teachers still learning from their associates.

Team teaching in college classes offers another kind of opportunity for students to participate in a situation where peers are learning from one another. For example, senior secondary education students on one campus have a seminar following their student teaching. Conducted by a panel of faculty members representing four academic areas, the seminar has the purpose of helping students increase their understanding of the place of their field of teaching specialization in a total high school program. It is not uncommon in this seminar for college teachers involved to find themselves in disagreement and to discover that they must engage in extended discussions to be sure they understand points of view and their implications. It is not uncommon to hear one faculty member say to another, "I wasn't aware of that. Where could I get more information on it?" When this happens, students are acutely aware of the fact that even the most learned professors must keep on learning from one another.

The daily experience of college students in their classes should make it evident to them that they can and should be learning constantly from discussion with others. Chances that this fact will be evident are better when college teachers are skilled in leading discussion in ways that not only students, but also they themselves, are learning from contributions to the discussion.

Selecting and Utilizing Professional Literature

One college teacher reported that he made a habit of taking into his classes about once a week what to him was an exciting, stimulating piece of professional literature and of telling his students why it was so stimulating. In so doing he tried to demonstrate to his students that he profited greatly from the ideas of others as he found them expressed in writing.

Another instructor said he tried to make sure during one of his courses that students had contact with what he viewed as sources of the most provocative professional literature. When pressed for a statement of criteria he used in judging "provocativeness," he indicated that he was always looking for books and periodicals that tended in the direction of philosophical analyses, or discussion of issues, or descriptions of practice that was frontier in nature. What this teacher did for his students was to suggest by example that one could be selective in what he chose to read and that each person should set criteria in terms of his own needs and interests.

To give students long bibliographies and to set course requirements so that they must "come in contact" with a wide range of professional literature may result in some desirable outcomes. Far better, however, is provision of more specific experiences with a few selected sources about which an instructor is enthusiastic and which have the quality of opening up problems, issues, and ideas rather than closing off exploration of alternatives and failing to offer variation in interpretation and application.

The professional, in whatever specialization, who views his preparation as finished when he completes the required degree, is in a sad state. This is no less true in teaching than it is in medicine where the need to be abreast of current findings is crucial. To expect to rely completely five years hence on what is known today is naïve. For competent practice in any profession, the practitioner must make use not only of what continues to be functional from his earlier study but also of the information accumulating rapidly at any given time. Beyond this general need to base practice on the best that is known, however, is the fact that a teacher who is not continuing to learn cannot be a dynamic, stimulating force in creatively helping others to learn.

CREATIVITY IN COLLEGE TEACHING

The purpose of this chapter has been to examine opportunities in the preparation of teachers that may help individuals to put creativity into their future teaching. Even the brief examination made here reveals the importance that must be attached to creativity in the teaching of college teachers as an influential factor in practices of their students when they become teachers. Within every college faculty there are those who have successfully developed qualities necessary for creative teaching and those who have not. Like others, college teachers are continuing to learn and can improve their practice.

In elementary and secondary schools teachers usually find themselves in settings where considerable emphasis is placed on their professional development. Generally, this emphasis is not one of coercion, but it is one of support, help, and cooperation. Conditions that surround school teachers are under constant study by specialists to discover what factors promote and what factors impede excellence in teaching. Conferences, workshops, study groups, curriculum committees, and a host of other activities provide the typical elementary or secondary school teacher with the stimulation and support that come from group efforts. For the individual wanting help, consultants are readily available. In fact, a staff of specialized personnel is usually employed and charged with responsibility for leadership in the improvement of teaching and in curriculum study and development.[2]

In most colleges, the picture is quite different. Although a college setting may be rich in human resources, printed materials, and research studies, other conditions surrounding the college teacher may actually prevent his utilization of such resources in the improvement of his own teaching. For reasons pointed out in earlier sections of this present chapter, the behavior of college teachers carries significant weight in developing teachers who will teach creatively in elementary and secondary schools. The illustrations presented suggest some of the ways in which college teachers demonstrate creativity in their own teaching as they help prospective teachers develop attitudes, values, knowledge, and skills essential to creativity in teaching. It would seem appropriate, therefore, to consider briefly a few of the conditions in collegiate environments that may facilitate full development and use by college teachers of their potential for creativity in teaching. Four factors have particular significance in analysis of the college environment: (1) faculty and administrative attitudes toward students, (2) concepts of teaching and learning, (3) curriculum organization and development, and (4) administrative policies related to the work of faculty members.

Attitudes of Instructors Toward Students

A college campus is like an elementary school in that an "atmosphere" can be felt almost immediately upon contact. An important ingredient in this atmosphere is the attitude toward students on the part of the faculty and administration. Students can be viewed as knowing very little, as having immature and not-to-be-trusted judgment, as lacking in seriousness of purpose, and as trying to "get away with" as little work as possible; or they can be viewed as budding scholars whose knowledge may be a source of learning for the faculty, as individuals in whom confidence can be placed because of their seriousness of purpose and their wisdom in decision-making regarding their work and their self-discipline.

[2] Chapter 8, "Responsible and Responsive Administration and Supervision," in this book presents an analysis of the particular ways in which such leadership personnel may promote creativity in teaching. Although the discussion is centered primarily on the work of such persons in elementary and secondary schools, what is suggested in Chapter 8 is pertinent to the work of leadership personnel in colleges and universities.

How students are perceived by the more mature adults in the college setting is apparent from such factors as the expectations the faculty hold of them, the degree of freedom granted to them in their work as well as in their social activities, and their participation in the affairs of the college community. Clear evidence of acceptance of and respect for students (or lack of these) is frequently found in conversations among faculty members, in their consistent manner of responding to students, or their tendencies to seek student advice at appropriate times. In some college policies, too, there are manifestations of an atmosphere of respect for students, collectively and individually.

The degree of real respect for students that pervades a college atmosphere is, of course, very important to the total quality of their education. Such respect has particular import, however, with reference to creativity in college teaching. First of all, the individual college faculty member is likely to adopt to some degree the prevailing attitudes around him. If the expectancy of the environment is that he will listen to and respect what students have to say, that he will learn to know students as individuals, that he will encourage freedom, and that he will often learn with students, the college teacher (with rare exceptions) will begin to deal with students in these ways.

Second, the college teacher who takes seriously the need to know each individual student and to respect his potential should have the support of a general atmosphere in which these things are expected. Otherwise there is danger that he may be viewed unfavorably by both students and staff colleagues. Third, and most important, without respect for students there is little chance for creativity in teaching, and certainly almost no chance for helping students to capitalize on their creative potential.

Concepts of Teaching and Learning Held by Faculty

If teaching is viewed as a process of transmitting information from the teacher to the student, both the teacher and the student have undesirable and unnecessary limits set on what and how they learn. For the teacher there are few procedures available that lend themselves to this narrow concept of teaching. Consequently, he may find himself confining teaching procedures to lecture and production of materials in print for use by students. The student, on the other hand, is confronted with the low-level goal of "learning" what has already been organized and interpreted by someone else. Thus he is deprived of the opportunity to explore the growing edge of knowledge in a field, to discover for himself new methods or approaches to particular information, or to question established generalizations.

When teaching is viewed as a process of providing the best possible opportunities for learning by students, a teacher is then challenged to examine all kinds of resources and procedures and deliberately to select those that would seem most effective in a given situation. His selection must take into account the individual students, the range of resources available, and other such factors. The very fact that the teacher, with this view of teaching, must consider individual students and a variety of procedures presents him with real possibility to be creative rather than to rely consistently on only two or three ways of teaching.

A concept of teaching encompasses a belief about learning and usually includes beliefs about evaluation of students' learning also. For example, college teachers may view students as successful in their learning in a college class when they are able to reproduce in writing or orally what they have read or heard. Other college teachers may view this level of learning as inadequate for college students and may, instead, expect their students to extend their learning beyond what is presently found in books, to acquire a method of inquiry basic to a field, and to apply that method in original study. If such expectations as the latter are held for students, both they and their teachers are more likely to exercise freedom and imagination in planning the range of experiences in a given course.

The intention here is not to suggest that there is one concept of teaching and learning that is valid above all others. Nor should it be inferred that creativity in teaching is possible within only one selected view of teaching and learning. It does seem clear, however, that the likelihood of creativity in college teaching is greater when the teacher's view of teaching places in the center his role in provision of learning opportunities. It seems clear, also, that the chances for creativity in teaching, and in learning by students, are best when the teacher's view of learning encompasses more than the acquisition of already organized subject matter.

Just as the prevailing faculty-administrative attitudes toward students influence the attitude of the individual college teacher, so the concepts of teaching and learning that prevail tend to affect the concepts held by any one member of the staff. Very seldom do college faculties consider such fundamental questions as what is teaching, what is learning, and what is expected of students in courses, in spite of the fact that answers to such questions are basic to their work. It would be well for college faculties to give time and energy to examination of their individual and collective concepts in these areas. In so doing, they might well look especially at conditions of teaching and learning that promise to facilitate creativity.

Curriculum Development and Organization

Procedures employed in continuous evaluation and development of college curricula often set the stage *for* or *against* creativity in teaching and learning. Those processes that would seem to promote creativity usually result from implementation of certain fundamental principles. Mention of only a few of these principles may illustrate their importance in relation to the central theme of this chapter.

Content and organization of a curriculum should be viewed as flexible and should be subjected to constant study and evaluation by all persons involved. Flexibility permits proper adjustment to the needs, interests, and abilities of both college teachers and students. The expectancy that a curriculum will be appraised critically and continuously calls for serious inquiry with respect to its merits, and, therefore, implies freedom for all those involved to make such inquiry.

Decisions of what shall be included in curricular offerings and how they shall be organized should be based on sound reasoning and on evidence, where evidence is obtainable. When college teachers and students are in a situation where they must examine their world, their aspirations, and their conceptions of teaching and learning as bases for decisions on the curriculum, they are drawn *toward* conditions that foster creativity and *away from* those that promote conformity with tradition and common practice. Moreover, because central figures in such examination are college teachers and their students, they are more likely to view their in-course activities as an important opportunity for inquiry of various kinds.

In some ways typical patterns of scheduling courses and allocating credits are unfortunate for the creative teacher. For example, the usual fifty-minute period may be too short a time for students and instructor to develop satisfaction from procedures other than lecture, recitation, and examination. Although this may be true in almost any college course, it has particular relevance for certain aspects of teacher education programs. A student who is pursuing an idea through observation in a school classroom often needs a continuous block of time that permits preparing for the observation, conducting it, and taking advantage of opportunity to analyze it immediately. The instructor who is trying to help students in building discussion skills so basic to responsiveness to people may need a period of time adequate for setting up a situation, tape-recording a discussion, and making analysis of the discussion with students. Procedures such as those implied here, and numerous others that could be mentioned, call for such flexibility in scheduling classes that longer periods of time are available when needed.

Perhaps the factor in curriculum development at the college level most essential to assisting teachers in being more creative in their work with students is the confidence placed in individual college teachers, their judgments, and their decisions. Surely when a college teacher feels that his colleagues and others trust him to carry out his responsibilities with excellence, he is more likely to have a sense of freedom in decision-making with respect to his teaching and to have more confidence in experimenting with his ideas.

Administrative Policies

Space does not permit, nor is it the intention here to present, a treatise on administrative policies at the collegiate level. However, there are certain commonly practiced policies in colleges that tend to distract faculty members from focusing attention on their work as teachers and that actually operate against creativity in teaching.

Chief among the policies that may impede improvement of college teaching are those governing promotions, merit increases in salary, and other rewards to individual faculty members. When the criteria stated in these policies place prime importance on the amount of publication and research done by faculty members (as they very often do) and fail to include quality of teaching as a central criterion, it is clear indication of what is valued most by administrators and others responsible for policies. To carry on research and experimentation can be a valuable creative activity for a college teacher. To organize his own insights and his interpretations of insights reported by others and transmit them through print is also a potentially worthwhile undertaking. Indeed, both of these activities may contribute greatly to the quality of an instructor's teaching. On the other hand, when time, energy, and attention of faculty members must be focused on activities that are external to their teaching, the chances are very great that even the college teacher who has ideas and wants to try them out in his teaching will find himself having insufficient time left for this purpose. Those responsible for developing and applying systems of rewards to college teachers must recognize the particular challenges with which they confront faculty members, and they must be certain that those challenges relate significantly to instruction, which is, after all, the core of the college program.

Recently there has appeared in college environments another condition for which administration is primarily responsible and which too often places unwarranted limits on the creativity of college teachers. Reference is here made to research grants from a variety of sources. It has been said that one must know how to prepare a request for such grants, and that "knowing how" means suggesting the study and design that is expected by the donor. In many instances of this kind individual college teachers or a group of faculty members may actually and consciously sacrifice truly creative approaches to their work because of the need to conform to what is expected by some person or some group outside the college environment. Another unfortunate situation exists when monies are available only in limited areas of research and experimentation. College teachers may find themselves having to give up what would be stimulating, exciting, and creative exploration because of restrictions placed on the use of research funds. All those who have decision-making authority with respect to allocation of research funds should examine with care what they may be doing to individual college teachers by the decisions they make. Somewhere funds should be found to encourage and sponsor studies in which individuals are interested and which do not necessarily meet stipulations often set down by outside grantors.

MARGARET LINDSEY

Concern for creativity in college teaching leads to regret that there has developed in higher education a tradition of almost no supervision of instruction. Supervision is used here to refer to the facilitation of the best possible teaching on the part of every faculty member. Individuals need to be able to discuss their own interests, not just with colleagues who are so consumed with their own ideas as to be able to give only passing attention as listeners, but with specialized persons whose function it is to encourage, to help, to offer suggestions, and to provide resources. There is reason to believe that college administrators would do well to consider adapting at the college level some of the leadership activities that have proved successful in elementary and secondary schools. There is little reason to believe that teachers cease to need help and support in the improvement of their teaching just because they are college teachers. This is especially true at present when literally thousands of new college teachers are going into practice every year, many of them with little preparation for the functions they are required to perform.

Conclusion

The foregoing brief analysis of some of the qualities needed if teachers are to be creative, and of ways their development might be fostered in preservice teacher education, implies certain generalizations about programs and personnel. In review, these might be stated as follows:

> Selection and organization of experiences to be provided in a teacher education program are based largely on a conception of the kinds of teachers and teaching needed in schools of today and tomorrow. Such a conception should put primary emphasis on the qualities that promote creativity in teaching.

> While these qualities include specific skills and bodies of information, they are composed largely of attitudes, values, and principles to guide behavior.

> The total program of teacher education should be envisioned as providing a wide range of experience in which individual students are helped in selecting those experiences meeting their particular needs.

Many channels should be open to students for seeking intimate and continuous guidance from day to day, both for personal and professional activities.

College teachers in teacher education teach a great deal by example. Students are helped in becoming creative teachers as they experience creative teaching in college.

Development of the qualities that make for creativity in teaching is the responsibility of all those who come in contact with prospective teachers.

Although direct approaches should be employed in helping students with concepts and skills that contribute to their full use of creative potential, much of what a student learns about teaching and teachers, himself, other people, ideas, security in uncertainty, and the need for continuing to learn, he gets through experience not directly designed for this purpose.

Educators who have worked with teachers at the preservice or the inservice level, and teachers themselves, know that four or five years of preparation for teaching, even when of the highest quality, results in a teacher who is left with much to be learned on the job. One of the central goals of a preservice program is to contribute to the development of teachers who will begin their professional work in the field with a desire and some ability to teach creatively.

8 RESPONSIBLE AND RESPONSIVE ADMINISTRATION AND SUPERVISION

Suppose you were an administrator or a supervisor faced with a faculty containing Peggy Brogan's Mrs. Wilson, Evelyn Wenzel's three "good" teachers, and Mary Harbage's Miss Jane Murdle, whom you are to meet in the next chapter. You might have on your staff also any of the teachers glimpsed briefly in other chapters. What would your expectations be? Would you hope to succeed in encouraging all to be equally creative, each in his own way? Would you give up on one to devote more attention to another who seemed especially promising? Would you expect all to abide by group agreements or would you recommend exempting one whose extraordinary originality seemed worth taking special risks to preserve? Would you expect to secure the benefits of a "team" without hampering the individual? Would you expect to encourage many teachers to take small steps forward and at the same time not hold back one who can progress in great leaps?

A teaching body is made up of individuals differing from one another in hundreds of ways, from their preservice preparation to their commitment to the profession and their concern for continued improvement on the job. Some have just left a teacher preparing institution; others are at different points on a continuum from few to many years of experience. Some of the recent entrants to the profession are inspired to teach creatively; others are unaware of opportunities in this direction. Some experienced teachers see themselves as possessing actual or potential ability to teach more creatively; others believe they do not have and could not develop such ability. The views of teachers as to what constitutes creativity differ, as does their tolerance of highly creative individuals in their midst.

Yet, these single members of the profession, with all their differences, cannot be dealt with as individuals alone, for teaching in modern times is increasingly a group-linked profession. Not only is a teacher responsible for *groups* of learning individuals, but he shares responsibility with a *group* of colleagues. The education of young people is entrusted to teams of professionals, usually working within highly complex organizations, with specialization and division of responsibility.

Teaching is group linked in another sense also. A teacher is caught up in a network of institutional policies and procedures governing his actions. He works with administrative and supervisory officers who have responsibility for enforcing such policies and procedures.

In a third sense, teaching is group linked in that the elements with which the teacher works—his tools (materials and equipment of all kinds), his working space, and his time schedule—are determined in terms of the needs and convenience of all in the organization.

In a fourth sense, teaching is group linked in that evaluation is in part based on the achievement of the staff as a whole, with individuals sharing in whatever praise or blame ensues.

The nature of the teaching profession and its responsibility makes it imperative that administration and supervision strive to build *groups* of people who have concern for the quality of the *total* effort and product.

A DUAL RESPONSIBILITY OF
ADMINISTRATION AND SUPERVISION

Administrators and supervisors are faced with a continuing problem with respect to fostering creativity in teaching. They are obliged to exercise at one and the same time a control function and a releasing function. These functions must be understood in their separateness and in their relatedness.

The Control Function

A group of people with a common function but with many specialized abilities and duties, to say nothing of differing perceptions of themselves, of one another, and of the job to be done, must be organized so that their efforts can be channeled efficiently. Group members must know what to count on in relation to general purposes and ways of working with students, patrons, and colleagues, time allocations, such as length of term, school day, or class, deadlines for the completion of records and reports, teaching load, and orderly ways of sharing space, equipment, and many of the tools for learning. Official purchasing must be planned in terms of available financial resources.

Setting up an organization and arriving at necessary agreements are only parts of the problem. No organization can operate without exercise of authority. The teaching staff may participate fully in setting up working arrangements, but the very people who help to make the decisions depend on certain officials to take final responsibility for implementation. Members of an organization need and want protection from themselves, so to speak, protection from human proclivities for procrastination, for interpreting regulations to suit individual convenience, for becoming negligent about routines out of boredom with those very routines. A certain amount and kind of uniformity and conformity are necessary and useful in a complicated organization. For enforcement purposes, self-control is most desirable, but it must be supplemented, in case of need, by control through an authority figure representing the group membership. One of the important functions of administration and supervision, then, is final enforcement of certain rules to make sure that the business of education will proceed in orderly fashion.

The Releasing Function

An equally compelling responsibility of school and college officials is to encourage individuals to improve on their own past performance, to envision better ways of teaching, and to experiment. This means removing all nonessential restrictions in order that individuals may be released to be true to themselves and their best ideas. It means, further, encouraging them to challenge restrictions that appear to present unnecessary barriers to creativity and to propose better arrangements to replace hampering conditions.

The Problem Restated

To foster creativity in teaching, ways must be found to encourage constructive difference within the limits of organizational requirements.

POSSIBLE LINES OF SOLUTION

When a problem is posed, several courses of action may be available. For the official interested in fostering creativity in teaching, the solution may lie in examining (1) the nature of creativity as a process, (2) perceptions as possible blocks to creativity, and (3) conditions that are believed to nourish and reward creativity.

Nature of Creativity as a Process

The seeming opposition between the control function and the releasing function of administration and supervision becomes less formidable when one examines features of the creative process. Creativity requires freedom—freedom to rebel against stifling conditions, freedom to make decisions differing from those made yesterday and differing from those made by others—but it is not unlimited freedom. Each individual must work within the limits imposed by his chosen medium. In creating, he must make *accommodation* to the nature of the medium—to the qualities that cannot be changed without destroying the integrity of the medium itself. Wood is not metal, a drum is not a reed instrument, words in print are not words as projected by an actor, a school is not a family home, nor yet is it a factory producing assembly line items. At the same time that the individual is accommodating to the limits of the medium, he must be testing the medium to make sure that the limits are real, not merely assumed. To achieve something new, he must *break through* incomplete or faulty perceptions of the nature of the medium.

For a teacher, the process of *accommodating–breaking through*, which is creativity, is a delicate one, since the education of human

224   ALICE MIEL

beings is at stake and mistakes may be costly. (Deliberately to avoid creativity in teaching is equally costly in terms of human development and therefore such an easy solution is not feasible.) The creative process is a difficult one for a teacher because the media—curriculum and teaching—consist of such elusive and shifting elements as time, space, people, and material resources, all of which have many possible uses in many possible combinations. These elements have their own inherent limitations—there are only twenty-four hours in a day, there is only so much space in a school plant, materials are never in endless supply nor can materials, even the best automated teaching devices, do everything. Personnel of a school and its patrons are as they are, with their hopes and fears, their talents and their lacks. All of these elements must be ordered and reordered for use of the total group.

No one teacher can, at will, break through all regulations without making it impossible for others to predict the nature of the medium with which they will be working. As indicated earlier, some restrictions are necessary to provide order for a group of professional educators sharing a common task. Such restrictions operate as an unavoidable limitation on the freedom of each individual for the sake of the greater freedom of each and all. The effect of useful (releasing) restrictions is to provide freedom for the individual to create. Some schools, however, have restrictions that are not necessary; their effect is to obstruct creativity in teaching. Those useless restrictions that continue because of inertia, because of failure to assess and replan the requirements of the organization, are unfortunate but can be removed with comparative ease. Those that result from the fears and faulty perceptions of people are more difficult to deal with.

Perceptions as Blocks to Creativity

Many a school official shows an understandable desire to have decisions made quickly and put into operation smoothly, to have an organization function as efficiently as possible. Wilhelms, in a column well worth reading in its entirety, uses himself as an example of an "over-anxious" status leader:

> ... I came to see that I was over-reacting. And my motives weren't as pretty as one might have hoped. I was over-reacting because I was over-anxious lest "my" beautiful organization be spoiled. The over-anxiety stemmed from a

subtle feeling that, with my genius, I should be able to build a perfect mechanism—and any flaw in it was a black mark on me.[1]

When an "over-anxious" administrator or supervisor must make a choice between releasing teachers to try out daring ideas and maintaining a safe, predictable institutional operation, the tendency often is to control too much. The anxiety of the official becomes a block to the creativity of others.

Another kind of block to creativity may be presented by the official who misunderstands the nature of creativity in leadership. The administrator or supervisor holds the same position with respect to teachers that the teacher holds in relation to students. Each must draw careful boundaries marking off his area for creativity lest he deprive others of their chances to be creative. The teacher who indulges in the luxury of making all the suggestions he can think of when children are trying to form a plan has stepped out of role. He may be exercising creativity as an individual but not as a teacher. The principal who has a dozen new ideas a week and who keeps the faculty busy carrying out his plans is imprisoning the faculty with the results of his individual creativity, but he is not serving creatively as an official responsible for fostering creativity in teachers. This is not to say that the administrator or supervisor should not share in producing ideas, but rather that all other staff members should also have this privilege.

Blocks to creativity may reside in teachers also. Many teachers cannot tolerate the unsettled feelings accompanying change, whether or not they themselves are closely involved. From the first questions raised about established procedures to the last stages of putting into effect new procedures, these less flexible teachers experience discomfort. Their defense against discomfort may be to give strong support to the known and to resist both the person and the idea representing newness. When the resistance is irrational and excessive, it may serve as a strong deterrent to creativity in others.

The administrator or supervisor is not necessarily obstructing creativity in teaching each time he exercises a control function, nor is he necessarily fostering creativity each time he dispenses

[1] Fred T. Wilhelms, "Leadership in Transition," *Educational Leadership,* XVII, No. 1 (October, 1959), pp. 39–47.

with a regulation. There is no evidence that creativity flourishes best in an organization with laissez faire as the attitude of its official leadership. A creative synthesis of the control function and the releasing function of administration and supervision must be actively sought.

Conditions Believed To Nourish and Reward Creativity in Teaching

Official leaders cannot "make" teachers creative either by requiring creativity in teaching or by the mere act of freeing teachers to be creative. The administrator or supervisor has only one channel of operation, and thus only one avenue for exercising creativity, in his own work. That channel is the *conditions* surrounding teaching. Since blocks to creativity may exist either within one or more teachers, within one or more officials, or within the working arrangements created among them, the school administration can help a teacher to remove blocks to his own creativity and can remove external blocks to creativity in classroom operations. The problem is *to create conditions that nourish and reward creativity in teaching.*

Conditions in educational organizations can be made to contribute more readily to creativity in teaching if there is understanding of the conditions generally agreed on as favoring creativity. Contemporary students of creativity in various fields of human striving present findings that may be translated into requisites for creativity in teaching in the following broad terms.[2]

1. To be creative in teaching, an individual needs a sense of purpose in living, including *commitment* to his work—his chosen arena of creativity. He must care greatly about the quality of opportunities for experience provided for those in his charge. He is helped, in this regard, by exposure to a model, a person who is himself demonstrating commitment.

2. To be creative in teaching, an individual must be willing to take risks. Therefore, he needs *psychological safety with freedom.* A feeling of safety is needed if the individual is to be able to toler-

2 The selected bibliography at the close of this book gives the names of many of these students of creativity. The analysis of requisites for creativity in teaching reflects in particular the agreements among the participants at the Granville, Ohio, Conference on Creativity. See mimeographed report edited by Manuel Barkan and Ross L. Mooney, The Ohio State University, Columbus, 1953.

ate uncertainty and to look for new answers, if he is not to conform compulsively, if he is not to deny *himself* by denying the evidence of his own senses. The concept of safety with freedom includes freedom, within reason, to time one's own changes, to decide when one will take certain risks with his security and his reputation as a teacher. A teacher is helped, in this regard, by a feeling of being completely accepted for himself.

3. To be creative in teaching, an individual must be approaching *total awareness*, must be receptive to feelings and experiences so that he can take in new information and see things in new relationships. A teacher is helped, in this regard, by being encouraged to be skeptical, to question what he observes, to see discrepancies between what is and what should be, and thus to see problems needing solution.

4. To be creative in teaching, an individual must achieve *engagement* in a problem. He must focus on a concern. A teacher is helped, in this regard, by being given autonomy in working on his chosen problem.

5. To be creative in teaching, an individual must have *increased consciousness of his own processes*. He must be in the habit of watching himself at work and of noting clusters of consequences, which are the meanings of his acts. While others may judge his work and be helpful in supplying evidence, he should have his own tests of his work. A teacher is helped, in this regard, by being expected to have the locus of evaluation inside himself.[3]

All of these conditions seem to be encompassed by one inclusive concept, namely, that a "safe-challenging environment" is favorable for learning.[4] The condition of safety helps the individual to feel that he has a comfortable and secure base from which to operate, from which to take risks in his own good time. In the same environment, however, there must also be challenge that invites the individual to leave the safety of the known and to taste the delights

[3] Where the locus of evaluation resides is an acid test of creativity according to Donald W. Berger whose definition appears in *Toward Better Teaching,* 1949 Yearbook of the Association for Supervision and Curriculum Development of the National Education Association, Washington, D.C., p. 121: "Creativity implies a fresh response, unique to the creator; it is characterized by personal initiative and conscious effort; it involves thinking and doing according to self-applied tests; and is finally judged as an accurate expression by the initiator."

[4] See Alice Miel and Peggy Brogan, *More Than Social Studies* (Englewood Cliffs, N.J.: Prentice-Hall, Inc., 1957), pp. 340–349, for a discussion of the significance of the concept of safety-challenge in the social learning of children.

of the new and untried. The challenge must be available for self-selection, just as the safety must always be available when needed. Therefore, the hyphen in the term *safe-challenging* is most important in expressing the relationship.

RESPONSIBILITIES OF ADMINISTRATION AND SUPERVISION

Within the framework of the five requisites for creativity just presented, it is possible to examine the responsibility of school and college officials in the provision of conditions conducive to creativity in teaching. These conditions are (1) a professional atmosphere, (2) a climate of psychological safety with freedom, (3) staff learning opportunities, (4) opportunities for decision making, and (5) opportunities for cooperative evaluation and self-evaluation. In addition, officials can serve creativity in teaching by promoting professional and public receptivity for new ideas. Each of these is an area in which administration and supervision have customarily functioned with more or less effectiveness. A look at this functioning in relation to its promise for fostering creativity in teaching should furnish a fresh look at familiar problems. A look at this functioning in terms of provision of a safe-challenging environment for teachers may suggest new criteria for judging ways of working in schools and colleges.

Creating a Professional Atmosphere

When a teacher is described as "professional," certain other adjectives come to mind—"dedicated," "devoted," "self-propelled." The teacher is dedicated in the sense of having decided to make teaching his main business in life and he is proud of that decision; he gets satisfaction not alone from his own teaching but from being a part of a larger group of people who care about their work. He is devoted to the welfare of his students. He needs no foreman to see to it that he turns out a good day's work. A teacher who is highly professional demonstrates the *commitment* required for creativity in any field. To be committed to one's calling and to work in the company of others similarly committed furnishes both safety and challenge to the individual in a group-linked profession such as teaching. The official leader has abundant opportunity to contribute to the professionalism of the setting for work.

Respect oneself as a professional person. An administrator who desires to create an atmosphere encouraging highly professional attitudes and behaviors on the part of teachers can begin with himself. He can be a model of professionalism for the teachers if he himself is deeply glad to be in education, if he holds his head high among other professional people in his community, and if his eyes are on the kind of school taking shape under his leadership rather than on the next promotion in sight. He will not imitate other managerial fields for the sake of prestige nor apologize for the particular place where he is serving society. By his own enthusiasm he will set a tone that signifies, "We here are engaged together in work so important that our society would suffer gravely without it."

Respect teachers as professional persons. If a teacher is to feel like a professional person, he must be treated as one. Until there is much evidence to the contrary, an administrator will do well to assume that an individual wants to be a good teacher. When the official consults the faculty and shares his thinking with them, he demonstrates confidence that he is dealing with a professional staff. This may have the useful effect revealed in a comment by a teacher: "Since my opinion was valued, it had to be valuable."

Respect for teachers as professional persons will forestall the use of them as errand boys or treatment of them as people with no plans for their own time—people who may be freely called to the office, interrupted by room telephone or intercom system, or required on short notice to attend a meeting. Teachers have a right to be resentful when they know that, with better planning, emergency measures would not have been required.

A way to show basic disrespect for teachers is to depend on coffee hours or an occasional social affair to make up for poor human relations. When adults feel manipulated like puppets or bribed like children, they cannot have basic respect for themselves or the official leader. Thus it becomes all the more difficult to feel committed to the profession represented.

Lack of respect for teachers as professional persons frequently stems from an underlying feeling that teaching is a lowly post to be escaped through "promotion" as soon as possible. The administrator or supervisor examining his practices in dealing with teachers will need to look into his own deepest convictions as to the worth of teaching.

ALICE MIEL

Encourage a businesslike attitude. Teachers are unusually dependent on the quality of professionalism around them. It is difficult to maintain a high degree of morale and commitment if most others in the faculty show even in small ways that they do not consider their work really important. Difficulties are compounded by a "don't care" atmosphere. Even under the most favorable circumstances it is not easy to take the risks involved in breaking new ground in teaching. If, on top of those necessary risks, one must also be in a small minority of the staff striving to break through established ways of teaching, the risks are increased. Colleagues may not want the minority even to try the new ways, let alone find them successful. Now, add as a third hazard the necessity of facing group pressure not to be "an eager beaver" about being on time for classes and meeting other obligations to students. While irresponsible attitudes toward a teacher's duties are by no means characteristic of the teaching profession as a whole, there are enough individuals who take responsibility lightly to make it advisable for administration and supervision to give attention to possible problems of this nature.

In exercising leadership in maintaining an atmosphere that may be called businesslike, school officials will do well to recognize that there must be enough flexibility to make intelligent allowance for individual differences and for unusual circumstances. Sometimes a teacher will accomplish more for students by spending an extra two minutes at the end of a coffee break clinching an exciting discussion than by appearing in the classroom on time. The one whom duty is always calling to abide by the letter of every regulation may be too compulsive to be highly creative. It is not desirable that teachers be alike in the ways they meet obligations to students, but it is a tremendous help if they are alike in caring that their efforts add up to good education.

It is desirable, also, that teachers have a friendly, relaxed relationship with one another, that they take time to play with ideas. A businesslike atmosphere would not preclude such a relationship and such use of time. It should preclude the kind of laxity that breeds more laxity until finally nobody cares about the job to be done. Administration can give leadership to a faculty analyzing its own ways of working and defining the conditions of work best suited to accomplishing what they believe is desirable for the educational program.

Teachers need to know that they can count on officials to ensure a fair division of labor and a reasonable fulfillment of responsibilities all around. Otherwise, working in an organization carries with it mostly barriers to creativity and few advantages. An affirmative program of encouraging teachers to share enthusiasm for their teaching, to "talk shop" on a constructive level, may help to bolster commitment. One New York City principal, inspired by the title of a play then current on the Broadway stage, posted a notice inviting the teachers in his building to "tea and sympathy." This was the first of many informal weekly chats, which teachers were free to attend if they liked. Many channels other than official staff meetings can be found by the leader searching for opportunities to spread the contagion of professional enthusiasm.

Conclusion. If a teacher is to be encouraged to teach more creatively, he must be helped to think of himself as an educator with dignity, rights, and responsibilities. An atmosphere of professionalism carries the message that it is safe and rewarding to show enthusiasm for one's work; it also carries the challenge of important work to be done.

Creating a Favorable Psychological Climate

For a psychological climate to be favorable to creativity in teaching, it must meet a teacher's needs for a feeling of safety with freedom. In venturing along more creative paths in teaching, a teacher's own reputation is at stake. He is known for certain kinds of successes; he can count on himself to produce in well-tried ways. He may be losing much that makes up the teacher he now is if he tries to cultivate a different teaching style. For this reason, freedom to create new responses to learners must be accompanied by a feeling that one will not lose all. Otherwise, the teacher will be reluctant to take the risks involved.

Safety with freedom to try new ways may take many forms, such as knowing that one can count on the interest, understanding, and support of others or knowing that one will have another chance. The official leader has it within his power to influence the psychological climate within a school, making it more favorable for creativity in teaching.

Demonstrate acceptance. Having a feeling of being completely accepted is a first requisite for a feeling of safety. Those who equate the term *acceptance* with *approval* find it difficult to see themselves completely accepting all other persons. Combs and Snygg have a brief and useful definition which makes a more reasonable demand: "Acceptance . . . is a dynamic word to describe an attitude of willingness to look at and consider the facts." [5] The authors go on to show that acceptance does not mean the same as resignation:

> It has to do with admission of data to consideration. A willingness to examine facts does not imply weakness and passivity. Resignation is an attitude of defeat. Acceptance is understanding without judging. It requires an openness to experience which provides the only sound basis upon which to progress. It is an attitude of taking people where they are and moving forward from this point . . . Acceptance is conducive to the exploration of personal meaning. It is not a substitute for it.[6]

Here, then, is what an administrator is asked to practice: a habit of looking to see what a situation or person or idea is made of, and going on from there in ways indicated by the facts observed.

Acceptance does not mean that there should or will be no disagreement on the part of the official with the actions and proposals of those with whom he works. The staff may contain a Mrs. Robbins who refuses to keep any of the school rules. The children are not supposed to use the only telephone, which is in the principal's office. Mrs. Robbins pays no attention to the regulation but brings a committee of children to the office and sees to it that one of them has the experience of using the instrument. Children are not supposed to be in their classrooms during the noon hour or at recess periods either. But in Mrs. Robbins' room those periods are some of the busiest learning times of the day. What does it mean to be accepting of Mrs. Robbins? First, the principal must take the behavior as given. It exists in fact. What is back of the behavior? The teacher may only be exhibiting a need to flout authority, which would suggest one line of further inquiry for the principal. She may, on the other hand, be struggling to achieve goals that school regulations seemed designed to deny. In that case, another line of follow-up is suggested.

[5] Arthur W. Combs and Donald Snygg, *Individual Behavior* (New York: Harper & Brothers, 1959), pp. 390–391.
[6] *Ibid.*, p. 391.

An administrator or supervisor will be demonstrating acceptance:

. . . if he listens to each teacher carefully to see what he is saying *now*, without prejudging that what will come from the lips of that teacher will be necessarily wise or necessarily foolish.

. . . if he takes a proposal for change as a sincere attempt to improve the school, not as an indictment of his leadership.

. . . if he can take a problem stated by a teacher as something to explore with him, resisting the temptation to bury the problem in assurances ("you are handling it beautifully; everything is going to be all right").

. . . if he can take deviate behavior as a signal to look both at the person and his purposes and at the situation and its possible limitations.

If an official can cultivate the ability to be accepting in these and other ways, he will give the individual teacher a feeling that there is a sincere attempt to understand him both as he is and as he would like to be and that new ideas will be listened to with respect.

Promote harmony among the staff. A strong, supporting group can furnish feelings of safety to a teacher as he tries new ways in teaching. The kind of harmony desired is not one of flabby agreement with any and every idea espoused by another. Wilhelms has described well a false appearance of harmony achieved by suppression of differences:

> Nothing is sicker than an organization in which the leader gets his way because the group feels that he means well, would be offended, or for reasons of personal inadequacy, needs support. Any good leader wants disagreement. But if only the useful disagreement could be got out in the open and put to work! Here probably is the very keystone of successful group action . . . [for] the sensed presence of the under-table communication remains a sapping, draining thing.[7]

Whether real opinions are being concealed from the official leader or from one another in the group, the result is equally "sapping." The harmony of a joint search for truth is the kind

[7] Fred T. Wilhelms, "Leadership in Transition," *Educational Leadership,* XVII, No. 1 (October, 1959), pp. 39–47.

needed for creativity in teaching. Such a search requires staff unity.

An official often inherits a staff that for one reason or another is divided into discordant cliques. A faculty such as the following, described by a teacher, is not uncommon:

> Mrs. C and I had a discussion this week about our faculty. We tried to analyze whether there was an "in" group and an "out" group as classified by social psychologists. Both she and I felt that only one teacher in the entire faculty could very definitely be considered "out." We identified a group of three middle-aged teachers who more or less keep together; a group of seven young teachers who might be considered an "in" group in that they constitute the largest-sized group; two or three teachers who seem to be aspiring to become a part of this group of seven (although at least thirty are not); four men teachers who have not formed any group but who more or less shift as "lone wolves"; and about five different groups of teachers who have one "good" friend. At least ten other teachers never eat in the teachers' lunchroom (a foods laboratory), remaining either in their own classrooms to eat or going to a restaurant, so that we see them only at faculty meetings and are not quite sure with whom they spend their time.

A faculty might possibly have such an informal social organization and still operate in their formal organization as a united group, accepting and supporting one another. However, further information from the same teacher gives some evidence that there is lack of harmony in this particular staff:

> While riding home from school with two other teachers we began discussing our school faculty. Miss D is a new teacher, and this was my first "social" contact with her. She told us that she felt that the faculty at our school was very unfriendly and that most of the girls had formed little cliques so that when she walked into the foods laboratory for lunch she often felt quite uncomfortable.

> Miss D said she had only one friend in the school and that our school is the only one she has ever been in where teachers do not even greet each other with a "Good morning" when they arrive.

Status systems growing up around faculty lunch situations are not unusual in a school or college but they have an unfortunate effect on faculty unity. An official would want to examine all evidences of division in a faculty to secure clues for promoting harmony. For example, the principal of the school just described might look at another practice dividing his faculty, as it appeared to the teacher reporting:

> Our principal seems to contribute to the general discord throughout the faculty by fostering a competitive attitude among the teachers. He has often praised the success of one teacher to another. This week, Mrs. S greeted me with the words, "Boy, I can really get to hate you! Mr. T keeps telling me to come up to see the store your children have built and to see how neat your room is." Even though Mr. T's indirect praise *may* help me feel a little more secure in my position, I do not believe that, given this way, it is worth the ill effects that it is working upon the staff and upon my personal relations with the teachers.

Reactions such as the foregoing show that officials must be wary lest praise pit one teacher against another. They must also note that recognition in the form of special assignments can set some teachers off from the rest. When one teacher proves to be especially capable, it is difficult to resist the temptation to turn over to him a great many important responsibilities.

Knowing how easy it is for individuals with their different beliefs and perceptions to fall into different camps, the administrator or supervisor desiring to create a unified and harmonious group must work actively to achieve this result. He must expect to take the lead in promoting acceptance within the staff—acceptance of self and of others. This is a beginning condition for learning to care—to care that each member of the organization has a chance to exercise his talents, to care about the feelings and accomplishments of each and all. In groups indulging in useless bickering or maintaining sullen silences, human energy is diverted from pursuing exciting ideas. Official leaders can set a mood by receiving contributions in an accepting way and by giving room for all kinds of opinions to be heard.

Reduce threats to a minimum. Interest in increased creativity in teaching calls for concern with the phenomenon of threat. Of this Combs and Snygg write: "... whatever seems to the behaver inconsistent with his existing perceptions of self may be experienced by the individual as threat. Whatever seems threatening to an individual in turn demands attention and produces a degree of tunnel vision in the perceptual field." [8] A few paragraphs later the authors continue:

> Under threat, behavior becomes rigid and less fluid or adaptable to changing requirements. People under stress seem less able to cope with ambiguous or unsolved problems. They feel a need to have things definite and sure and in clear figure even though this may mean sacrificing accuracy.
>
> Unfortunately, the restricting effect of threat in the phenomenal field simply complicates the resolution of problems. For adequate perception we need, not a narrow field of differentiation, but a broad one. Too narrow a field from which differentiations may occur results in repetitions of the same behavior time after time.[9]

This description of the effect of threat explains the importance of a climate of safety with freedom—freedom from needless, damaging anxiety, which deflects teachers from constructive use of their talents.

Three supervisory officers were taking considerable risk in dealing with a new teacher in ways that caused him to write as follows:

> As I started teaching my immediate and continuing problem was one of classroom control and management. In the latter part of the third month, I was observed briefly by the "helping teacher." She left me with the suggestion that I use oaktag rulers for penmanship exercises and that I display "eyewash" around the room in expectation of the supervisor's visit, with—as an afterthought—the supporting rationale that such display encourages the children.
>
> The supervisor made an unexpected visit soon after, leaving as comment the suggestion that I improve my handwriting on the chalkboard and that I concern myself with my control problems. No suggestions, just, "We hope you do better."
>
> In January the principal observed one lesson and in the conference immediately following, comments centered on

[8] Arthur W. Combs and Donald Snygg, *Individual Behavior* (New York: Harper & Brothers, 1959), p. 170.
[9] *Ibid.*, pp. 171–172.

motivation. Concluding the conference the principal told me that I would have a different grade level the following term, and she hoped improvement would be evident. She said she would give me observation opportunities in other classrooms. She mentioned that no teacher had ever before been involuntarily transferred from her school. Here the tone changed to "coercive."

A few days later the supervisor visited for the second time, found "improvement" in the lessons and said it was evident I was still having a control problem and that "they" felt very concerned about it—period!

These supervisors no doubt felt they were being helpful to a new young teacher, but if they had been able to read the young man's account they would have gained some insights. Fortunately for all concerned the teacher apparently was able to maintain his balance and use the "help" for all it was worth, for he wrote:

The suggestions of each supervisor have value, and I believe that I have improved, but it was difficult trying to straddle three different thoughts which had not been related to each other before being presented to me. If nothing else, this indicts our organizational arrangement as inefficient.

I am aware that my not finding professional favor may possibly resolve itself irrationally in interpersonal friction. This I intend to avoid as much as possible.

Many supervisory activities not intended as threats are perceived that way even by relatively secure teachers. Teacher intervisitation, judicious transfer of teachers to other schools to secure better balanced staffs, and supervisory visits and conferences designed to help a teacher may be perceived by the teacher involved or by his colleagues as evidence that the teacher is considered weak. Thus these devices may be threatening. If administrators wish to avoid putting needless strain on teachers, they must learn to read signs of threat and must practice viewing actions and situations through the eyes of the teacher.

Maintain reasonable limits. Important to a climate of safety with freedom is clear understanding of what one may and may not do. It is plainly the responsibility of administration to make existing limits known to all teachers. For example, teachers must know what materials are furnished and the procedures for getting their share. They need to know if money is available to spend for supplies with the help of students. They need to know deadlines. The final authority for enforcing limits also rests with administration and supervision. If the enforcement is judicious, all can have the security of knowing boundaries within which they are expected to operate. A related responsibility of official leadership is equally important, however. Administrators must take care that limits are reasonable. Many of the regulations imposed by officials reduce sharply and unnecessarily the chance for teachers to handle situations creatively. Note the following set of rules handed to new teachers by the principal of an elementary school:

1. Handwriting must be practiced for fifteen minutes every day.
2. Group all your children into three ability groups.
3. Every class must have a physical education period each day for fifteen minutes where skills are taught.
4. We expect discipline in this school. Rooms must be quiet and children are expected to walk quietly in the halls. To help with this, the teacher should lead her children to the door each time they leave the building.

Unless there is demonstrated need for uniformity, limits, to be reasonable, should contain some flexibility, some room for exercise of judgment. It is reasonable to require that all first grade teachers in a school system teach manuscript rather than cursive writing. It would be unreasonable to set a particular point in a particular grade when all children would be made to drop manuscript writing and learn cursive. It is reasonable to require that all teachers in a high school use the same grading system. It would be unreasonable to legislate against additional ways of communicating with parents which some but not all teachers might wish to try.

Because it is easy for one or a few persons to make errors in setting limits, a good safeguard is to arrive at limits cooperatively. This process can include examining the accumulated limits with an eye to cutting through those that are outmoded or unduly restricting or for any other reason unnecessary. Teachers should be working with their official leaders in a search for the fewest basic agreements needed to allow the institution to maintain itself. They should be challenging limits that appear to be contributing nothing except holding back the creativity of individuals. Is it really necessary for each teacher to write out his plans for a week ahead and file them with the principal for the one reason that a substitute teacher may one day need them? Or might a group of teachers devise quite a different type of requirement if they took as their problem, "What is the best way to make sure that a substitute could easily take over for one of us at any time?"

Whether or not teachers help to set limits, they will need to have easily consulted sources of written information on existing regulations, policies, and procedures. A well-run school or college has an efficient communication system as one way of preventing waste of time and energy for members of the organization. This convenience is lost, however, when teachers' lives are so governed by minute rules for everything that there is little room left for their own judgment.

Conclusion. A teacher can feel on safe ground and free to use his talents creatively if he feels, "I am accepted for what I am. People around me care what I think and what I want to accomplish; they will listen and they will help. Certain details are settled for all of us by common consent, and beyond that I am released and encouraged to be my best self."

Creating Staff Learning Opportunities

Feelings of commitment and safety with freedom are in a sense conditions that must both precede and accompany a condition of central importance in creativity. This is the condition of openness to new experience, which allows the individual to become immersed in the stuff with which he will create, which lets him turn the stuff over and look at it in many ways, and which sends him searching for new information. Administrators and supervisors have available many ways of helping teachers search and question.

Arrange for easy access to new information. Of great importance is a place where teachers can easily find recent books, pamphlets, and professional journals to browse in or to borrow for more careful reading. Because there is such a constant flood of reading material, teachers appreciate having their attention called to a special piece that is noteworthy for some reason or other, especially if it is not made required reading. A school official might make it a practice to look for the offbeat piece, the writer who is challenging a popular position, the scholar who is feeling his way with a new theory, the writer who has the gift of making his reader think. Often a well-selected quotation from such a piece will invite teachers to read further.

In selecting titles for a professional library, it is well to include material from other countries and authors representing disciplines related to education. Useful also is opportunity for gaining up-to-date information in various content fields. Bulletin boards in teachers' lounges can be used for sharing items found by different teachers. Teachers can learn much from one another if they share the different enthusiasms they usually represent.

Another way of bringing sources of information to teachers is to arrange conferences where challenging people may be heard in person. It is especially important that teachers hear specialists in various lines of work in the community if these individuals themselves have broken through to new ideas in their fields and are enthusiastic about the meaning of new developments for education. Trips by groups of teachers to study community conditions and processes can be revealing also, especially if there is cooperative planning of the objectives of the trip so that curriculum implications will be in the forefront.

Question current arrangements and practices. Meetings of a faculty as a whole or in subgroups can be used by the official leader to set an example of questioning and challenging the ways that have become comfortable and taken for granted. The official will want these sessions to be occasions where teachers freely bring up points that trouble them. This is not easy to achieve even though there has been good hard work invested in establishing a supporting climate. To encourage teachers to exchange ideas freely, the status person present may relieve the tension somewhat by having problems brought up first in small groups so that when reported to the total group they are surrounded by anonymity. If the group leader and the group members pass the test of acceptance of problems on such occasions—"it is all right to have a problem, we need to know what it is made of, what could all of us do about it?"— it will become increasingly easy for teachers to speak freely in the total group.

It is especially important for the group to have patience and go two-thirds of the way in understanding the group member who cannot be clear because he is himself out at the edge of his understanding. Only in an atmosphere of mutual search and real desire for communication can the "wild" ideas be stated that may lead to a whole new look. Only thus can teachers build respect for and skill in the process of digging out their own meanings.

Another way of encouraging open looks at situations is a fact-finding approach. The official leader himself may collect facts that raise certain questions or he may involve the staff in designing and carrying out such an inquiry. When teachers are faced with an array of facts that disturb present perceptions, the door is often opened for examination of previously untouched ideas. Thus, one advantage of the child study movement has been that teachers acquired new information which they could not then pretend *to themselves* that they did not have.

Sponsor new professional adventures. A good way to develop openness to experience is to help the individual have an experience in which he can get a different view of a familiar landscape. When a teacher is in a position to look at the curriculum as a whole, old information falls into new relationships and calls for new information. Representing the school on a responsible school or community committee, interpreting the school program to the public through speaking or writing, attending a state or national conference with a definite responsibility for contributing to the insights of the stay-at-homes, all give opportunity to acquire a new view. Teachers will profit from sharing in some of the learning experiences available to administration and supervision, such as taking responsibility for foreign visitors, sitting in on a case conference, helping to induct new teachers, following a high school student through a day at school, spending a day at a level of the school most remote from one's own, planning ways to assess the hard-to-measure objectives, and many more.

A different kind of adventure, central to a purpose of developing more awareness, is for members of a faculty to set out as individuals, each to take the first steps in learning a new field inviting creativity, with the idea of studying themselves in the process and exchanging experiences. A group of teachers might also use the brainstorming technique popularized by Osborn,[10] both for the practice it gives in stretching the imagination and for the good ideas that might result in relation to the problem selected. Such a problem might be anything from thinking of ways to reach the

10 Alex F. Osborn, *Applied Imagination* (New York: Charles Scribner's Sons, 1957, revised edition).

parent "who never comes to school" to ways to reach the boy "who isn't interested in *anything*."

Conclusion. The purpose of the learning opportunities suggested here, and of others to be developed as the education profession becomes more creative along this line, is to give teachers experiences out of which ideas grow and to develop in teachers the habit of questioning techniques that have always worked, the habit of keeping their minds open to new kinds of learning opportunities for their students. People are being helped to change the pictures in their minds, helped to get rid of "don't ever—always" thinking (don't ever use workbooks, always have arithmetic early in the morning). Intake of newness is required for output of newness.

Providing Opportunities for Decision Making

Creativity requires full and genuine engagement in a problem. For the teacher this means being involved in making the decisions necessary for structuring a learning environment. Arranging learning opportunities is the focus of the teacher's efforts, and in order to put creativity into this task the teacher must have autonomy. In exercising his autonomy, he takes into account the resources he has and the limits within which he must work—what the students are like, what materials are available, what others want him to accomplish. Then he makes decisions tailored to the requirements of the situation. Some of these decisions are made in anticipation of the teaching-learning situation, some are made necessarily in the interacting situation. Here is a most difficult point for the administrator or supervisor, for here he must step aside. He can share in decision making up to a certain point, but beyond that only the teacher can decide and further help must be indirect.

Work through channels of organization. One form of indirect help comes through using regular meetings of a faculty to do basic planning as a framework for individual teacher planning. A faculty may adopt certain emphases for a year or may isolate one problem to which all agree to give serious attention. Such a basic group can also listen to individual teacher plans and help to improve them. Plans for simple tryout of a new idea or for more carefully structured action research may be up for discussion. Whether one or a few are to engage in this venture, they will be helped both by the ideas they will gather and by the sympathetic understanding they are more likely to encounter as they meet small or large failures along the way. Their successes, too, will more likely be hailed with pleasure when the plans have been given an open hearing. There will be less likelihood that others on the staff will look on the experimenting teacher or teachers with suspicion and jealousy as people in special favor with the administration, people getting more supplies and help and attention than the rest. The experiments in progress will seem to be owned by the whole staff. Nonexperimenting colleagues may be built into the plan for gathering evidence or may serve otherwise as resource people. Thus it can be expected that the staff will want to keep informed on how things are going.

Not always will the tryout be a defined experiment or action research project. The official leader will want to build a climate where there is an assumption that many teachers will be trying new ways in many areas whenever they feel ready to do so and often without consultation, especially when changes are minor. Self-selected, self-timed, and therefore steady and gradual curriculum change will be in process. The whole staff will then expect faculty meetings in which there are frequent progress reports and which turn into clinics as a tough problem is brought up for general consideration. The whole staff will be engaged in a treasure hunt for materials useful to one another when they know what various colleagues are working on.

Work for uncommitted time. All writers in the field of creativity stress the need for time to reflect, organize, and evaluate information, hunch, and plan. This has been called perceptive waiting time. In the busy days led by teachers and their official leaders it seems next to impossible to set aside time for such a purpose. A few ways that have been tried may suggest others.

Faculty meetings were mentioned previously as a useful channel for promoting creativity in teaching. It is desirable that such sessions be scheduled at least partially on school time and that they be long enough for genuine group thinking. Some of this time might well be set aside for apparently idle exploring. Schachtel has something to say about idleness in this connection:

> Compared, for example, with the strictly purposeful modern manufacturing process, which regulates uniformly every movement of machine and human hand in order to avoid any waste motion and thus produce the finished product in the shortest possible time and with the smallest expense of en-

ergy, the creative process, and especially its earlier phases, may seem like an incredible waste . . . But even if the work of art, of poetry, or creative thought is acknowledged as a worth-while end in itself, expanding as it does the range of conscious human experience, the perspective of the performance principle may lead to the view that there is something "regressive" in the period of free, mobile, and open play of the mind, the senses, the hand with the many possibilities and aspects of the objects only some of which may enter ultimately into the creation. Yet, it is clear that the incubation period as well as the period of execution of the work are equally important, and that the former provides the foundations for the latter.[11]

Another way to provide time for a "free, mobile, and open play" of the mind and senses is to build into school calendars days for which teachers are paid but which are beyond the days when children must by law attend school. Some may be days before school starts in the fall, some may fall at the end of the year, some may be scattered through the year. Certain school systems employ teachers in summer months to work on curriculum problems. Whole days free from work with children should lend themselves to free-wheeling and browsing among ideas. Often both teachers and officials become restless if they cannot show tangible results of such days—definite plans made, materials prepared, resource persons used, and the like.

Stock and Thelen no doubt had such restlessness in mind when they wrote as follows:

> In general, our experiences with training groups bear out the notion that creativity is the result of prevention of inhibition and threat on the one hand, and of stimulation, motivation, and clarification on the other.
>
> The group must be motivated, it must want to solve the problem, and this means that it probably needs to have first-hand experiences that put the members under tension. Then there must be the opportunity to discharge the tension by grappling directly with the problem, rather than, for ex-

---

[11] Ernest G. Schachtel, *Metamorphosis* (New York: Basic Books, Inc., 1959), p. 246.

ample, by fighting the leader, scapegoating a member, or shifting responsibility to something outside the group. To grapple directly with the problem requires alternation of solitude, during which one collects his thoughts and hopes for insight, with stimulation and sharing, during which ideas get kicked around, elaborated, and defended—this is the process of finding new meanings that would not occur to one by oneself. To engage in this latter process with others requires conditions such that one not only can take the risk of sticking his neck out but will, in fact, be rewarded for so doing. Risk-taking seems to be easiest when the group is not too deadly serious, because a serious group is too conscious of time-wasting: it is too intent on the goal to be able to back up and approach it by the kind of circling maneuvers through which new ideational territory can be discovered. The group must also be under pressure, so that there will be expectations of performance and reward for performance, but it should probably arrange the pressures for itself through consideration of deadlines for each step; and these deadlines should be easily modifiable through orderly processes of examination of progress, difficulties, and energy and time resources. We note that these conditions for creativity are also conditions for getting work done, and we propose that constant talk about whether the group is creative may simply add to its anxiety without increasing creativity over and above the amount that goes with effective working.[12]

If the profession itself becomes convinced of the value of time spent in "circling maneuvers through which new ideational territory can be discovered" with a view to later use in solving some of the problems of teaching, the public, too, may be helped to value such time use by its teachers.

An individual teacher often needs to find time to stand off from the scene of action to gather himself together. He may need time to think over the behavior of one child so that before that day is over he can try a new way of reaching him. No teacher should have to go through a complete school day without a break from work with the students. High schools and colleges can arrange free periods merely by having a large enough staff. In elementary

12 Dorothy Stock and Herbert Thelen, *Emotional Dynamics and Group Culture* (Washington, D.C.: National Training Laboratories, 1958), p. 257.

ALICE MIEL

schools cooperative planning should yield ways of handling the pupil load so that different teachers in turn may have time released for reflecting while the data gathered continuously in the teaching-learning situation are fresh. Planning certain large group experiences, using special resource teachers at times, hiring one or two floating teachers, working as teams with various individual responsibilities assigned, have all been tried.

At the college level, colleagues might carry extra heavy loads for part of an academic year reducing the teaching load of one staff member at a time in order that he may write or do research.

Work for decisions that release rather than hamper. At this point it should be necessary only to repeat an earlier caution against making an individual within an organization subject to decisions that are too minute, too numerous, too hampering. What a difference it can make in opportunities to exercise creativity if groups in their decision making consciously set about to discover how much latitude can be allowed, how many ways can be declared "right" for reaching desired goals. Such decisions give the individual the comfortable feeling of reasonable limits already discussed while at the same time inviting responsible choice and therefore experimentation to discover best ways.

Give opportunity to select and learn to use new tools. Study of new materials—books, films, television programs, science equipment, projectors, recording equipment—with a view to making decisions as to purchase and use is another way to foster creativity in teaching. New materials often suggest new ways of helping students learn. Planning training sessions for developing skill in using new kinds of materials, and using old materials in new ways, should heighten the effectiveness of all purchases. "Doing" workshops of this type furnish another avenue for fresh ideas.

Provide necessary administrative support. When teachers are increasing the creativity in their teaching, needs arise for materials, books, films, and other things that cannot be anticipated. Administrative arrangements should be geared to honor emergency requests within reason. This may mean a general overhauling of policies on ordering supplies, booking films, deciding what to decentralize and what to house centrally, what kind of delivery system to have, how much uncommitted budget to set aside.

New ways of teaching may call for a different kind of staff involvement in budget preparation and cooperative planning of ways to find resources for dealing with the unexpected. Here in itself is a large field for creativity.

New ways of teaching may call also for an overhauling of old policies and procedures with relation to what shall be taught, when, and how. It may call for revisions in stated aims and in guides giving suggestions to teachers.

Conclusion. In teaching, the actual creation comes at the point of making decisions about learning opportunities of students. Giving teachers chances to learn the skills of intelligent decision making, surrounding individual decision making with thoughtful group planning, and assuming responsibility for changes needed to implement new decisions are services that can be rendered by administration and supervision.

Encouraging Cooperative Evaluation

Just as the teacher makes the final decisions in the teaching-learning situation, so must he also make his own judgments about the adequacy of his decisions. Evaluation of decisions made in teaching is always difficult. A teacher can never have the satisfaction of standing off to take a look at a tangible and durable finished product and to say, "There it is. I made it and it is good." The product of a teacher's creativity is a constellation of opportunities for educative experience always blending into new opportunities. The hard work of polishing such a product must always be performed by trying next time to operate a little more perceptively. Nevertheless, a teacher must know how to study his own results and his ways of achieving them if he is to be able to improve. In this process he will want evidence of his own and of others to help him judge how the learners are using opportunities provided and what they appear to be *becoming.* This view of the evaluation problem places two types of responsibility on the official leadership.

Reduce official judging to a minimum. In the running of a school system there are occasions when judgments have to be made by a school official with respect to a teacher. At the end of each probationary year one person or a group of responsible officers must decide on retention or dismissal. After the probationary period of two or three years has passed there is occasional need to make a judgment about a teacher who is a candidate for a promotion or who at that date may have to be dismissed. If all official judging is confined to those occasions and if such judging is fair and open as far as the subject is concerned, a wide field for self-evaluation and cooperative evaluation is opened.

Have a broad program of self- and cooperative evaluation. Because of the fleeting nature of his created product, a teacher has special need to learn whether or not there is continuity in the enterprise in which he is working, whether or not his efforts and those of his colleagues are adding up to something worthwhile. For this reason, he needs to be part of a larger program of evaluation, one that involves many persons having opportunity to judge the results of the school program over a period of time.

As with group planning discussed earlier, cooperative group evaluation is a training ground for building the attitudes and the competence required for the individual to evaluate himself realistically. "How are *we* doing?" can be a major concern. Groups can ask: "What are we doing to ourselves? What are we overemphasizing? underemphasizing? What evidence do we have? Where can we get more? In what unusual places might we look for evidence?"

Such concerns lead inevitably to the related question, "How am *I* doing?" If a teacher is trying something new, he can be helped to use a process of collecting and studying evidence of change in student behavior as a way of going beyond playing by ear. The official leader can set an example by not insisting that inappropriate evaluation instruments (for example, certain standardized tests) be depended upon as a major source of evidence. The official also can refrain from pushing for early results and, instead, help the teacher and his colleagues to realize how long it may take before a difference can be detected. The administrator or supervisor will want to help a teacher build respect for different kinds of evidence, including the teacher's own observations and feelings, and to use this evidence in his continuous planning.

Conclusion. Evaluation has for its purpose the gathering of evidence that allows one to plan ahead more intelligently. It has a forward look and it is a necessary part of the creative process. A person who stays at the mercy of the judgments of other people is in a poor position to venture out into the unknown where events must be judged while they are in progress and where the outside judge cannot always be on hand.

Deutsch has suggested that "the last stage in the creative process is perhaps that of receptivity." [13] He refers to the step from invention to innovation, the complex problem of changing human habits on a wider scale. If general patterns of decision about learning opportunities appear promising when tested, receptivity of others is a necessary condition for spreading the basic idea to other teachers. In a profession like teaching, it is important that advances be consolidated and widely used. This does not mean that changes that have been successful for some can then be ordered into existence. But administration and supervision can help promising ideas about teaching to live and prosper. This is a responsibility that a group-linked profession like education need not and probably should not leave with the individual creator.

Another responsibility that goes beyond the individual creator is securing public acceptance of new ways of teaching. This is a political problem that requires the attention of the profession as a whole and especially of administration and supervision.

Oral and written reports to school and community groups can give recognition to those trying to break through to better ways of teaching. At the same time, such reports help others to grow along with the individuals searching for new insights. Written reports in professional journals give additional satisfaction to those whose work is reported and to their colleagues and patrons. At the same time, the ideas are made available to a wider group of teachers, and help the progress of American education as a whole.

If teachers can find the time and have enough skill to enjoy writing about their own work, they reap extra benefit from analyzing their work for others. However, it is often better that an administrator or supervisor write the account on the basis of much study of the situation than to have it go unreported. Sometimes a team writing job is feasible, with the official leader assuming responsibility for adding information and making generalizations that those deeply involved may be too modest or too close to the scene to include. In such reports it is important to give evidence of the value of the educational change described and to help the reader to distinguish between the basic ideas that may be trans-

13 Karl W. Deutsch, "Creativity in a Scientific Civilization," in *Changing Attitudes in a Changing World* (New York: Bank Street College of Education Publications, 1958), p. 32.

ALICE MIEL

ferable to another school and the details that could not and should not be copied. The most useful of these reports will be those that help a whole profession to break through encrusted ideas and get off some of the plateaus on which education comes to rest with great frequency.

The problem of getting receptivity for new ideas in education is complicated and should not be left to the individual teacher. Here is a responsibility to be shared by the entire profession. Administration and supervision may be expected to spearhead efforts in this direction.

Recapitulation

The rightful function of school and college administration and supervision in promoting more creativity in teaching is a dual one of providing at the same time safety and challenge. As the official leader helps teachers to feel a sense of commitment to an important profession and as he helps them to agree on a general direction of efforts, feelings of both safety and challenge are enhanced. Specifically, safety and challenge are being provided when:

. . . *teachers feel accepted and recognized.* They know that individual differences are expected and respected. Each is helped to feel, "I have worth in myself." Each is listened to with a view to mutual understanding. The fine points that account for high quality in learning opportunities are observed and valued. Each teacher knows that his best will be recognized.

. . . *teachers have an organization within which to work.* They know what they can count on. Limits are known and reasonable; teachers have participated in setting many of them. They know the limits will be enforced with intelligent allowance for individual differences. They know also that they have channels that make it legal and expected that they will challenge existing arrangements. They have machinery for carrying on a process of planning-evaluating. They have spokesmen who can make authoritative statements for them, statements that are based on common agreements.

. . . *teachers are encouraged to discover better ways of teaching.* They know that there is general encouragement of examined change. They are helped to engage in a process of problem discovery and solution. Through lifting small dissatisfactions to the level of conscious problem attack, whole new vistas are opened up. Teachers are encouraged to deal with the current and the controversial, to venture into uncharted territory where instructional materials have not yet caught up with events. They are given the support of suggested policies and procedures for dealing with the unknown. They are helped to do action research on their teaching.

... *teachers have sources of new ideas.* Conferences, speakers, discussion and study groups, films, school visits, trips, printed materials, and television programs are available as sources of ideas for what schools might be. Images of alternative ways of teaching are secured not only through the printed and the spoken word but through observations in classrooms where new ideas are at work.

... *teachers can select, plan, and time the specifics of their own changes.* They are invited to make their own decisions and evaluate the consequences. Curriculum guides and other means of showing official expectations have many options built into them, including the choice of devising one's own alternatives. Teachers know they have time to develop new understandings and skills.

... *teachers have help in making changes.* Resource persons are available to supplement the skills of the teacher. Policies and procedures with respect to securing and using instructional materials are geared both to predictable and emerging needs.

... *teachers are informed of others' attempts to improve teaching.* They know who is doing what and why. They know about changes while they are in progress. If and when a change is adopted on a wide scale, they understand and feel ready.

In working to achieve a safe-challenging setting for teachers, the official leader is working on a problem of providing for ordered freedom. He does not have the choice of being either a maintainer of the status quo *or* a change agent. The official's creativity resides in the responsible and responsive ways he helps teachers to be themselves, yet to conform—to find their own meaning in teaching, yet to contribute to others' search for creativity. Partly he will help teachers to accommodate their teaching, as far as necessary and useful, to the expectations of the profession, the public, and its children. Here long experience and time-honored goals will be weighty. For the rest, the official will help teachers break through ways that have outlived their usefulness because they are based on information now known to be inadequate. In this sense, creativity in administration and supervision, leading to creativity in teaching, for the sake of creativity in human living, is a never-ending challenge.

9 SELF-EDUCATION IN CREATIVITY

Nick gave the big center table an extra polish. It was almost four o'clock. Anytime now the teachers would be stopping by and he wanted their special spot to be ready. It wasn't that their daily visits helped the business a lot. A coke, a soda, and a few cups of coffee didn't put much money in the cash register. But Nick liked having them—liked it so much that he would even give them separate checks.

They came in tired, but usually left all in a rush, with a laugh and a cheerful goodbye. While they were here, talking and interrupting each other, time flew. They surely gave some of the other teachers a going over—not every time, but once in a while.

Sometimes he looked at them and wondered—they didn't seem to be much alike. They were all spread out from young through middle age. They taught different grades and subjects. In fact, one didn't teach at all. Sometimes six, sometimes eight of them came. Once in a while there were more. "The regulars" were his favorites—Mary Ann, who taught beginners; Jerry, who worked some place in the middle; Sally, who had an older group; Jo, who didn't work in any one classroom but took her art materials to several; and Lois, the principal of Barber School, who sometimes found an office dull.

If the teachers had known about Nick's wonderings they could have given him some clues as to why they met at his combined soda fountain and delicatessen. Here they traded rides. Lois brought Mary Ann and Jo this far. Then Jerry took them home. Of course there was the pickup a little food gave them in the late afternoon. And, if any of them hadn't planned dinner too well, Nick could always supply some menu fillers. But it was more than food that brought them here. Nick's place had become the bridge from one part of their lives to another. Four o'clock was a good time to look at the school day's triumphs and despairs, getting them into focus—being not quite so triumphant nor so despairing.

Nick knew they enjoyed each other; that was obvious. He didn't realize that they sparked one another, that they gave and received support, security, and confidence, as each ventured into new ways of teaching and living. These were fundamentally good teachers who worked with a high degree of confidence. And such teachers are never content with themselves and their teaching; they search for ways to grow and improve.

Nick gave a satisfied nod as he looked over the table—spoons, napkins, sugar, and the chili sauce just in case Jerry wanted some French fries. The worn green Plymouth stopped in front of the shop. Nick hastily put an "Out of Order" sign on the juke box. His teachers weren't going to be disturbed. As they came in, they were deep in their favorite topic, creativity.*

"We've been reading, talking, dabbling, and getting all excited about creativity in teaching. Don't you think it's time we tried to do something about it, or stopped all this talking? Let's consider it seriously."

"I have an idea about starting. I've underlined some sentences in the book, *Creativity in Teaching*. I noticed, Sally, that you talked back in some places along the margins. And didn't I see a quote from it on top of your desk, Jo? Let's start with one of these."

"Wait a minute, wait a minute. Before we jump into this, let's

---

* The following bits of conversation were taken from many sessions at Nick's. Some things were said aloud, others within.

look at some of the basic 'whys.' What's back of this? Is creativity getting to be a cult—or does it have a place for all of us?"

"Here we go again—talk and more talk."

"Now, Jerry, don't be so impatient. I agree with Lois. We'd better see if these ideas fit us and we fit them. Do you remember, Mary Ann, when you were little and tried to make the paper doll dresses from the *Ladies' Home Journal* fit the dolls in the *Woman's Home Companion?* Sometimes it worked and sometimes it didn't. Maybe creativity belongs to us or maybe it doesn't."

"I can't agree. There can be a place for it in every life no matter who a person is or what he does. Life hands us a series of situations which have to be resolved in some way. There are impulses, longings, needs, seeking outlets. We can either deal with these in a routine way, ignore them, or try to find imaginative and creative solutions. I'm sure that problem solving can be artistic creation."

"Is that why we want to find out about and be committed to this idea of creativity? We would expect you to be, Jo, but all of us are interested."

"Remember, first I'm a teacher and then I'm an artist. And I've never been satisfied with what I can do, either way."

"I know partly why I want to find out about creativity. I wrote a poem once—don't laugh—it was lovely. I think I found out what a touch of inspiration means in creating."

"We wouldn't laugh. Creativity must be like living on tiptoe, or being on the very top of the mountain."

"Yes, but that only for a while. There also have to be weary hours of doing and searching."

"Of course, if you know the skills and techniques involved, then the quest is less difficult. You have to learn."

"Deep down weariness can be a part of it, I'm sure."

"But after that wouldn't there be a feeling of freedom? This idea, this thing that had captured you, had held you enthralled, but as it came into being you were released."

"Look, each of us knows something about the feelings that go with creativity. Haven't you been so absorbed in the wonder of your class at times that you've kept your eyes away from the clock, knowing that if you looked and realized the time you would break the spell?"

"If that's the way you feel, you'd better look the clock square in the face and prove to yourself that you aren't controlled by it."

"For me the feeling, the desire, the need to say something starts slowly. Then the swiftening tempo almost takes it out of my control. Some place along the way, though, I get discouraged and give up. My half-done masterpieces fill a whole desk drawer. I don't know how to get started again."

"Every artist, writer, illustrator, designer, musician, dancer . . ."

"Wait, aren't you going to count us in?"

"Give me time. Every musician, dancer, and teacher knows the deep inner satisfaction of expressing something creatively—the joy of communicating with others. Only we don't know how to make it happen often enough for ourselves and for others; and how to sustain it if it does happen."

"I have an artist friend who would add that the expression, whatever it is, must be done in harmony. There has to be a creation of order, of design."

"You mean like the way a good jazz band weaves harmony? They create designs out of chaotic sounds—it all comes together in a perfect blending."

"I'd better get home and design a dinner or there will be no harmony at our house tonight! Shall we decide to work on this?"

"Yes, let's. Only please, Mary Ann, go gently. I'll never forget what happened with that unit on animals. Such barking, yowling, and even braying! Could you just dip your toes gently in being creative? Don't get submerged."

"I'll remember. But while I'm remembering I'm going to hold fast to a phrase from a book I read: 'Creativity is a potential in everyone, it can be encouraged and fostered. And its purpose is to enable people to live more fully.' How can I start gently with an idea as big as that one? I'll try!"

"This could be a real adventure . . ."

* * *

The next day Nick shook his head as he watched his teachers come in. Sally seemed discouraged. Mary Ann drooped. Lois' eyes were smudged with weariness. Even Jerry looked as though the day had been too much for him. Nick paused for a moment. Hadn't he heard that sugar was a pick-up? Quickly he heaped a plate with fresh doughnuts and firmly placed it in the center of the table.

Mary Ann smiled faintly, took a bite and said, "Well, if problem solving is artistic creation—and I'm quoting you, Jo—then this day gave me more chances to be a creator than I wanted or could manage. Some things I whipped through without thinking. But one time I was stopped cold. I had no pattern, no way of knowing what was best."

"What happened? It sounds catastrophic."

"Beth ranted, raved, and carried on like mad. She yelled, stamped her feet, and started to tear up the doll clothes. I still don't know what triggered it, or why it happened."

"What did you do?"

"Do? I didn't know what to do. I was so stunned I just sat and watched. After a while she eased out some and when I quietly started folding up dresses and things she began to help me. I'm somehow glad I didn't order her to stop. She might not have been able to and then both of us would have been in a spot. I still don't know what Beth was fighting."

"I had a big surprise today too. I was all excited about getting some creative writing started. The students had some wonderful ideas that popped as we talked. I guess I really got going, for all at once Janie said in the nicest possible way, 'Please, will you stop talking and let us write?' I tried to thank her with a smile. Didn't say another word!"

"It's too bad that more of the students can't say in words what they are feeling. Janie is lucky. We have to be able to read gestures, facial expressions, and other signs of meaning for those who aren't articulate. We probably make mistakes in interpreting—or even worse, don't read the visible entreaties and warnings."

"Yes, but we could get better and better at reading what signs we see—and we could try to develop more Janies. How have you helped her get to the place that she can ask you, the teacher, to keep still?"

"I'm not sure but I think it's partly because I'm very careful in reacting to what any student says. I think they all know that I respect them—their own individualities. I know Janie. I value her. I listen to her."

(*I'm glad they didn't see me with Pete. If ever there was an example of communication gone completely wrong, that was it. Pete was angry and so was I. And we both showed it.*)

"I wonder if Mike was trying to tell me something today and had no words. He kept insisting that he had to have a clean sheet of paper. I looked and only one edge was mussed. I didn't let him get another."

"Don't you ever want to make a fresh start on an unsmudged page? It's one of the things I have to do. How my sister fusses at me for all the half-written sheets that turn up in the wastepaper basket. And yet even as she fusses she understands."

"Ruth certainly had a crammed piece of paper in study hall. It was probably a love note from Don. Anyhow she was reading it. I suggested primly that this was a study hall and that she should get to work. Afterward I had to admit to myself that Ruth would have started to work, with no suggestion from me, just as soon as the letter had been read. I get extremely moral about study hall. It must be what the name *study* hall suggests to me, remembering the way teachers made me conform when I was in high school. Ugh."

"That will give us something to think about for next time. . . ."

* * *

"I have a starter question for us today. What is our part in the student's creativity? How have we, the teachers, been involved in those moments at school when we are sure that beauty and meaning, awareness and expression have come together, so that uniqueness and creativeness have resulted?"

"We may have been the catalysts . . ."

"We are the ones who set the conditions—the scene shifters."

"We may have cleared the way."

"But it may be that we only respond to what is happening—are only aware of it. We could be nothing more than fortunate bystanders."

"Does it make any difference exactly what we are—just so we are there and respond in a needed way?"

"Yes, it does. It can't be left to chance. Unless we know what we are doing, how can we improve? It isn't enough to always 'play by ear.' It may work now and then. But we need to know how to woo creativity deliberately."

"We must have a high degree of sensitivity and awareness, or we won't understand enough to help; the moment will pass."

"Yes, and there must be a way of developing more of this awareness and sensitivity, as well as gaining more problem solving knowhow."

"I think it comes partly by learning to observe, to watch, and to gather meaning as you do it. Every once in a while you have to stop and examine a situation. You need to know how it got to this stage and where it might be going. You try to grasp the essence of it all in a breath—while looking at the past and sensing the possible consequences of any next move. The more aware you are of the essence of 'now' the better chances you have of doing the best thing."

"Actually, Mary Ann, when you didn't do anything about Beth's tantrum, you may have been giving both of you time to look at what was happening."

"And time for more than that. I caught a glimpse of what Beth might be feeling. She was so full of anger and frustration that any words of mine would have been futile."

"I should have taken time to look at the way David and Tommy were feeling when I insisted that they had to work in the same group. It wasn't five minutes until they were in a near fight. This right after I had said, 'Of course you two can work together!'"

"Yet you know how you would feel if you were told you had to spend an hour every day with our Dragon, Miss Murdle."

"That's what I'm trying to say. I should have stopped long enough to see what the boys might be feeling."

"I wonder what happens to Jack when I keep telling him to hurry, hurry, hurry? He isn't made that way."

"After a term with Jack year before last I think I can tell you —it doesn't do a thing. Jack being Jack, he probably goes on at his own leisurely pace. You know, I envy him. I'd like to relax half that much."

"Aren't we inconsistent though? You envy and yet you want to push Jack. I take delight in the fact that Marty dances and skips through life. Her tempo is swift and bouncy, and yet I primly and righteously insist that she walk."

"I wonder. We keep trying to motivate them—or is *push* a better word?—into a mold. It's one that could be outdated and fashioned after our own childhood. We try to make them deny their own uniqueness—their own age—and we know that it is wrong to do it. It's important that each one develop as an individual. Think of all the effort we waste."

"I keep trying to get my class excited about what *I* think is great art. I lug paintings and prints back and forth, try to display them beautifully—and those preadolescents walk right by them. I'd save myself a lot of trips to the museums if I gave it up." (*My mold. My idea. Is there some way to make it their exhibit?*)

"That's like my class; only *they* are the ones who are pushing and I'm dragging my feet. They are determined to have a circus unit. I can think of all sorts of reasons that we shouldn't. Truth to tell, I'm ashamed to let them start. In my book, circus units are passé. Only thing is, the children don't know about my book!"

"Aren't we being a little hard on ourselves? We seem to insist on stopping to take a long look at things that don't suit us. Wouldn't it be better to focus on the times when children have been able to interpret and organize—grow and leap ahead—the times when creativity has been the essence of the moment?"

"The moment—or longer—for creativity can be sustained. It took a whole period for Tommy's stubby fingers to find a mother giraffe and baby in a mass of clay."

"Jerry, you can't mean the Tommy I know, fighting, whining, the nonreader, the fighter, the boy whose hands were never clean and whose shirt tail was always flapping?"

"Yes, that Tommy. Only this time it was different. I wish you could have seen Jo. Without a sound she stopped to watch him, and slowly the others in the class put aside their work and watched too. I was so thrilled to be there."

"What became of the giraffe family, Jo? I want to see too."

"They are being glazed and fired and then Tommy and I will put them in the display case. Everyone should enjoy such loveliness. I long to keep them myself, but they are not mine to have."

"No—but you and I and all that class will always have the wonder of it. Who else remembers such a time?"

"During rhythms one day Jean began to dance in the true meaning of that word. This was more than rhythmic response, it was interpretation. Instead of stopping the music at the end of the inevitable sixteen bars, I slid into another melody. I'm not sure who was leading. We seemed to be improvising together. It was exciting and beautiful stuff."

"Like the jazz band someone mentioned, you two wove harmony, together."

"Ellie often weaves harmony. Only she does it with color. If she comes to school under a cloud, she can lose it at the easel. Her blending of color and space brings her release. Quite seriously I feel that she should study design some day."

"You know what we're doing? We are pulling all of our examples from the 'arts.' Surely children can be creative in other ways. I don't want to be counted out and I certainly can't draw, compose, dance, or write."

"I know of an example—Jon, with his ability to take giant strides, to sum up and generalize all in a second."

"Yes, he even does it as he puns. I'll never forget his pre-Easter announcement, which came like a flash, 'When an Easter egg is dyed it's dead.' I laughed, he laughed, and the rest of the class just looked on politely."

"Richard never does anything that swiftly; he is ponderous and slow going. But the results of his silences are such that the whole class waits expectantly and patiently. Wouldn't have missed Richard for anything."

"My class waits expectantly for the results of Nora Ellen's thinking—but it's the opposite kind. She sweeps through all barriers and first thing they know she has the children organized and in action. Isn't that being creative?"

"Right. I've been trying to think of an example outside of the arts, and my thoughts keep coming back to Tammy. Don't know. Wore my best dress yesterday, the one with the velvet trim. Tammy stood by me. He touched, felt, rubbed, and stopped just this side of tasting it. He knows all about velvet now. I stayed very still until he gave me a satisfied smile and walked away. Creative? I don't know. He gathered lots of meaning."

"Allen is creative in expressing himself. He is completely unafraid of letting his own feelings show. No one ever laughs at him when he tells of his love and admiration. He feels, he recognizes his feelings, and he expresses them. His talking about being thankful was one of the most beautiful things I have heard. After he had started, the others were released to add their thoughts. If ever I need a knight in shining armor, I'll remember Allen."

"It is almost impossible for teen-agers to express themselves in words. Yet sometimes there is a wealth of meaning in their rather guarded statements. When Terry finished *The World of Caesar Augustus*, I could tell by her eyes that she was thrilled. Yet all she said was, 'Children were being taught *Do unto others* in different countries all over the world at the same time!' She had found a new kind of understanding, had brought meaning to her world from that of Caesar Augustus. Those books are wonderful ways to organize the past so that you can get hold of it."

"I'll elect Nancy for one who is most creative in everyday life.

She always knows how someone else feels. She comforts the sad and rejoices with the happy. When I spilled my milk she sent Heidie to get a cloth, Tammy to get another bottle of the stuff, and she made sympathetic sounds and then said, 'Will your mother scold you about your dress?' When I was more than a little embarrassed, she took over and helped me out of the situation."

"And I'll take over for Lois. She's restless and it's way past five. Time to get dinner started. Let's break it up for tonight . . ."

* * *

"Just a cup of coffee today, Nick. And don't give Lois any French fries until she loses a pound—that new suit has to fit. Look, since that good session we had last time, I've been wondering what keeps us from having more creative experiences both for ourselves and our students? What are the blocks in the way? Isn't that worth talking about?"

"It certainly is, for if we can recognize the blocks, then we have taken the first step in finding our way over, under, around, or above them. But can we manage this alone, even when we know what stands in our way?"

"Well, not always by ourselves—but sometimes, yes. The important thing is to take that first step."

"You mean to tell me, because I find the school system's policy on reporting to parents one that practically denies any creative approach, I can get going and change it! All of us together couldn't manage that."

"Oh, I'll admit that there are some blocks an individual can't remove. Administrative policy is not under our control, but we have to do what we can while trying to keep from being too frustrated by what we can't change."

"How long has that report card committee been at work?"

"I've been on it for two years now and even though it is hard to believe, we are making progress. Don't look that way, Jerry; we are!"

"And meanwhile I try to put children into neat little slots marked A, B, C, and D. I can't stand pinning labels like 'Excellent' and 'Stupid' on people."

"But, in addition to the A, B, and C labels, can't you manage a short conference with each parent?"

"I write a little note on a card and slide it into each envelope.

That adds a personal touch and lets me say something to temper the D's and A's."

"That's better than blowing your top about the tortoise-like committee."

"And what's more, doing that, you are getting yourself ready for the new type of reporting. That's the direction in which we are moving, snail-paced though we may be."

"I guess part of my trouble is my unwillingness to go on without having it settled exactly how we are going to grade and report. I waste a powerful lot of energy just fussing about it."

"All of us waste ourselves when we aren't able to tolerate ambiguity. We push too hard to have things settled and all at once they are—but maybe the wrong way."

"And yet you can't keep putting off. Isn't there a time for decision and action?"

"There is. Waiting for it a bit can make you doubly certain when it arrives. Something says very clearly, 'You have waited long enough. The time is now.' Just like the phrase 'The lamp is lighted' in *The Lost Prince*."

"The time element comes up so often as we talk—time to decide, time to wait . . ."

"These all have to do with a sense of time—an awareness of when it is appropriate to act, when we need to hurry, to wait, to lag. But most teachers would say that the greatest stumbling block in dealing creatively with situations, people, and materials is the lack of time."

"Yet we all have the same amount. Some of us make it more difficult to manage by putting it into tight little boxes called hours and half-hours and letting them dictate to us."

"And then we pack these little boxes full to overflowing with trivia."

"Trivia—are you sure?"

"Not for you maybe, but for some, yes. I'm afraid trivia make Murdle feel so very important. Being very busy and very important are synonymous to her."

"And to be engrossed with trivia is to be very secure and safe?"

"Too secure. Too safe. There isn't time to adventure with the new and different. With safety you cling to your comfortable, outmoded pattern."

"And it's not only legal to do things differently; it's crucial. We have to experiment and try."

"You mean we don't have to teach subtraction by the take-away method for now and all time? Don't we have to conform when there is one best way?"

"Best? Are you positive? Until you experiment, you can't be sure. And then, when you are sure, you don't dare stay persuaded. There might be another 'best' if you keep looking. Openness could be a key to creativity!"

"But we do have to conform."

"Maybe, but I'm making a plea for intelligent nonconformity."

"Like . . . ?"

"Like if you can't see any good reason for children eternally marching into school, to a class, to the—"

"A fire drill?"

"Now, that isn't fair. Of course you conform in a fire drill."

"But not to the extent that you take the children to a blocked exit just because it is the assigned one."

"Right. But all this getting into line to go some place makes no sense to me at all. And if it isn't sensible to conform, then you try some discriminating nonconformity."

"And with your class it has certainly worked. It is a joy to watch your group walking quietly around the building chatting to each other. The dividend is obvious."

"Yes, Kelly's children do precision marching from one spot to another. But once they get out from under her eye they break loose."

"There's a lot of contrast in degrees and kinds of discipline in our building."

"I need to find a type of discipline that works well for me. I know it has to be internal but I have such trouble making myself read all the references, keep all the records, try all the suggestions."

"Part of the problem is that we keep making long lists of what we think we 'ought' to do. It wouldn't hurt to sort through that long list under 'ought' and see how many items actually belong there."

"No human being could skim, much less read all the articles in *N.E.A. Journal, Elementary English, Educational Leadership, Childhood Education*, and a dozen others, and yet we all feel a bit conscience-stricken as we watch the unread copies accumulate."

"It's silly to fuss at ourselves about things like that. We should learn to forgive ourselves as well as others. Best we go through each magazine, pick out an article or so, look for the topic, writer, or paragraph that says, 'This is worthwhile' and put the rest aside with no qualm of conscience, no self-condemnation."

"I've marveled at the way we manage to keep at this concept of creativity. Haven't we applied one kind of self-discipline?"

"Yes. The concept is important enough that we are willing to commit time, energy, and thought to it."

"We not only became interested; we may even be seeing ourselves grow through it."

"A worthwhile commitment plus helping each other has created momentum."

"Just as the artist's product takes over and tells him what to do, so the idea of doing something about creativity is dictating to us. Isn't that right, Jo?"

"Um?"

"Lois?"

"You aren't listening!"

"Halfway I am. Was thinking how tired I was when school finished this afternoon. All those faces and voices that had been at me all day—a steady stream of children, teachers, parents. Sometimes by dismissal time I feel pulled apart. A half-hour ago I would have said that weariness kept me from being creative—but I'm not tired now."

"The details you handle in a day could make anyone tired."

"Part of my weariness is akin to boredom. There is such a fine line between the two that at times they merge."

"Could there be some comfort in the fact that because you handle so many administrative details others are freed for more creative activities?"

"That's part of my responsibility, but I keep thinking I must be doing things in a way that is depleting, plus doing things that never really need to be done. 'Scuse me from the conversation while I mull this over a bit, I'll catch up with you later."

"Deplete—that's the word that describes the way I felt after Pete and I had a battle royal. I didn't tell you the other day, but I thought of it when you were talking about Beth and the temper tantrum. Pete lost control and I was angry with him. I'm ashamed of having lost my temper—and I was completely exhausted when it was over. Pete was too. It went on and on. But today I'm reporting progress. Another scene was in the making and I held fast and weathered it in calm. I waited, got myself in hand, did what seemed best. I have a feeling that I saved two important things —time and energy. Neither Pete nor I was exhausted. This crisis passed quickly."

"Do you realize what you've been saying? You've pointed out the important fact that we can free two vital elements—energy and time."

"It's interesting, Mary Ann, that you are learning to delay action, for your own tempo is swift. Now you are able to respect the timing of a situation as well as that of another individual."

"Felt sorry for Richard the other day when he said, 'I never do anything fast enough to suit anyone!' Maybe I'd better apply your ideas of respecting internal timing to my work with him."

"I told you this was a progress report. I haven't yet reached the stage where I can say with Thoreau, 'Time is the river in which I fish,' but I might get there."

"That's an optimistic note to end on today . . ."

* * *

Inevitably there came an afternoon when "the regulars" were fed up with everything. What Nick had hoped would be another exciting or at least a comfortable time degenerated into a gripe session. In spite of the extra cups of coffee, the extra attention he gave them, the gloom was slow to lift. Things got off to a bad start. As they came in Sally dumped a heap of papers on the chair beside her, from which they promptly slithered to the floor.

"Look at them. Just look at them. Ugh. I'm so tired of correcting spelling, putting in punctuation marks, and reading the same old stuff over and over, I could scream. They don't care what kind of papers they turn in. There's my evening right there on the floor, all of it. And there will be another set tomorrow, and another, and another—ad infinitum. Sometimes I wish I taught first grade—no papers, no grades—"

"Don't you think we do any evaluating in first grade? I want you to know—"

"If someone along the way bothered to teach something it would help. It seems each group knows less than the last one."

"I like that. What do you think we do all day?"

Nick quietly picked up the papers and put them in a neat stack by the cash register. The silence was vast. Cautiously he filled each coffee cup. Unable to stand the quiet, he dropped a coin in the juke box and pushed No. 6D. The strains of "The Chipmunk Song" filled the room. It was Mary Ann who laughed and started the talk going.

"I was feeling just like Alvin, ready to growl at any one of you. Lois, I've often wondered what principals do with requisitions. Do they store them away like chipmunks store nuts? I asked for a library table and chairs last May."

"Yes, I store the duplicates away in the bottom drawer after I send them in to the central office. Please believe me when I say I cringe every time I see them there. Keep on ordering—someday they will come."

"I'd say, Mary Ann, that you were 'making-do' with what you have very well. The library shelf the boys built is a good substitute."

"And how did you get permission to build it? I've asked and asked if I may paint that ugly piano in my room. I'll buy the paint. People keep quoting rules, rules, rules to me. No permission."

"That rule about painting furniture came into effect when one teacher let her creativity run rampant. She painted every chair, every table a different color. The room looked like a blazing rainbow, well off key. The effect was ghastly."

"But I'm going to make it a soft muted green. Wouldn't that blend in, Jo?"

"Fine, and if you want something more practical than moral support, I'll even spill paint on top of the piano. Then it will *have* to be finished."

"We're talking about intelligent nonconformity again. We've looked at a rule. Found it to be applicable in some cases and silly in others. I'm going to take a look at all the classroom rules I make and see how many of them are worthy ones and which ones I'd better set aside."

"I learned that lesson the hard way my first year of teaching. Reached the far end of my patience one day and said I would punish the next child who whispered. Wouldn't you know it would be Eugene—the quiet, the good, the meek. I hadn't learned yet that I could tell a group of children that I had made a mistake. I punished him and then we had a good cry together. All that misery for one whispered conversation that I wouldn't even notice now."

"I get so bored in teachers' meeting that I could, at my age, start whispering or writing notes. I've even considered growling."

"That would startle us. Some afternoons I'd welcome a growl to break the boredom."

"Meetings aren't that bad in every school. I'm interested in our experiments in group dynamics."

"Even though you aren't doing anything exciting or interesting in your school, Jerry, couldn't you do some of the observing and recording that Lois and her group are trying?"

"What would I observe? How the teachers' patience and the seats of their skirts and trousers are worn thin? Always it's the same. Mr. Highland makes a set of announcements—ones we have already read in the superintendent's calendar. Then he talks about order in the halls, behavior in the cafeteria, safety on the playground, and finishes up with one of the standard jokes."

"Once in a while we have a guest speaker, just as though we didn't have any ideas of our own. I feel sorry for them. There we sit, poised for flight. Promptly at 4:30 watches are obviously checked, coats are pulled a bit closer around shoulders, and general restlessness takes over."

"You might try getting yourself on the committee to plan the meetings."

"Yes, and I might grow wings and fly to China. What committee? There isn't any."

"A committee isn't the answer unless it's one that does something. We've had a steering committee for curriculum outlines for the last five years. The steering takes us in circles."

"I feel safe in Junior High, for Mr. Watts keeps saying that as soon as he gets the reports from the elementary curriculum group, we will start redefining ours. Things are so nicely unsettled now."

"Seriously what should I do? The meetings bore me beyond endurance. Maybe in a few years we can have another approach to them, but meanwhile do I have to sit there and get all vitriolic and volcanic inside?"

"Why not write like mad and fury all the time. Everyone will think you are taking notes."

"Write what?"

"Oh, try a poem."

"I don't feel poetic."

"Well then, how about working on a house plan or sketching the speaker?"

"I could try—but a fine bit of art work would be produced while I was gritting my teeth."

"If it's really taking that much out of you, then try pulling yourself away, intellectually and emotionally. It can be done. I tried to like Kelly. I made an effort to get to know her. To be with her still makes me want to kick the cat or hit someone over the head. I've simply set her aside in my life. She is apart from it and I don't let her penetrate my defenses."

"That could be dangerous if you did it too often, but in rare circumstances perhaps it's all right."

"At least Sally made a try at getting to know her—and she did reserve judgment until she had investigated further."

"And now I'm going to drop a bombshell. I made a skeptical try at getting to know Murdle, and it worked! Asked her to let me borrow the recipe for potato candy—the one thing she lets her group make in the entire school year. She wrote it out in great detail—when to have the children wash their hands, how long to boil the potatoes in relation to their size, how to mash the sugar in and everything. She wants to know exactly when we are going to make it so that she can stand by to help. I'm amazed. I'm wondering, could Murdle in all of her officious busyness and self-righteousness possibly be lonely? I may bring her along some afternoon when we are due for a mild session."

Murdle? Here? Nick dropped the glass he had been polishing for the last five minutes. This was too much. His domain was about to be invaded by the Dragon—and the teachers were bringing her. At least he would get to see this disturbing creature.

* * *

The next afternoon two cars drove up in front of the shop. Nick looked intently at the neat, spare figure emerging from the Chevrolet. Miss Murdle? She looked a little older than the others, or was that because of the way she fixed her hair? Not as up-to-date as his teachers, but not too bad. She crisply ordered tea with milk and gave Nick a brief smile as he set it before her. The smile surprised him. For a time the teachers indulged in mild chit-chat.

"Hardly worth a working man's listening time," thought Nick. It was Sally who started things going.

"You know, Miss Murdle, I've always been half afraid of you, and here you are just as pleasant as can be."

"Please, call me Jane. Afraid of me? Oh no!" (*I'm the one who is afraid.*)

"I don't think Sally means afraid exactly."

"Yes I do, Jerry, and I used to be afraid of you and your bluntness. A spade is too spady when you talk, until one knows you."

(*Well, what have I been saying to ruffle our Sally? I pride myself on being honest, but . . .*)

"Actually, aren't all sorts of fears the basis for many difficulties we have with others? Sally was once afraid of Jerry's tongue, but now she understands. Fears could keep us from doing a more adequate job of teaching. Even this thing of creativity could be curbed by fears."

"Fear of the new, of change."

"Of our abilities, and shortcomings."

"Being so afraid of failures that we hide them even from ourselves rather than taking a good long look at the why of the failure."

"My private skeleton-closet has not only my failures hidden in its darkest corner, but also some of my successes. Isn't it as bad to be afraid of one as the other? I was taught that it wasn't quite nice to let your real reactions show."

"I'm glad my reactions weren't taught out of me. When I'm glad, I obviously rejoice. When I'm sad, my unhappiness shows. Maybe too much. When I'm afraid, I try to see why and get over it. At least, I'm true to my feelings. There is one degree of fear though, the one akin to terror, that I can't yet manage. It simply immobilizes me. I freeze. I'm not even mildly intelligent."

(*I learned that kind of fear when a teacher ridiculed me before the whole class. Never again did I trust an adult in a position of authority. I've shown her though. I'm a better teacher than she ever hoped to be.*)

(*Wonder what Murdle's thinking. She has been so pleasant and now that grim set look has suddenly taken over.*)

"It's hard for adults to admit that they are ever afraid. How much easier it would be for children if we could say, 'I, too, have known fear.' There is some courage to be gained in even talking about it. When I'm afraid I try to think of the most dreadful possible eventuality. Always, I know I could face it, so I manage."

"I make myself see the thing through that frightens me. It takes grim determination. After I've 'managed' a few times, then it becomes easier. Driving a car in five o'clock traffic was extremely disturbing to me when I first came to the city. I made myself drive, day after day. I don't enjoy city driving even now, but I hold my own." (*What a silly example to pull out, but I want them to like me and invite me again, and I must talk some.*)

(*Hold your own, Jane Murdle? I'd say you do that and more.*)

"I believe that Janet manages to get through an oral recitation in much the same way. The other day in class we were discussing Caesar's campaigns. Janet is very shy, but she forgot herself enough to say that Caesar had certainly made some mistakes. Someone asked, 'Such as?' Poor Janet. Her voice quavered. She turned scarlet but she answered."

"Or Sid. He was once so overcome to find that he was reciting that he sank down farther and farther until he was sitting on the floor by his chair when he finished."

"Didn't anyone laugh?"

"They did not. We all shared his misery and were glad that he made it. For Sid it was a giant step. Now he feels 'free to come and safe to go.' "

"And when students feel that way there is no fear. Let it be cast out and there is room for so many feelings that lead to better doing." (*There, I've talked twice.*)

"No one dares live with many fears. Tension comes and goes— and it has its place. But the deeper kind of terror immobilizes, as Mary Ann pointed out."

"Isn't one way of getting ahead of fear to move forward where we have both knowledge and skill? In some area each one of us moves in high confidence. That can be our bridge to take us safely into the unknown. The knowledge of what has gone well in the past helps us in the future."

"Can't the bridge be a symbol sometimes? I used to borrow my mother's bracelet to wear on a day I was having exams. No one, in my opinion, ever dared give her a low grade, and I felt safer with a symbol of her success on my wrist."

"That's like a list of 'Talkable Topics' I took along on my first date. It was insurance against an anticipated vast and deadly silence during which I was sure I would perish. The crumpled piece of paper stayed untouched in my pocket all evening. Didn't need it, perhaps because I had so carefully prepared it."

"For a teen-ager you were very wise. I remember a phrase in a book on creativity, 'She garnered her world about her?' In a way, that was what you were doing. I often mark time for a while as I organize my thinking, bring my experience into focus, and prepare to attack some unsolved problem."

"I didn't have much of a world to garner together when I faced my first third grade class. No student teaching at all, and the few courses in education hadn't quite 'taken.' I was virtually scared to death the first morning. The only security or bridge I had was the fact that I knew and loved children's books. Somehow I was certain that if things got out of hand I could always start to read aloud. Once in a while I'd reach out and touch *Pinocchio* as I went by my desk. It was the only familiar thing in that alien world. Books were the bridge to teaching for me."

"And you have certainly used them well. Now you help others find and use them. Isn't it our job to help children find their bridges to other experiences? The young ones are eager to try the new, but the middle graders are more wary. If we could keep them reaching toward the unknown with a degree of security, the growth potential would be terrific. They might never need to be afraid—if we helped at the right time. I've got to do a lot of thinking about building bridges . . ."

Nick beamed at all of them. Things had gone so well. He could afford to think about this bridge business and his hope of opening another shop. He put the thought aside and carefully made out each check. As Miss Murdle reached for all of them he shook his head in a warning "No." The Dragon wasn't so bad. In fact, he rather liked her. She must not do the wrong thing. His teachers always paid separately. Jane Murdle joined the others at the door. (*I never thought that I might frighten anyone. Do you suppose I really do? Surely not. But just the same it might be good for me to watch myself.*)

* * *

MARY HARBAGE

At the next session, it was Jane who cut through the small talk and brought the conversation into immediate focus.

"I've been thinking about our last talk. Had to ask Mary Ann several questions to fill in background. You talked about fears and I think I understand how this subject ties into the over-all one of creativity. I was shocked to know that Sally had been afraid of me. I *had* to think about it. I *had* to watch myself and other people to see if there might be any justification in this. I'm amazed at what I discovered, and not just about fears either. Some of my knowledge can't help but make me a better teacher. I'm wondering if you have talked about self-understanding as a help to creative teaching."

(*Welcome to the group, Jane.*)

"We have implied it again and again. It's a good topic for us to explore together."

"Each of us needs to be able to say, 'This I am now, as far as I know. These are my strengths and weaknesses. And I'll try to behave in terms of this knowledge.' "

"I know a 'for instance.' If an organization asked me to manage their finances for them I would decline. I don't do that systematic sort of thing well, I don't enjoy it, and what's more I don't want to learn to."

"And on the other hand if you were asked to help plan a program for this organization, your imaginative approach would be helpful."

"I think so." (*I said it aloud, admitted something good about myself!*)

"Let me tell you what I'm trying to find out about myself and my teaching. I have a hunch, and I believe in trying to prove my hunches. I think I make some serious mistakes when I teach history. I'm excited about it. I'm filled to the brim with it. I go too fast, I assume too much, and I'm inclined to overgeneralize. I plan the courses and I try to crowd every detail into one semester. We go like the wind. Last year I balked like a mule at having to teach remedial arithmetic, I was very uncertain about how to start. We went slowly. The students helped in the planning. I worked hard, for I couldn't pose as an authority. It turned out to be a most exciting class for the students and for me. I'm trying to decide why it was so special. Now I'm teaching two sections of the history in different ways. One is the old 'cram-the-course-full' method. In the other I'm helping the class develop plans. I hope I'll know more about my hunches soon—"

"Maybe following through on hunches is one way of finding out about the untried and unknown of myself. I want to find my furthest reaches."

"With your adventurous spirit you will always be able to find a horizon. I can take only so much adventuring at a time. I need to know when to withdraw for my own safety, to pull away into security."

"Everyone has to do that emotionally, and I have to do it physically. I had to learn a long time ago to recognize and behave in terms of symptoms of plain physical weariness. It's a great disadvantage to look as strong as a horse. I get so many jobs handed to me. Now I know that when I'm too tired my coordination begins to slip, my spelling disintegrates, and I've got to rest—or fall apart at the seams. It adds up to a reality and I have to live with it."

"I'm learning a lot about myself and the way I work. It sounds strange, but when the going is too difficult I can be refreshed and ready to go at it again if I read some light love story."

"I used to think I couldn't start any big job until all the little ones had been taken care of. I didn't want to live with that kind of reality, so I began to make a list of all the other tasks needing to be done and sternly told myself to get on with the main one. It works pretty well."

"I'm wondering a little about a sort of ritual I go through before I start writing. All the pencils have to be very sharp and neatly lined up in a row. The eraser must be close at hand. A stack of clean paper in one spot and the outline in another. Only then can I start."

"I can tell you a sure cure for that. Get a summer job on a newspaper. Last July and August all my rituals went out of the window in the stress of meeting a deadline. Copy had to be ready at a certain hour. The discipline of a press is a rugged experience, but a learning one."

"I know *I* couldn't work against a deadline and yet *you* can. I don't always like what I find out about myself."

"No one does. I'm ashamed of the fact that I feel a twinge of envy when the principal praises another teacher's work very highly.

Someday, if I keep growing up, I'll be able to rejoice wholeheartedly at the success of others."

"I took a good step forward when I no longer resented the fact that my father called my sister 'Partner.' For years I felt that it was pointing out an inadequacy in me. Then, all at once I found I was enjoying the fact that they had this kind of relationship."

"Again, it's like stopping and savoring the full meaning of a situation. Then you know how to go on. The other day a friend phoned to ask me a question. In the very asking the appropriate answer was implied and I gave it. It wasn't correct at all. I doodled on the telephone pad for a few minutes, called the person back and said, 'I'm sorry. I answered your question incorrectly. I should have said ———' There was quite a silence, a little laugh, and a quick 'Thank you.' I felt I had taken a step away from automatically handing out the pat formula as an answer."

"We no longer use pat formulas with each other and are getting so we resist using them with others. Good for us!"

"We do help each other, don't we? Our courage, our insight, our awareness, and sensitivity are all heightened."

"Caution lights blink faster for me."

"The green go-ahead shines more clearly."

"Here, we have discovered that it is safe to be honest."

"And we are encouraged to keep trying; at least I am. Had a story back from an editor. This time no rejection slip but a real letter making concrete suggestions about changing it in places. I felt encouraged and settled down to rewrite it. May even take a course in writing next summer. Somehow I've got to learn the skills of the trade, need to master the tools."

"Just as I had to find out in detail how to refinish an antique after I went on an auction buying spree last vacation. It wasn't enough to want to know how—I had to learn the skills. I'm still in an apprentice state, but I'll make it."

"You all have helped me keep things in focus—in fact, I find perspective easier."

"I need to be blasted at every so often and I get it here. But someone who cares for me has to do the blasting or I can't take it. I know you all like me—and what you tell me is said honestly and kindly."

"I like to have a little praise now and then. Usually with you

I either get it or find I no longer need it. My worth to you is implied in the way you listen."

Miss Jane Murdle opened her purse, extracted the exact amount of change and said, "That's what I meant when I said self-understanding helped. As you know yourself and as you know others, you think and act in terms of your needs and theirs. It's much more intelligent . . ."

* * *

By spring vacation Nick sensed that the teachers were beginning to feel more confident about their experiment. Now they were sure they were on the way. It hadn't been easy. Some days seemed dedicated to backward steps, but as the teachers looked over records they were sure of positive gains. It was Jane who had insisted that they must make notes on their experiments and efforts and now they blessed her for the suggestion. As they looked back they were sure that they and their students were "becoming"—becoming more fulfilled as they faced and adequately dealt with the ups and downs of daily living.

Mary Ann knew that the circus had been one of the most rewarding units of the year—filled with good fun and good learning. George had gained badly needed status with the group. Linda had found a degree of poise and David had become able to talk comfortably with others since he had successfully handled his role of ringmaster. In fact, the group had come into their own through the one-ring extravaganza.

Sally's teen-agers had completely taken over the selection and arrangement of the art display. They transported every piece, too. No longer was the borrowing done just from the art museum. Sally was amazed at their display on "Design in Daily Use." She was even more excited when individual students showed her some of their treasures. The climax came when five of the boys took her to the parking lot to see their hot rod and explained just how this gorgeous thing had been created out of a "heap."

The teachers agreed that they had made the greatest gains as they had worked with time, space, and weariness. Inventories and work diaries of what-had-been-done-when had led to discussions about what was really rewarding to both teacher and students. There had been some shifting of plans, changing of schedules, and even dropping of time-honored activities. Sally had agreed to give up the daily drill assignments, and Jane put aside the workbooks. Together they were trying new ways of evaluating pupil progress and few of these infringed on after-school hours. Now Sally felt that the day had twenty-eight hours in it.

When Lois had studied her inventory she decided that, as a principal, she was doing clerical work that other people were trained to do and, what was worse, were paid to do. She took the others on the staff in on her findings, gauged their reactions and started some reorganization of office chores. What a joy it was to have free time for working with teachers.

Those routine tasks that the teachers couldn't eliminate, couldn't skip—those were the ones they learned to whip through with a minimum of energy expended. A great deal was done to put unpleasant jobs into pleasurable backgrounds to make the going easier.

Neither Beth nor Pete had had a temper tantrum for weeks. Mary Ann was teaching herself to give children time to work things through. "White space" in time was as important as white space on a page. It had paid dividends in the improved classroom situation.

One afternoon as Jo faced what was probably the ninety-seven-thousandth dirty paint jar of her career as an art teacher, she firmly put it aside before giving way to the desire to hurl it through the window. She *could* not, she *would* not spend the rest of her life washing paint jars. Sitting down at the desk she wrote this ad for the school paper:

Earn that extra money!
Easy work! Short hours!
Inquire at the Art Department
Friday 3:45 P.M.

Jerry hadn't growled during a teacher's meeting but in the midst of a very dull one had got up and quietly left. Strangely enough, he hadn't been too angry or upset, just determined. He stayed out-of-doors all afternoon, then started the next day by asking Mr. Highland for a conference. It wasn't easy for Jerry to explain to the principal why he had left the meeting, and it was even harder to do it in a quiet and tactful way. No great change had been noticeable at the meetings in the following weeks, but Mr. Highland had asked several times if there were any questions. And each time it was Jerry who made a valiant try and was beginning to get others involved in a mild type of discussion.

The attack on space by Nick's teachers started when the long-awaited library table and chairs were delivered to Barber School. Such excitement! As usual, the teachers went at the problem as one. Floor plans were made and discarded. Bits of cardboard representing tables, desks, chairs, bookshelves, and even a piano (muted green in color) were moved about within rectangles representing an office, an art room, and classrooms. And from room arrangement they had to go on and consider equipment and supplies. What was needed? Where should things be kept?

Weariness? They weren't sure just what had happened to it. Of course, they got tired but the worn-out-dragged-down feeling seemed to have disappeared—for always, they hoped. Work was more exciting now and, at times, actually seemed to refresh them.

So many others were now involved in the search for creativity, one could hardly count them. Several staffs were planning study groups; one P.T.A. had asked for sources of help; and there was even talk of a school-wide workshop. The students had always been part and parcel of it all—the inspiration, the example, the participants.

The regulars couldn't get to Nick's quite so often these days but managed to hold Thursday after school free for their get-together. They agreed, as they looked back over the year, that they had often stumbled, they had wasted lots of time, they had groped a bit—but they had never given up. Some wonderful big things and many small satisfying things had happened. More times of beauty, meaning, and fulfillment had been recorded.

Nick knew that this was the last Thursday his teachers would come; school would soon be closed. What summer plans his teachers were making! Already he was looking forward to the fall sessions and all the tales that would be told. Mary Ann was going to school at some place that sounded like a loaf of bread. Anyhow, since her story had been accepted, she was going to study to be a writer. Wasn't that a funny time to start to study—after she had something published? Never would he forget the afternoon she came tearing in waving the magazine with her name and her story in it. That had called for an extra round of coffee (plus one tea) on the house.

Jane was going to school to work on a "Master's." Lois said

she just wanted to sit on the front porch awhile and then leisurely clean house and leisurely take a short trip. Jo had the car all packed for a summer of sketching and painting in the Smokies. Jerry's car was already bulging with camping equipment. Evidently he was going to explore the U.S. and Canada, with a side trip into Mexico. And for Sally the great summer was at hand. She was going to England to soak up history at its source.

*   *   *

They came in a little quieter and more slowly than usual. It was Mary Ann who noticed the roses in the middle of the table.

"Oh Nick, how lovely! And on our table too! I wonder what I really like best? This afternoon it was children. Saturday night it was music, and right this instant it is the perfection of a rose. My day seems very full."

"Beauty always reaches out to you, Mary Ann, and you respond. It sparks something in you. I wonder what has sparked each one of us. What has made it important to us to keep trying to be better people as well as better teachers? What provided the impetus? We have to know so that we can find it again and again."

"Do you remember that afternoon months ago when we talked about a touch of inspiration? I think that is what I have to have. I listened to a speech once and in spite of the audience around me I felt that the speaker had been thinking just of me as he planned his talk. He had known that in the audience there would be someone with more troubles than she could bear. He talked. I understood and I began to do things differently because of his words."

"That's something like the time I went to my first national conference. I was young and filled with wide-eyed wonder. Here were the people I had heard and read about—in person! I had a bad case of hero worship, but it helped me. I tried to emulate them."

"I know what you mean. At one of the big educational meetings you can get swept out of your ruts. It's an exciting feeling."

"I guess my unfailing source of inspiration is the out-of-doors. Hills, trees, sky, the sea—these I turn to again and again."

"I know inspiration when I match my mood of happiness, sorrow, or serenity with the words of a poet. Whatever I am feeling is given back to me—more beautiful."

"And not just in poetry. You can find it in prose too. I remember when I first read these words in Elizabeth Goudge's *Green Dolphin Street:*

> The whole universe was stilled as listening for a voice. For the space of one heartbeat there was peace on earth. For one fraction of a moment there was no deed of violence wrought on earth, no hatred, no fire, no whirlwind, no pain, no fear. Existence rested against the heart of God, then sighed and journeyed on.

I stopped and savored the words then. Ever since, when I sense deep peace, the passage comes to mind."

"When a span of time is almost unbearably filled with happiness or beauty, I remind myself that no matter what life may bring, I have had and known this moment. It can never be taken from me. Then I go back to it again and again in memory."

"And in the same way when life is full of hurt and problems, almost more than you can take, you hold fast and face it through because you know 'This too will pass' and somehow you will be stronger for it."

"I watch for it, whatever 'it' is, in children's faces."

"I find it in a stranger's smile."

"A beautifully set table."

"The feel of cool fresh sheets."

"A well-made pun."

"A tremendous piece of machinery doing the work of a hundred men."

"Do you know what we are saying? That the source of our inspiration could be almost any place. It could be found at any time. And it could be a simple satisfaction or something of splendor and magnificence."

"It depends on us—our sensitivity, awareness, openness, perceptivity. We have to catch it on the wing or set it up deliberately."

"As good old Hockett and Jacobsen taught us in our student days, we have to enter the main stream of life."

"That could mean—accept the invitation."

"Try out the new ideas."

"Go to the exhibit."

"Yes, and it means keeping a sense of adventure alive, holding on to a zest for living."

"You have to sniff, read, talk, listen, hear, feel, and see—and do it consciously."

"And if you do it that way you'll gather more and more meaning about life."

"This all sounds so exciting, so enthusiastic. Don't forget there are times when life becomes a dull, plodding affair."

"Can't you put something into it? You have to live looking ahead."

"Buy a ticket for a play."

"Plan a trip."

"Promise yourself a bunch of the first spring violets."

"Run away for a day."

"Don't forget there are many times when you are going to have to pull away from activity, from people, so that you can organize, put together, savor all the multitudinous facets of living."

"But, after you've pulled away, then you have to turn toward people again. You search through so many to find the few who become a cherished part of your life for always. With them you dig deeply, and you know them well."

"And in the search you will find individuals who are wonderful, or entertaining, or kind, or exciting."

"Not to mention caustic, cruel, dishonest."

"There aren't many of those. And you never let the few keep you from the many who are rewarding to discover."

"While getting to know all these people and doing all this living, best keep some inner citadel free, some refuge within yourself. You can't maintain this intensity in living all the time."

"A whole day alone."

"A long country walk."

"Spending five minutes with your elbows on the window sill, looking at nothing."

"A good quiet think."

"And then, when you are ready—back into the stream of life. It's like an ebb and flow."

Mary Ann pulled a book from under her purse. "Anne Morrow Lindbergh in *The Steep Ascent* has said it for us, has told us that to be fulfilled we can't say 'No' to life.

> People "died" all the time in their lives. Parts of them died
> when they made the wrong kind of decisions—decisions

against life . . . When you denied life you were warned. The door clicked and you were safe inside—safe and dead . . .

You knew for yourself when you were turning against life— and when you were going with it.

And to that I want to add that you not only 'go with life' but you do it consciously and sensitively. Then you become more of a person; you are more fulfilled."

"And as we work with children we are helping them 'become.' We can open up new ways, new situations for them. We can help them to be open to life, to reach beyond what they now know of it. It is our job to create the many learning situations, both for ourselves and for them."

Lois murmured, "Going with life, full of awareness and openness. That's what we've been doing. Once started, there's no turning back. It's too much of an adventure. Wonder where it will lead us next?"

There was the flurry of getting their books and purses sorted out, finding the exact change, wishing Nick a grand summer. Then suddenly the shop was very quiet. As he cleared the table Nick thought, "Luck to you all as you go with life." He hung up his apron, locked the shop, and reached in his pocket for the car keys. This was a time to go adventuring, the day to find the right location for his new shop.

BIBLIOGRAPHY ON CREATIVITY

BIBLIOGRAPHY ON CREATIVITY

Selected on the Basis of Implications for Teaching

Anderson, Harold H., editor. *Creativity and Its Cultivation.* New York: Harper & Brothers, 1959. 293 pp.

Fifteen addresses presented at the Interdisciplinary Symposia on Creativity at Michigan State University are contained in this volume. Each writer suggests ways in which creativity can be fostered to make individuals more effective in today's world. Among the contributors to this volume are Erich Fromm, Rollo May, Carl Rogers, Abraham Maslow, J. P. Guilford, and Ernest R. Hilgard.

Association for Supervision and Curriculum Development. *Toward Better Teaching.* 1949 Yearbook. Washington, D.C.: The National Education Association. 282 pp.

Within a context describing the components of better teaching, the authors of this yearbook have identified the task of fostering creativity as one of the aspects of good teaching. Chapter V contains many examples of ways that creative teachers have given children opportunity for creative expression in the classroom. The last pages of the chapter describe the kind of classroom that fosters creativity.

285

Bartlett, Frederic. *Thinking: An Experimental and Social Study.*
New York: Basic Books, Inc., 1958. 203 pp.
Bartlett has some new and refreshing ideas about the nature
of different kinds of thinking. He attempts to describe the
thinking process in what he terms "open" and "closed" systems. The concluding chapters on "adventurous thinking"
have many implications for the person interested in creativity, for in these chapters are described the theoretical bases
and certain experiments the author has performed to help
in understanding thinking in "open" systems. The thinking
of the artist, the scientist, and the person engaged in everyday living are described.

Buber, Martin. "Productivity and Existence," in *Identity and
Anxiety, Survival of the Person in Mass Society.* Maurice R. Stein,
Arthur J. Vidich, and David Manning White, editors. Glencoe:
The Free Press, 1960, pp. 628-632.
In a brief chapter, Buber discusses the potential for intense
creative living in each individual. In an age in which much
emphasis is placed upon productivity, individuals tend to
produce without adequate "inner development." The truly
creative person experiences so strongly that his "experiences unite into an image that demands to be set forth."

Cooper, Russel M., editor. *The Two Ends of the Log: Learning
and Teaching in Today's College.* Minneapolis: University of
Minnesota Press, 1958. 317 pp.
Included in this work are addresses given at the Centennial
Conference on College Teaching sponsored by the Association of Minnesota Colleges. In a brief but pithy chapter,
Morris I. Stein describes the implications of the creative
process for the development of a college environment designed to foster creativity in students.

Ghiselin, Brewster, editor. *The Creative Process.* New York:
Mentor Books, 1952. 251 pp.
In this symposium, thirty-eight highly creative individuals
discuss how new ideas are born and developed in fields of
art, literature, music, science, and psychology. The methods
of mastery of necessary techniques and knowledge and the
kinds of qualities that the creative person must possess in
order to bring good ideas to fruition are described in the
words of these thinkers.

Guilford, J. P., Benjamin Fruchter, and H. Paul Kelley. "Development and Applications of Tests of Intellectual and Special Aptitudes." *Review of Educational Research*, XXIX (February 1959), 26-41.

The structure of the intellect is highly complex. Tests of an open-ended nature are revealing a set of mental operations that the researchers call "divergent thinking" or thinking that goes searching, changes routes, and yields multiple answers. The relationship of divergent thinking to creative performance is discussed. The article contains a review of current tests and an extensive bibliography.

Hayakawa, S. I., editor. *Our Language and Our World*. New York: Harper & Brothers, 1959. 402 pp.

In this compilation of articles from *ETC.: A Review of General Semantics 1953–1958,* Hayakawa has included several selections related to the study of creativity. "The Significance of Being Unique" by Earl Kelley and "Toward a Theory of Creativity" by Carl Rogers contain brief but penetrating statements of the viewpoints of these writers. Although the ideas of Rogers may be found in other works, he makes a unique contribution in this book by concluding his chapter with a group of hypotheses that he suggests for testing.

Keniston, Kenneth. "Alienation and the Decline of Utopia," *The American Scholar*, XXIX (Spring 1960), 161-200.

Keniston, in a clear, concise article, describes the apparent apathetic behavior of today's young people and attempts to explain the reasons for the lack of commitment to the improvement of society. It is important that the concept of commitment be reconstructed so that creative persons will feel free to voice their aspirations and hopes for society without being stifled by cold indifference.

Kubie, Lawrence S., M.D. *Neurotic Distortion of the Creative Process*. Porter Lecture Series 22. Lawrence: University of Kansas Press, 1958. 151 pp.

Kubie challenges the assumption that psychological illness is necessary to the creative process. In a penetrating discussion the author explains his theory of thinking that causes objects to be seen in new or different ways. Especially pertinent to the individual interested in creative teaching is Chapter III, which deals with implications of Kubie's ideas for education and the process of maturing.

Mearns, Hughes. *Creative Power: The Education of Youth in the Creative Arts.* Second revised edition. New York: Dover Publications, Inc., 1958. 272 pp.

In an expanded version of a work first published in 1929, Mearns describes his methods and theories of stimulating creative expression in children. The book contains much illustrative material gathered from the author's classes in creative education at the Lincoln School of Teachers College, Columbia University, and from other teachers interested in helping children develop their creative potential.

Moustakas, Clark E., editor. *The Self: Explorations in Personal Growth.* New York: Harper & Brothers, 1956. 284 pp.

Included in this work are articles of nineteen writers on the nature of personality. Unlike many books in this area, this volume focuses on the structure of the healthy personality rather than the ill or abnormal one. Chapters by Rogers, Mooney, and Maslow are particularly appropriate to the subject of creativity. Rogers and Maslow discuss in a concise manner characteristics of persons capable of creative activity. Mooney lays groundwork for creative research.

Murphy, Gardner. *Human Potentialities.* New York: Basic Books, Inc., 1958. 340 pp.

In an age in which the stature of man is often belittled, Murphy describes the kind of person man may become. Especially appropriate is Part III in which Murphy discusses the necessity of the freeing of intelligence if man is to break away from the mold of culture. Perhaps Murphy's most useful contribution to the literature on creativity is his discussion of the creative individual in the society of which he is a part, a society demanding balance and order as well as new and divergent ways of thinking.

Osborn, Alex F. *Applied Imagination.* Revised edition. New York: Charles Scribner's Sons, 1957. 379 pp.

Principles and procedures of creative thinking are presented through homely examples from many fields. The technique of brainstorming is emphasized.

Patrick, Catherine. *What Is Creative Thinking?* New York: Philosophical Library, 1955. 210 pp.

Patrick presents a survey of much of the research on creative thinking in many fields of human endeavor. The creative process is described with illustrative material drawn from the lives and works of scientists, writers, and musicians. Patrick discusses the age of productivity and conditions for creative thought. Her conclusions are that the creative process is the same in all fields and that the home and school can do more than they are now doing to encourage creativity in the young.

Ruesch, Jurgen, and Weldon Kees. *Nonverbal Communication, Notes on the Visual Perception of Human Relations.* Berkeley: University of California Press, 1956. 205 pp.

To study this book of telling photographs is to have an experience in new ways of seeing.

Schachtel, Ernest G. *Metamorphosis.* New York: Basic Books, Inc., 1959. 344 pp.

Focusing on man's unrealized potential, Schachtel describes causes of much of man's "embeddedness" in the familiar. Chapter X, "Perception as Creative Experience," is a discussion of the necessity of openness for creative experience.

Smith, Paul, editor. *Creativity: An Examination of the Creative Process.* A Report on the Third Communications Conference of the Art Directors Club of New York. New York: Hastings House, Publishers, Inc., 1959. 210 pp.

The creative process is discussed by representatives from business and industry, the arts, education, and science. Even though the knowledge demanded in each field varies, the contributions of the various writers indicate that the approach to new ideas and new knowledge in each field is similar.

Stein, Morris I., and Shirley J. Heinze. *Creativity and the Individual.* Glencoe: The Free Press, 1960. 418 pp.

Summaries of selected literature in psychology and psychiatry. The selections are organized around the following chapter titles, "The Criterion and Other Problems in the Study of Creativity," "The Creative Process," "Heredity,"

"The Nervous System," "Age," "Early Experiences," "Religion," "Cognitive Factors," "Personality Characteristics and Motivating Factors," "Psychopathology and Other Illnesses," "Statistical Studies," "Stimulating Creativity," and "Symposia and Surveys of the Literature." Excellent source of abstracts of reports on a wide range of research as well as of theoretical and speculative papers.

Summerfield, Jack D., and Lorlyn Thatcher, editors. *The Creative Mind and Method*, a supplement to *The Texas Quarterly*, Summer, 1960. Austin: University of Texas Press. 118 pp.
  The nature of creativeness in American arts, sciences, and professions is explored in fifteen essays by leading figures in those fields. Included also are records of two small-group discussions led by Lyman Bryson, whose commentary unites the whole book.

Taylor, Calvin W., editor. *The 1955 University of Utah Research Conference on the Identification of Creative Scientific Talent*. Salt Lake City: University of Utah Press, 1956. 268 pp.
  Although the twenty-one reports compiled in this volume are essentially about creativity in scientific areas, many of the articles have value for those interested in creativity in teaching. Especially appropriate are articles by J. P. Guilford, Frank Barron, Morris I. Stein, B. S. Bloom, Brewster Ghiselin, and Calvin Taylor. Writers deal with such topics as the relationship of intellectual factors to creativity, the disposition to originality, the creative process and its relation to identifying creative talent, and problems in identifying creative students.

——————————. *The Second (1957) University of Utah Research Conference on the Identification of Creative Scientific Talent*. Salt Lake City: University of Utah Press, 1958. 255 pp.
  This volume contains the sixteen reports presented at a follow-up conference of the Utah group. Many of the same contributors to the previous volume also have articles in this one. In addition, Ross Mooney discusses "A Conceptual Model for Integrating Four Approaches to the Identification of Creative Talent." Frank Barron presents some thoughtful ideas on "The Needs for Order and for Disorder as Motives in Creative Activity."

Taylor, Calvin W., editor. *The Third (1959) University of Utah Research Conference on the Identification of Creative Scientific Talent.* Salt Lake City: University of Utah Press, 1959. 334 pp.

This report on the third of a series of biennial conferences contains nineteen research papers, four committee reports, and a transcript of a spontaneous discussion by the total group on "Some Concerns about Certain Factors in the Creativity Movement." The committee reports deal with criteria of creativity, prediction of creativity, the role of educational experience in the development of creative scientific talent, and environmental conditions affecting creativity. Especially pertinent for educators are the papers by J. W. Getzels and P. W. Jackson on the highly intelligent and the highly creative adolescent and E. Paul Torrance on creative thinking in the early school years.

Torrance, E. Paul, editor. *Creativity.* Minneapolis: University of Minnesota, Center for Continuation Study of the General Extension Division, 1959. 140 pp.

Torrance has included in the first part of this mimeographed volume the addresses of such people as Calvin Taylor, Ned Flanders, Robert Wilson, J. W. Getzels, P. W. Jackson, and Viktor Lowenfeld, presented at the Second Minnesota Conference on Gifted Children. In the latter part of the book are accounts of the Minnesota Studies of Creative Thinking.

Von Fange, E. K. *Professional Creativity.* Englewood Cliffs, N. J.: Prentice-Hall, Inc., 1959. 260 pp.

Although this book is written from the viewpoint of an instructor in creative engineering at the General Electric Company, the work is designed to interest all those desiring to understand better the creative process. In addition to dealing with the steps in creation, certain chapters describe such topics as convincing others and dealing with resistance to change.

Wilt, Miriam E. *Creativity in the Elementary School.* New York: Appleton-Century-Crofts, Inc., 1959. 69 pp.

Focuses on helping children create with words, with their bodies, and with their hands. Attempts to show "the common denominators of all creative endeavor in the elementary age group—i.e., readiness, activities, media, self-evaluation, and adult acceptance."

Zirbes, Laura. *Spurs to Creative Teaching.* New York: G. P. Putnam's Sons, 1959. 354 pp.

With much illustrative material drawn from her wide experience, Zirbes has set out to "spark" the teacher to think about more creative ways of working in his own situation. The first chapters contain definitions and descriptions of creative teaching. Included in these chapters are contributions of other writers interested in creative education. The remainder of the book deals with the application of the principles of creative education to social studies, language arts, reading, arithmetic, music, and art. Chapters are also devoted to creative approaches to preservice and inservice teacher education.

INDEX

INDEX

A

Acceptance, 233, 251
Administration:
  as professional function, 3
  dual responsibility of, 222-224
  learning from policies of, 217-219
  perceptions of, 225-227
  support from, 247-248
Adopt-a Ship Plan, 174
Alberty, Elsie J., 151
Alice Adams, 169
Ambiguity, tolerance of, 27, 228
American Council on Education, 169
Antioch College, 161
Anxiety, 201 (*see also* Fears, Threat)
Approaches:
  analytic, 129
  intuitive, 129
Approval, 233
Arendt, Hannah, 37
Ashton-Warner, Sylvia, 51, 53, 58, 59, 60, 66
Associates, learning from, 209-211
Atmosphere, professional, 229-232
Attitude:
  businesslike, 231-232
  learning from instructors', 213-214
Awareness (*see* Openness)

B

Barkan, Manuel, 227
Barriers to creativity, 20, 217-219, 225-227

B

Bennett, Arnold, 153
Berger, Donald W., 228
Blocks (*see* Barriers)
Brainstorming, 27, 242-243
Brown, A. W., 83
Brown, Margaret Wise, 170
Bruner, Jerome S., 107, 129

C

Carin, Arthur, 101
Caring:
  as integrating force in living, 51
  as something to be learned, 52
  as way of finding meaning, 50-66
  shown by respect, 58-59
Challenge, 228, 251-252
Change, encouragement of, 251-252
Charlip, Remy, 171
Clark, Harold F., 24
Class size, 72
Climate, psychological, 232-241 (*see also* Atmosphere)
Closure:
  as act of self-discovery, 39
  as aspect of creative process, 24, 38-40
  as responsibility of creator, 39
  criteria for, 39
Colorado State College of Education, 161
Combs, Arthur W., 155, 233, 237
Commitment, 227, 229
Communication:
  nonverbal, 200-201
  to inform, 252

Conditions:
for creativity, 227-228
for safety-challenge in teaching, 251-252
Consciousness of process, 228
Content:
creativity in development of, 74, 108-112
defined, 73
development of, 73
feeling, 120-129
flexibility of approach, 129-134
informational, 112-117
skill, 118-120
types of, 73, 108
Core curriculum, 150-152
Corwin, Norman, 128
Couch, G. B., 83
Creative behavior:
as risk taking, 89
characteristics of, 48, 63
related to problems, 63-65
related to values, 65-66
Creative process:
American vs. European view, 23
as transaction between self and environment, 40
complete cycle of, 54
defined, 6, 7, 79
democratic view of, 7
major aspects of, 24
nature of, 224
study of, 23-24
Creative teaching:
as energy-giving, 52
as style of one's own, 67
defined, 7-9
generalizations concerning, 50
involving both skill and art, 54-55
nature of, 224-225
qualities of, 184-185
responsiveness as material for, 79
Creativity:
a quality in each individual, 7, 61, 81
a quality that can be enhanced, 7
as deliberate choice, 8
as judged by product, 6, 7
as making of forms, 32
barriers to, 134-137
by-products of, 7
demanded by human situation, 15
elements of, 182
evaluation of, 8

in college teaching, 212-213
in development of content, 74
in living, 15-21
in relation to areas of sensitivity, 62-63
in relation to intelligence, 33-34
in teaching, 7-8
need for nurture of, 81
pressures against, 20, 217-219
requirements for, 137
Curriculum:
core, 150-152
defined, 4
development as professional function, 3, 4
learning from development and organization of, 216-217

D

Death Be Not Proud, 128
Decision making:
for self changes, 252
opportunities for, 243-248
releasing through, 247
Denver, Colorado, Public Schools, 146, 147, 148, 153, 157
Design in teaching:
aspects of, 71
interrelationships in, 75
Deutsch, Karl W., 143, 163, 250
Dewey, John, 145, 176
Dice, L. Kathryn, 152
Dickhart, Audrey, 110
Diederich, Paul, 142
Discipline:
as aspect of creative process, 24, 36-38
as mediation between focus and product, 37
as responsibility, 36
in relation to focus, 36
in relation to school requirements, 37
in relation to school schedules, 37-38

E

Edman, Irwin, 31
Encounter:
as source of meaning, 17, 19-20
creative quality of, 84
levels of, 85

Engagement (*see* Focus)
Environment (*see* Atmosphere)
Evaluation:
cooperative, 248-249
official, 248-249
responsibility of creator, 228
self-, 249
Experience, analysis of direct, 196-198

F

Fears, 201-203 (*see also* Threat)
Films:
Alice Adams, 169
as materials, 169-170
The Informer, 169
Focus:
as anticipation of product, 30
as aspect of creative process, 24, 29-35
as commitment to definition of outcome, 34
as differentiation, 30, 34
as engagement, 228
as giving form, 31, 34
as mediation between raw experience and disciplined work, 37
as plan for continuing a transaction, 34
as refining of data, 30
as structure, 31
as test of meaning, 30
as way of dealing with wholeness, 31
as way of ordering experience, 31, 35
hypothesis as, 30, 32
in alternation with openness, 29, 34
Freedom:
as condition of creativity, 227-228
with safety, 237
Functions:
control, 223
in education profession, 3, 6
of promoting receptivity, 250-251
releasing, 223-224

G

Getzels, J. W., 33
Gordimer, Nadine, 57
Guidance as professional function, 3
Guilford, J. P., 25
Guthrie, A. B., 169

H

Hagaman, Neva, 146
Hanna, Lavone A., 146
Harmony, 234-236
Henry, Edith M., 172, 173
Hilgard, Ernest, 27
History as a discipline, 33
Hobelman, L., 43
Hopi Indians, 161
Huebner, Dwayne, 139
Human Comedy, 128
Hutchinson, Eliot Dole, 176
Hypothesizing as focusing, 32

I

Image:
concepts, forming, 189-190
from college experiences, 190-192
from example, 185-190
primary, 185
through administrative policies and procedures, 191-192
through content, 190
through modification of teacher education program, 191
through procedures, 191
Imitation, 22-23
Individuals, study of, 198-199
Information, access to, 240-241
Informer, The, 169
Integrity:
as fundamental in relationships, 80
as synonymous with unity, 82
defined, 81
in purposes, 91
mutuality as element in, 81
respect as element in, 82
Interaction, classroom pattern of, 72
Intergroup Education, Study of, 169

J

Jackson, P. W., 33
Jennings, Frank G., 22
Johnson, Crockett, 171
Joyce, James, 30

K

Kelley, Harold H., 91
Kornberg, Leonard, 4, 72-73
Krauss, Ruth, 171

L

Language skills, improvement of, 199-200

Learning:
by teaching, 208-209
emphasis on, 4
from administrative policies, 217-219
from associates, 209-211
from attitudes of instructors, 213-214
from concepts of teaching and learning, 214-216
from curriculum development and organization, 216-217
from professional literature, 211-212
new tools for, 247
opportunities for staff, 240-243
view of self in, 207-208
Lewin, Kurt, 155
Limits, 238-240
Literature:
as material, 128, 167-170
children's, 169-170
professional, 211-212
Young Scott Books, 170
Lodge, Helen, 169
Lowell, Amy, 168
Lurry, Lucile L., 151

M

Maslow, A. H., 54, 61, 63
Materials:
films, 169-170
for designing in teaching, 71, 74
free and inexpensive, 141
graphic and plastic, 171-173
humble, 163-168
inventiveness with, 162-163
learning to select and use, 247
liberal amounts of, 141
literary, 167-170
recordings, 170
May, Rollo, 23
Meaning:
as key to saving time, 144-145
as product of interaction, 79
as related to perception, 100
created in encounter, 17, 19-20
defined, 73
Media in teaching, 8

Millard, Cecil, 81
Model (*see* Image)
Mooney, Ross L., 23, 145, 147, 154, 227
Moreno, J. L., 154
Morrison, A. W., 83
Mumford, Lewis, 37
Murrow, Edward R., 170
Mutuality, as element in integrity, 81-82

N

Nonverbal communication, 200-201

O

Ohio State University Laboratory School, 160
Open Road, Inc., 160
Openness:
as aspect of creative process, 24-29, 84
as habit to be sought, 27
as quality of encounter, 84
as threat, 25
as total awareness, 228
in alternation with focus, 29
relation to defensiveness, 24, 25
relation to definition, 25
relation to judgment, 24
relation to structuring, 24
resulting in increased awareness, 89
risk taking as condition of, 89
Opportunities for experience:
as product of creativity in teaching, 8
curriculum defined as, 4
Organization:
channels of, 243-244
for safety-challenge, 251
usefulness of, 223
Osborn, Alex F., 27, 242
"Our Five Senses" unit, 146-148
Overstreet, Harry and Bonaro, 50

P

Pepinsky, Harold B., 25-26
Perceptions as possible barriers, 225-227
Potentiality, utilization of, 192-195